Routledge Revivals

Selling the Welfare State

Originally published in 1988, this book offers the first comprehensive and critical analysis of the privatisation of public housing in Britain. It outlines the historical background to the growth of public housing and the developing political debates surrounding its disposal. The main emphasis in the book, however, is on the ways in which privatisation in housing links to other key changes in British society. The long trend for British social housing to become a welfare housing sector is related to evidence of growing social polarisation and segregation. Within this overall context, the book explores the uneven spatial and social consequences of the policy.

Selling the Welfare State:

The Privatisation of Public Housing

Ray Forrest and Alan Murie

Routledge
Taylor & Francis Group

First published in 1988
by Routledge

This edition first published in 2011 by Routledge
2 Park Square, Milton Park, Abingdon, Oxon, OX14 4RN

Simultaneously published in the USA and Canada
by Routledge
270 Madison Avenue, New York, NY 10016

Routledge is an imprint of the Taylor & Francis Group, an informa business

© 1988 Ray Forrest and Alan Murie

Publisher's Note

The publisher has gone to great lengths to ensure the quality of this reprint but
points out that some imperfections in the original copies may be apparent.

Disclaimer

The publisher has made every effort to trace copyright holders and welcomes
correspondence from those they have been unable to contact.

ISBN 13: 978-0-415-61624-9 (hbk)
ISBN 13: 978-0-415-61625-6 (pbk)

SELLING THE WELFARE STATE: THE PRIVATISATION OF COUNCIL HOUSING

In social, political and economic terms, the most important element in the privatisation programme of the Thatcher governments has been the sale of publicly owned housing. This book offers the first comprehensive and critical analysis of the privatisation of public housing in Britain. It outlines the historical background to the growth of public housing and the developing political debate surrounding its disposal. The main emphasis in the book, however, is on the ways in which privatisation in housing links to other key changes in British society. The long trend for British social housing to become a welfare housing sector is related to evidence of growing social polarisation and segregation. Within this overall context, the book explores the uneven spatial and social consequences of the policy. Issues of local democracy and autonomy, centralisation and the public expenditure background are also examined. The book also provides an up to date and detailed assessment of the operation and impact of the policy itself. Whilst critical of the original claims made of the policy and the ways in which it has been pursued, the book argues against any narrow assessment of the pros and cons of selling council housing. The pattern of housng access and opportunity has been affected by council house sales. However, explanations of what is happening in the British housing market demand a broader based analysis of contemporary social change.

Ray Forrest is Research Fellow at the School for Advanced Urban Studies and Lecturer at the School of Applied Social Studies, University of Bristol. Alan Murie is Senior Lecturer at the School for Advanced Urban Studies

Selling the Welfare State:
The Privatisation of Public Housing

RAY FORREST AND ALAN MURIE

ROUTLEDGE
London and New York

First published in 1988 by
Routledge
a division of Routledge, Chapman and Hall
11 New Fetter Lane, London EC4P 4EE

Printed in Great Britain by
Billing & Sons Ltd, Worcester

British Library Cataloguing in Publication Data

Forrest, Ray
    Selling the welfare state: the
    privatisation of public housing.
    1. Public housing — England 2. House
    selling — England
    I. Forrest, Ray II. Murie, Alan
    333'1'1   HD7334.A3
    ISBN 0-415-00531-0

Contents

Tables

Figures

Preface

Contrary to popular belief, the sale of council housing in Britain has a long legislative, political and policy history — almost as long as the history of council housing itself. For those who have not followed the debate with close interest we have provided some historical background in Chapters 2 and 3. Those more familiar with the issue may wish to omit these chapters and concentrate on the remainder of the book. In the bulk of the text we attempt to provide a comprehensive account of the social, spatial and fiscal implications of the changes which have affected council housing in more recent years.

The book draws together, updates and develops material which has been published in various forms over the years. It also provides a substantial amount of new analysis of empirical evidence and offers new insights and perspectives on housing and social change in contemporary Britain. Whilst this material is principally concerned with the sphere of housing, its relevance goes beyond this and forms part of a much broader analysis of social and economic transformation. In this sense it should not only be of interest to a specialist housing audience but also to those in Britain and elsewhere with an interest in the changing nature of welfare provision in both industrialised capitalist and state socialist societies.

In addition to the material which is referenced in the bibliography, the book draws on a series of unpublished studies in Birmingham, Carrick, Derwentside, Hackney, Hounslow, Hyndburn, Liverpool, New Forest, Norwich, Plymouth, Slough, Solihull and Sutton.

Acknowledgements

This book is based on research which was carried out over a number of years. The principal funding was provided by the Nuffield Foundation through two research grants: *Residualising the Public Sector?* (1981–2) and *Monitoring the Right to Buy* (1982–6). Some sections of the book have also been informed by more recent work supported by the Economic and Social Research Council (in particular Chapter 9).

In the course of the research numerous people have provided information, comment and assistance. We should thank particularly the officers and members in our case study authorities. We should also thank Stephen Merrett for some valuable and detailed comments on Chapter 10.

We also wish to express our thanks to the research secretaries at the School for Advanced Urban Studies for typing this manuscript and associated material over the life of the research.

1

Introduction: Privatisation and Housing

Privatisation has become a dominant theme in politics and policy in many countries. It has risen to the top of the British political agenda (Ascher, 1987) and has achieved, it is argued, 'the largest transfer of property since the dissolution of the monasteries under Henry VIII' (Pirie, 1985). It has generated considerable academic literature and debate and is a regular theme in newspaper, television and radio presentations. Many of these contributions acknowledge that what has been labelled as privatisation is a very mixed bag. Different contributions have focused on the formation of a company and sale of at least 50% of the shares to private shareholders (Beesley and Littlechild, 1983); the privatisation of public enterprises or the public sector of industry (Heald and Steel, 1981; Heald, 1985); on contracting out of public services (Ascher, 1987); and on the transfer of service or goods production activities (Dunleavy, 1986). Any such focus leaves out the largest transfer of assets which has occurred as a result of public policy. At least until the end of 1986 the sale of council housing had generated more receipts than all the other sales of assets combined. It has involved over one million households in the acquisition of a substantial, individually owned and controlled capital asset.

In social, political and economic terms, the most important element in the privatisation programme of the Thatcher governments has been the sale of publicly owned dwellings. This book provides the first comprehensive analysis of this major component of privatisation. It offers a critical assessment of the original claims made of the policy and the ways in which it has been pursued. The main emphasis, however, is on the relationships between privatisation in housing and other broader dimensions of social and economic change. In this sense the book argues against any narrow assessment of the pros and cons of selling council housing. Patterns of access and opportunity have been affected by council house sales but explanations of what is happening in the British housing market demand a broader based analysis of contemporary social change.

The lessons and questions raised in relation to the privatisation of public housing are not easily transferable to others, but are important for any overall assessment. Heald and Steel (1982) have identified four main objectives in privatising public enterprises: enhancing freedom; improving efficiency; reducing the public sector borrowing requirement; and tackling the problem of public sector pay. The first two objectives are characterised as philosophical and the third and fourth as more pragmatic. For council house sales it is the first of these which most nearly reflects initial objectives while the third emerged as of major importance later.

Although privatisation of public enterprises had been a major theme of the Conservative government of 1951–5, Heald (1985) refers to the radicalisation of the Conservative party during its 1974–9 period in opposition; and to the 'hostility to public sector unions after the humiliations suffered by the Heath government'. He also identifies the inability of policy makers to devise a viable framework for economic and financial control as supporting the ideological motivation for privatisation.

Heald and Morris (1984) also refer to four classes of privatisation activity — denationalisation (selling off nationalised industries and withdrawal from comprehensive provision); substitution (of customer fees for tax finance); liberalisation (relaxation or abolition of monopoly powers of nationalised industries); and contracting out (arrangements for work in services which remain the responsibility of public authorities to be carried out by private firms). The background to the largest privatisation programme is different. Sales of council houses have taken place and been discussed for as long as council housing has existed and the sale of council houses occurred between the wars. Local enthusiasm for sales also predated the radicalisation of the 1970s or the anti-municipal stance apparent in the 1980s. Nor has the form of privatisation which has initially been embarked upon been principally about introducing competition. While that has been a dominant theme in contracting out and in discussion of the efficiency of services and industries it has not featured in the same way in housing.

Not surprisingly council house sales do not fit neatly into any of the classes of privatisation referred to earlier. Council housing has never been a monopoly service, customer fees (rents) have always operated and contracting out in construction of dwellings has been normal. Pirie's (1985) list of different methods of privatisation reflects his broader definition of what is involved. He refers to selling the whole of an enterprise, selling complete parts or proportions, selling and giving to the workforce and the public, charging, contracting out, diluting the public sector, deregulation, repealing monopolies, encouraging exit from State provision and providing rights to private substitution. He lists council house sales under 'buying out existing interest groups' when it would be more appropriate to talk of selling and giving to users (rather than the public or the workforce). But if the sale of council houses is to be treated alongside other forms of privatisation it is important to acknowledge the range of questions surrounding it. The sale of council houses does not only involve sales to users: vacant dwelling sales have been a continuing feature and privatisation of estates is a growing one. And selling council houses does not mean the severing of relationships with government. Government regulation and subsidy (if only through tax reliefs) involve elements which could be presented as similar to the hybrid privatised enterprises which continue to involve substantial government shareholdings. Privatisation in housing more generally involves deregulation, increasing the role of private sector institutions and developing partnerships between public and private sectors (especially with private sector finance). In some of these cases issues of efficiency are involved. However, at least in relation to the sale of council houses to sitting tenants, it is aspects of choice and of ownership and control *per se* which are more likely to be involved.

Selling council houses is not only of interest in relation to discussion of privatisation. It involves an important element in restructuring the housing market and a re-organisation of the welfare state. Especially in the decade after 1945 there was a general consensus that state provision of housing was an essential element in the general attack on poverty and ill health and in the development of a more equal society with greater equality of opportunity. As with the development of the welfare state in general council housing both before and since that period was subject to a variety of attacks. However, in the general restructuring of welfare in Britain the demunicipalisation of council housing has been among the most dramatic changes. And just as the development of public housing and of the best examples of public housing (including the new towns) attracted considerable attention from other countries and influenced policy development there, so the privatisation of council housing has

3

attracted the same attention.

In spite of this a wide-ranging published consideration of the restructuring of council housing is not available. There is a range of questions about what it involves and represents and about its impact. There are important questions about local autonomy, ownership and control, gainers and losers and the impacts on home ownership as well as on council housing. In a period of increased concern for the problems of inner city and similar neighbourhoods, the impact of a policy which changes the structure of housing opportunities is of enhanced importance.

Particularly since 1979 privatisation has entered the popular consciousness as shorthand for a variety of policies aimed at re-asserting market forces and rolling back the frontiers of the state. This broader philosophy has been developed by the Conservative party in government. On coming to power, the notion of a return to the 'free' market was a matter of rhetoric rather than explicit policies. Indeed, the sale of council houses was an exception in this respect, representing the vanguard of what was to become a much more pervasive strategy associated with cost cutting, efficiency and less tangible notions of individual freedom and the perceived debilitating effects of dependency on paternalistic, oppressive bureaucracies. A view of council housing estates as corrosive islands of socialism has been translated to a perspective of an overextended state, stifling freedom and entrepreneurial flair and inculcating a habit of dependency. Where deregulation has occurred, for example in urban public transport or planning legislation, the aim has been to remove the fetters on private capital rather than on individuals. Thatcherism is certainly not libertarian and some accounts emphasise the growth of a coercive state and greater restrictions on individual freedom (Dearlove and Saunders, 1984; Hillyard and Percy-Smith, 1987).

The most prominent features of the Thatcher administration's privatisation programme have been *denationalisation* within the public market sector with the sale of shares in public enterprises such as British Gas, British Airways and British Telecom *and* the sale of council houses. In terms of cash receipts, the value of sales and the number of households directly affected, the sale of council houses represents the most significant single element in the govern-ment's privatisation policy. Until the sale of British Gas its claim to be by far the most important was difficult even to challenge. Within the welfare state it is housing which has been most affected by this new philosophy. The key institutions of the welfare state, such as the National Health Service and state education, may be facing financial stringency but they remain largely intact as state services. The contraction of the state housing sector through privatisation and reduced investment and the more general exposure of housing provision to market forces has been more striking. No other welfare programme has been cut so substantially. As O'Higgins (1983) noted: 'Housing is not only the welfare programme suffering the largest cuts, it is also the only programme where cuts have been overachieved. . .' The results in terms of investment and subsidy can be briefly summarised. Public sector dwelling starts and completions have fallen dramatically. Council house building has declined to its lowest peacetime level since 1925. The availability of council housing to rent has contracted for the first time. Exchequer subsidies for council tenants in general have been drastically cut and council rents have risen dramatically. Those dependent on state benefits in housing increasingly face a stigmatising, means-tested regime. And the general thrust of housing provision has been towards commodification — the reassertion and extension of a market ideology (Murie and Forrest, 1980; Forrest and Williams, 1981, 1984; Harloe, 1981).

Whilst council house sales have been the most important aspect of privatisation, developments such as rent deregulation, the shift towards privatised forms of residential accommodation for the elderly and recent measures to encourage the disposal of whole council estates to private developers and quasi-private trusts have also developed. Far from the Right to Buy representing the thick end of the privatisation wedge, in retrospect it may be seen as the precursor to the complete dismantling of the council housing sector and the removal of housing provision from the control of locally elected bodies. Why this has been possible is open to some speculation. At this point it is appropriate to note that council housing, unlike the other major elements of the welfare state, has always been a minority provision for the working classes. There is no middle-class vote in council housing. When there has been a risk of or actual opposition by vociferous middle-class interests, as in proposals to alter the basis for student grants or to reduce investment in the National Health Service, the government has been forced to backtrack or tread warily.

We have shifted a long way from the academic debates of the 1960s and early 1970s when critical analyses of contemporary capitalism emphasised a relationship between the welfare state and the capitalist economy which was both symbiotic and contradictory. Capitalism could neither live with nor without the existence of a pervasive and burdensome welfare system. Moreover, what was then the new left generated powerful critiques of the possibilities of socialist transformation through welfarism. The welfare state was said to be ineffective, inefficient and the repressive and more likely to stabilise than undermine the system. And it was the middle classes who were reaping the greatest benefits from state education and the National Health Service.

Within Britain, council housing found itself in a particularly exposed position. It was a highly visible part of the welfare state. And this visibility was real rather than metaphorical in the form of the mass, high rise housing which dominated the inner areas of some of the major cities. It mattered little that the vast majority of council dwellings were houses with gardens and that unpopular dump estates were the exception rather than the rule. Council housing provoked images of drab uniformity, long waiting lists, insensitive bureaucracies and second-class citizenship. Basic housing standards may have been raised but the approach of local bureaucracies derived from the market and private landlordism.

In short, it seemed to have little to do with socialism. Such criticisms found a new and 'unwelcome ally in the antiplanning and antistatist ideologies of the new right' (Szelenyi, 1981) with notions of self-help, decentralisation, and self-determination being translated into the democracy of the free individual competing in the free market. For the right, home ownership represented decentralisation and self-determination in its purest form. The creation of a property owning democracy was a central part of the ideological crusade of the Thatcher administration — and council house sales were the principal mechanism in achieving this social revolution. The left found itself politically and theoretically compromised. It was clearly stretching credibility to mount a spirited defence of what had been the object of such harsh criticism. Consequently there was little possibility of any mass mobilisation in defence of council housing. Those tenants able to buy and occupying desirable dwellings were being offered an attractive opportunity. Those living in the less desirable parts of the council sector, on the inner and outer city estates of high rise flats and run down houses, were unlikely to take to the streets to proclaim their deep seated faith in collective public provision. For them the issues were more likely to revolve around what had been built, what they had been allocated and what rent they paid, rather than the speculative consequences of selling council houses. Whilst it might have been accurate to suggest that the sale of council houses could only make things worse, it was too abstract and remote an argument to win strong and widespread sympathy. Those tenants who had benefited most from public provision, those in spacious well-built houses on cottage estates stood to gain most from the sales policy. And those who had experienced a different phase of council housing, a more residual downgraded form of provision, had little to express but disenchantment. It is somewhat ironic that whilst the negative residual image of council housing provided much of the justification for its erosion and disposal through sales, the very viability of selling council houses was dependent on its earlier achievements as a relatively privileged, high status form of provision for the skilled working classes. In other words, the fact that large numbers of public sector tenants were living in highly desirable dwellings which they were keen to buy was an indication of what council housing was and could have been rather than an indictment of what it had become.

Writing in 1987 over a million council houses have now been sold and academic debate is more likely to be pre-occupied with the limits to the contraction of the welfare state rather than the consequences of its further expansion. And political positions, on the left at least, have been diluted to the extent that it is difficult to imagine the fierce controversy over council house sales which was much in evidence in the 1960s and 1970s. The electoral and ideological impact of two Thatcher administrations has been such that disagreements over the sale of public sector dwellings are more likely to focus on the fine detail than to be matters of political principle. Indeed, at the level of national politics there is a high degree of consensus on the issue. And a measure of the change in the political climate and attitudes towards housing provision is that anyone who argues for a sustained programme of council house building is liable to be branded subversive, militant and an electoral liability. Council housing, it seems, is a tenure of the past.

Despite this apparent political consensus over council house sales, with the major parties firmly committed to a future vision of some form of mass home ownership, the questions surrounding selling council houses are as great as ever. Whilst for some, resistance to disposing of council dwellings was a matter of ideological purity, more reasoned disagreement with the policy derived from the context in which it was occurring, the terms of disposal and the lack of compensatory policies. Council houses have always been sold. Birmingham, for example, was building for sale in the 1920s. But it was also building substantial numbers of properties for rent to those who could not afford to buy. One of the significant changes which occurred in the early 1980s was that for the first time the number of sales outstripped the level of new public-sector building. This gap has continued to widen and 1980 marks more than a symbolic watershed in the restructuring of housing tenure and the effective end of the expansion of council housing. In housing policy terms this development reflected the channelling of political and fiscal energies into the expansion of home ownership generally, and the sale of council houses specifically, to the neglect of other aspects of housing provision. Arguably more pressing needs have taken second place. With evidence of increasing homelessness, lengthening waiting lists, mounting problems of decay and disrepair in the housing stock and a general squeeze on local authority resources was it logical or defensible to give council house sales over-riding priority? This was, for example, how Norwich City Council saw the position. Not only had central government introduced a statutory right to buy in the Housing Act 1980 which removed any local authority discretion, it was also encroaching on hallowed constitutional ground in introducing legislative measures which threatened local government autonomy in more serious ways. As Norwich saw it they were not only being forced to sell council houses but they had to prioritise the processing of those purchases above all else (see Chapter 9). Increasing centralisation is therefore one aspect of the broader significance of the history and development of the sale of council houses.

The recent history of council house sales is also one of greater incentives to purchase. When the disposal of council dwellings had to be at market value very few properties were sold. It was then argued that some parallel should be drawn with the privately rented sector and the sale of properties to sitting tenants. Typically, such properties commanded a lower market value. This was one justification for the introduction of discounts of 20 or 30%. Another argument centred on providing some compensation for years of wasted rental payments. Curiously, those who now advocated sales on such terms were rather close to those who had previously condemned the unspecified numbers of oversubsidised, featherbedded tenants in the public sector. Given that logic, those with long tenancy histories in the better quality dwellings should be compensating the state. With the legislative procession of the 1980s such dubious justifications for discounts have long been forgotten. The Housing Acts of 1980, 1984 and 1986 have raised discounts from a maximum of 50% to 70%. What began as a policy represented as providing cheaper access to home ownership for those tenants who wished to take up the opportunity has degenerated rapidly into an inequitable, complicated package concerned with a variety of objectives. Those tenants who stubbornly refuse to exercise their right to buy face ever increasing rents which in some cases take the costs of continued renting beyond the monthly mortgage payments. But the wider issue relates to the disposal of public assets at below market value. It should be a matter of some concern to ratepayers and taxpayers that by 1986 discounts on council houses amounted to some £5.6 billion (*Hansard*, 1986, vol. 105, col. 42).

The undervaluing of state assets is not, however, confined to council housing. Similar calculations have been made regarding the sale of British Telecom, Amersham International, Jaguar, British Gas and other such recent disposals. A property owning democracy is now embraced within a broader vision of popular capitalism. As the Financial Secretary to the Treasury remarked in 1984: 'Our aim is to build upon our property owning democracy and to establish a people's capital market, to bring capitalism to the place of work, to the high street, and even to the home' (Mr John Moore quoted in *The Economist*, 21.12.85). Given the fiscal significance of council house sales it is curious that in general debates on privatisation or in the presentation of public accounts the disposal of such a significant block of public assets is rarely mentioned. The implication is that council house sales, unlike say the sale of shares in British Telecom or British Petroleum, is a social policy rather than one which is economically driven. Whatever the original aims and justifications for selling council houses the importance of the proceeds from tenant purchase has not been lost on the Treasury. And the general tone and shape of the policy has been increasingly dictated by economic rather than housing policy considerations.

The proceeds from asset sales have become crucial to government public expenditure planning and have disguised real increases in public spending due largely to escalating unemployment. By 1989–90 privatisation proceeds are expected to contribute £5 billion to total planned expenditure. The significance of council house sales in this equation is illustrated in Table 1.1. From a total of over £16 billion from various assets sales between 1980–1 and 1985–6, housing proceeds (of which some 90% accrue from local authority asset sales) account for over half. Moreover, between 1987 and 1990 the proceeds of housing privatisation are expected to contribute a further £5 billion. To make a further comparison between 1980 and 1986 gross capital expenditure on public rental housing amounted to some £5 billion, less than half the total proceeds from housing asset sales.

Table 1.1: Privatisation proceeds, 1980/1–1985/6

	£ million
Amersham International plc	64
Associated British Ports Holdings plc	97
British Aerospace plc	389
British Petroleum plc	551
British Sugar Corporation plc	44
British Telecommunications plc	2703
Britoil plc	1053
Cable and Wireless plc	1015
Enterprise Oil plc	382
National Enterprise Board/British Technology Group	257
National Freight Company	5
Crown Agents	7
Crown Agents Holding and Realisation Board	18
Forestry Commission	82
Land Settlement Association	20
Lease on motorway service areas	52
New Town Development Corporations and Commission for New Towns	126
North Sea Oil Licence Premia	349
Property Services Agency	5
Sale of Commodity Stocks	36
Sale of oil stockpiles	107
TOTAL	7362
Housing (principally council house sales)	9055
TOTAL	16417

Source: HM Treasury (1987) *The Government's Expenditure Plans 1987–8 to 1989–90*, cm. 56-II.

There is another important aspect which differentiates housing capital receipts from the receipts gained from the sale of other assets. In the latter case cash receipts (say from the sale of shares) accrue directly to the Treasury. With the sale of council owned dwellings, it is councils which receive the capital receipts. The Treasury does not receive any cash sums but is able to take the sums received into account in calculating the level of new borrowing required by local authorities. These receipts are important in holding the Public Sector Borrowing Requirement (PSBR) down or giving the Treasury more room to manoeuvre within an existing PSBR level. Treasury restrictions on local authority use of capital receipts have become greater since 1980 and have resulted (along with local authority decisions on spending) in a substantial accumulation of receipts. The political and electoral significance of council house sales clearly extends beyond the confines of housing policy and

10

beyond the assumed political impact of an increased level of home ownership.

The privatisation of council housing remains a live political issue although we have moved a long way from heated debates about the pros and cons of selling council houses. There are now new pressures and new rationales for transferring the public stock to individuals and private capital. Whereas privatisation in other areas has progressed from institutional capitalism to popular capitalism, from benefiting Jeremy to benefiting Sid, the privatisation of council housing has, if anything, moved in the opposite direction. With the prospect of decreasing sales to individual tenants, fiscal and political imperatives dictate the development of new forms of mass disposal. Those who stubbornly refuse to exercise their statutory right to buy may find themselves returned to a privately rented sector from which a previous generation of council tenants had escaped. Much of the justification for selling council houses derived from the evident desire among public tenants to become home owners. There is no evidence that public tenants would prefer to rent privately. Indeed, the reading of any study of tenure preferences would indicate the almost universal unpopularity of private landlordism. Whilst the advocates of council house sales found it appropriate to quote such findings when the policy was exclusively concerned with the promotion of home ownership, there is predictably little reference to such studies to buttress a renewed enthusiasm for private renting.

This book draws upon research on council housing and council house sales which stretches over more than ten years. In that period the political and socio-economic context has changed dramatically. There is now little disagreement that council housing serves the most vulnerable and marginal groups in society. The quantitative and qualitative erosion of the public housing sector has been paralleled by the growth of an underclass of economically and socially excluded households. They are increasingly concentrated in a downgraded public housing sector. Speculating on the future impact of council house sales in 1976, from an analysis of a limited number of early sales and in a quite different economic context, it was suggested that disposals on a substantial scale would alter the role, nature and geography of public housing. The public housing sector would shift towards 'a residual or poor law service offering undesirable, second best properties to poor people'. The report continued:

> Such a situation is not unlike that in the USA, where public housing tends to be poor quality housing concentrated in inner

11

city neighbourhoods and both used by and identified with the poor, with racial minorities and with welfare and problem households. The recipe is one for social segregation and stigmatization. (Forrest and Murie, 1976, p. 33)

What may have seemed like scaremongering then is almost conventional wisdom now — at least in relation to certain of the large council estates in England's major conurbations and the overall direction of change. Policy developments, the uneven impact of recession and transformations in Britain's economic structure have produced a complex mosaic of inequality and social polarisation and the relationships between marginalised groups and housing tenures is by no means straightforward.

The selective nature of council house sales has coincided with reduced investment and reduced general subsidy. As is made clear in subsequent chapters, these processes have altered fundamentally the status, quality and geography of public housing. Whatever the past failures of public housing, direct state provision achieved considerable success in eroding the connections between low income and poor quality housing. These connections are now being reasserted. The system-built, high-rise council housing in the major conurbations is now deeply implicated in a broader analysis of the urban problem. Not only is council housing increasingly guilty through its perceived association with a new underclass but its conception, construction and design are now blamed for social disintegration and anti-establishment behaviour. Rising crime rates, the widespread urban riots of 1981 and 1983 and events at Broadwater Farm have encouraged a renewal of interest in the relationships between environment and behaviour. It has not taken long for Coleman's (1985) detailed analysis of design and social malaise to feed into ministerial statements such as Pattie's that 'Council housing breeds slums, delinquency, vandalism, waste, arrears and social polarisation' (*Inside Housing*, 1986). Moreover, housing and urban problems have been brought nearer the centre of the political agenda through critical reports highlighting the extent of urban deprivation, the lack of investment in the physical fabric of dwellings and the chaotic and inequitable system of housing finance (Church of England, 1985; National Federation of Housing Associations, 1985). In the same year a report published by the Department of the Environment estimated that £19 billion was required to refurbish the existing housing stock (Department of the Environment, 1985).

Central government responses to some of the growing problems of urban deprivation have been well publicised. Ministerial fact-finding visits, the inner area programme, the development of a priority estates programme and the setting up of an Urban Housing Renewal Unit by the Department of the Environment have combined to create the impression that substantial resources are being channelled into the most deprived estates. But throughout this period of growing inequality, urban decay and rising homelessness the government's housing policy priorities have remained elsewhere, namely the sale of council houses. The allocation of resources for other initiatives has been trivial by comparison to the cash generated from the disposal of council dwellings. The political and bureaucratic energies devoted by central government to the success of the sales policy have been unprecedented in the housing field.

It must be stressed, however, that the housing sphere has been affected by the profound changes in the social and economic structure of Britain. The gap between rich and poor has widened and the poorest sections of society are experiencing multiple disadvantage. As producers they are excluded from the labour market. As consumers they are on the periphery of the housing market and have lifestyles increasingly divergent from the majority. They are the long term unemployed, the young never-employed, the early retired and economically redundant. A recent study of four peripheral council estates concluded with a disturbing description of peripheral isolation, entrapment, immobility and decline.

> The most striking common factor in all four case studies is the high level of social and economic deprivation, all of them having roughly three times the national rate of unemployment in 1981. Even though the average proportional increase in unemployment during the 1970s was no higher than the national increase, it has been suggested that because unemployment was already high the income of the outer estates has decreased even further relative to the national average, and that in some sense, all four estates may now have to be regarded as 'subsistence' communities, with very low disposable incomes. The estates have all 'converged' to almost the same very high levels of unemployment and have possibly reached a basic level of dependency, where unemployment and/or receiving state benefits is a majority condition and where further increases in unemployment may make less and less difference to the local income (CES Limited, 1984).

A decade ago perspectives on council housing and council tenants

13

would have been very different. A longstanding criticism of the public housing sector was that it failed to cater for those in most severe housing need. Few commentators now argue that council tenants are oversubsidised, earn high wages and drive expensive cars. Rather, the dominant image is of pauperisation. Resources have in fact been withdrawn at the point where they were increasingly likely to benefit the poorest sections of society. In this sense, one is tempted to raise images of deserving and undeserving categories and of discrimination on grounds of race and gender.

It is these sorts of issues which are most fundamental in assessing the impact and significance of the sale of council houses. In the chapters which follow we explore the origin and nature of council housing and the political, legislative and fiscal dimensions of the sales policy. There is a detailed assessment of the national, regional and local geography of council house sales. In the final chapters issues of local democracy, local autonomy and the broader future of a social housing sector are examined. These are important issues in their own right but the book is not simply about the consequences of council house sales. It is also about power and powerlessness. It is about reshaping welfare provision in housing and in other spheres. The title of this book conveys a relatively simple message. However both the financing and construction of council housing have always been privatised and the erosion of direct state provision through council housing has involved a reorganisation of state subsidy and involvement in housing rather than a withdrawal.

2

Council Housing — Historical Roots and Contemporary Issues

The background to the development of council housing and housing policy in Britain has been the need to subsidise housing costs. This has been necessary to achieve objectives relating to the supply of dwellings and their standards and to enable producers to obtain an acceptable rate of return on capital. Housing is a durable, fixed location commodity. Both shortages and improved standards of housing have maintained costs at a high level relative to incomes. In this situation various forms of subsidising and spreading costs have developed. Tax reliefs, loans and grants for housing purposes and subsidies for local authority house building have all represented mechanisms to relieve the problems of a quantitative shortage of housing, problems of sub-standard houses in the stock and problems arising from the gap between what many householders could pay and the cost of providing adequate housing. Public sector housing in Britain has been the product of subsidising dwellings rather than people — object rather than subject subsidies. It has provided high quality housing for the working classes. It has also contributed to the number of dwellings built, the standards they were built to, the speed of replacement of obsolete stock and the raising of general housing standards.

The growth of council housing through the 20th century has been an important factor in changing the social and political environment in Britain. It has represented a significant change in ownership and control and has facilitated a substantial improvement in and redistribution of housing resources. However the establishment of council housing as a major tenure form has not occurred as a result of any general support or acceptance of the desirability of state provided housing. The collapse of investment by private landlords and the destruction and disruption occasioned by two world wars

15

have increased the role of council housing beyond the original intentions of the policies. Nevertheless the expansion of council housing has consistently only formed part of a wider restructuring of the housing market. The period of growth of council housing has also been a period of growth of individual owner occupation. And throughout most of that period the principal preoccupation of governments has been to facilitate private rather than state controlled production and consumption of housing.

THE ORIGINS OF COUNCIL HOUSING TO 1919

The various available discussions of the origins and development of housing policy and of public housing in Britain emphasise its slow and tentative growth (Gauldie, 1974; Merrett, 1979). Powers to provide housing developed slowly and only following the failure of other mechanisms to deal with problems associated with the supply and quality of housing. Local authorities did not respond enthusiastically to powers as they developed. In general they remained opposed to direct provision of houses and to rate-funded subsidy. Without such subsidy local authorities could only meet the costs of building activities by charging rents in excess of what the poorly housed could afford.

Accounts of the development of public intervention in housing usually start with descriptions of the urban squalor associated with the industrial revolution. Population growth, migration and rapid industrialisation were not catered for through managed town expansion. Industrial pollution and living conditions posed a threat to the general health of the whole population, to productivity and to social cohesion. In view of 19th century housing conditions it is often regarded as surprising that a genuine housing policy did not emerge sooner. The earliest interventions were public health measures. By 1875 legislation detailed standards and procedures relating to nuisances. By 1890 a reformed local government system had public health powers concerned with the interior arrangements of houses, ventilation of rooms, paving and drainage of premises, an adequate water supply for water closets, the structure of floors, hearths and staircases, the height of rooms, the identification of dwellings fit for human habitation and the construction, use and repair of houses. However the public health Acts did not include any powers to deal with slum areas or to combat problems of shortages and over-crowding by building dwellings. A more direct housing policy —

involving intervention through direct provision or subsidy was not embarked upon energetically until other options had been attempted and private investment had declined.

The structure of private landlordism proved inappropriate for the needs of a rapidly urbanising society. As Daunton (1983) states:

> Private landlords did not fit easily into either the Conservative or Liberal view of taxation which developed up to the First World War. Essentially, house-capitalists were without a political base in either of the major parties of pre-war Britain, and they became even more marginal with the post 1918 realignment of politics. (pp. 294, 295)

A marked decline in private investment in the provision of housing was evident long before the introduction of rent control in 1915, and had led to proposals for Exchequer subsidy of housing as early as 1909 (Wilding, 1972; Orbach, 1977). The decline in investment in private renting was associated with the effects of public intervention in raising standards and reduced profitability given that the rent paying capacity did not increase. It is also associated with the emergence of new markets for capital and ones which yielded a higher rate of return. Against this background the failure of new forms of tenure to fill the emerging gap was important. The voluntary sector model dwelling associations failed to generate a sufficient return on capital even though rents were too high for low wage earners. The contributions of the building societies, mutual aid organisations and employer housing schemes were not sufficient.

The earliest housing legislation is the Lodging Houses Act 1851 which provided powers in respect of lodging houses. Subsequent legislation extended to local authorities powers to enable them to clear and improve individual slum dwellings and then areas of unfit dwellings. Obligations in respect of compensation and rehousing developed haltingly and much local authority clearance activity in the last third of the 19th century was not accompanied by rehousing provision. The most widely used piece of housing legislation before 1919 was the Housing of the Working Classes Act 1890 which consolidated measures (but still did not impose a duty) in relation to slum clearance and gave powers for local authorities to provide separate houses or cottages (not just hostels) for the working classes (not just linked to slum clearance rehousing).

The period before 1919 is marked by a reluctance to envisage a permanent role for the government in housing. Legislation was permissive and unsupported by Exchequer subsidies, and for example, dwellings constructed in redevelopment areas were to be resold within ten years. By 1914 only some 24,000 dwellings had been built by local authorities. The rate of building had increased in the years 1912–14, but without subsidy to bring rents within the reach of lower income households direct public provision made little real impact on slum dwellers. Dwellings built by local authorities in the 19th century were intended for the working classes but in practice poorer sections of the community could not afford unsubsidised rents (rate borne subsidy was not substantial) and it was the 'affluent' working class who benefited — the less affluent merely moved on to properties elsewhere in the private rented sector with lower rents. The reluctance to incur the costs and responsibilities of providing dwellings in the 19th century is normally associated with attitudes to property and the structure of local government prior to the 1890s. In addition, questions of subsidy of housing involved attitudes to poor relief, dependency and commitment to family and work.

Continuing industrial development not only generated additional housing needs but also operated to reduce the existing supply. The building of railway systems which cut into the centre of cities through residential areas sometimes actively reduced dwelling supply, exacerbating problems of housing shortage and overcrowding. Even the tentative steps of government had something of this effect. Those steps which can be regarded as progressive were often a mixed blessing in that they pushed up costs. Without any comparable increase in rent paying capacity, intervention to raise standards (and therefore costs) reduced the rate of return on private investment in rented property.

HOUSING POLICY BETWEEN 1915 AND 1939

While it would be wrong to minimise the changes in housing and housing policy prior to 1915 the period since then has been one of more dramatic and marked transformation. However, the changes in the period since 1915 have been more directly associated with the impact of State intervention. The development of individualised private ownership, of public housing provision and of the associated institutions and arrangements has dramatically affected the housing environment. At the turn of the century the great majority of dwellings in Britain were rented from private landlords. By 1938 only

18

58% of dwellings in England and Wales were owned by private landlords. Just less than one third of dwellings were owner occupied and 10% publicly owned. Over 50% of owner occupied dwellings in 1938 were pre-1914 dwellings and as many as one million rented dwellings were sold to owner occupiers in the period up to 1938 (DoE, 1977). Certainly the very rapid growth of owner occupation was only made possible by such sales and the slower growth in public housing was more affected by differences in new building rates.

Exchequer subsidy for council housing was introduced in 1919 and altered the financial environment for local authorities' building activities. But this did not result from a change in the climate of opinion in favour of state housing. Rather it was a response to the threat of civil disturbance and the political situation immediately following the First World War. Lloyd George's pledge of homes fit for heroes is the most generally quoted slogan associated with postwar social reconstruction. Historians of the period discuss the pledge not just in terms of political opportunism but of the threat of industrial and political unrest both during wartime and with demobilisation from the armed services. The housing programme was at the heart of a programme of social reform. While 'slums are not fit homes for the men who have won this war' it was also believed that 'the money we are going to spend on housing is an insurance against Bolshevism and Revolution' (Swenarton, 1981, p. 79).

Although the response to these threats in 1919 was a general identification of housing as the first problem to be faced, the policies developed to deal with it were seen as transitional and temporary. As building costs fell back to their normal level so the need for an extraordinary intervention would pass. Policy makers were not equipped with analyses which identified a change in the rate of return on investment in housing-to-rent relative to other types of investment. This change had already reduced the rate of investment by rentier landlords before the war and continued to do so subsequently (with the added impact of rent controls). But many policy makers between the wars expected investment by rentier landlords to recover and indeed Daunton (1983, p. 298) argues that state housing had the mundane purpose of 'easing the adjustment of rents to a market level'. In this he takes issue with the view that the origins of council housing were primarily political and ideological. He argues that they were a more mundane, short-term economic response to the problems of scarcity rent levels. Moreover the

19

reluctance to sustain investment in public housing was also associated with an increasing commitment to owner occupation.

Against this background the housing programme introduced under the Housing Act 1919 as an insurance against industrial unrest was cut back and then abandoned on grounds of high cost. The Housing Act 1923 (the Chamberlain Act) which replaced the 1919 Act had as its central objective the promotion, through subsidy, of speculative building of small working-class houses either for sale or rental. It also provided subsidy — at a reduced rate — for council house building. While some 153,700 council houses were built in England and Wales under the Addison Act between 1919 and 1923 only some 75,300 dwellings were built by local authorities under the Chamberlain Act between 1925 and 1933. It was the Wheatley Act with its more generous Exchequer and mandatory rate subsidies which 'established the local authorities as part of the permanent machinery for providing working class houses'. Under this Act, introduced by a minority Labour government in 1924, 504,500 dwellings with higher standards rather than lower rents were built between 1924 and 1935.

Statistics of this type give an impression of consistent and sustained growth of council housing. Such an impression is misleading. The 'violent instability' in the output figures for local authority building is attributable to cuts in subsidy in 1926, 1927 and again in 1928 (Merrett, 1979, p. 49). Local authority housebuilding plans were affected by these cuts, by labour shortage and by uncertainties arising from the consequences for rents of changes in costs and subsidies. In order to reduce costs there was considerable experimentation with new building methods, materials, reduced standards and the building of flats and maisonettes. At the same time considerable effort was expended on reconditioning older properties rather than on new council building and steps were taken to encourage private investment through rent decontrol and subsidy to private builders. Changes in the numbers, design and standards of council dwellings built indicate the lack of consistent support for council housing in the period.

The lack of sustained support was most clearly indicated by the abandonment of council house building for general needs and its replacement, following the Housing Act 1930, by slum clearance. Moore however has demonstrated that rehabilitation or reconditioning were a consistent element in providing housing at an even lower cost. He states that 'the reconditioning programme of the twenties and early thirties reached proportions which have not been equalled to this day' (Moore, 1980). He quotes Bowley's figure of 300,000 houses made fit for human habitation *each year* between 1919 and 1930 through reconditioning and forcing landlords to carry out or pay for repairs and alterations. He argues that reconditioning increasingly came to be seen by government as a direct alternative to slum clearance and new building. Council house building was not the central element in policy and it was not the shift from general needs to slum clearance building which marked the most significant policy change. In general after 1919 a principal preoccupation was to cut the role and the cost of council house building and find alternative ways of providing a housing policy for the working classes. In this sense the shift to slum clearance after 1930 was not a shift to a residual policy. Such a shift had occurred much earlier and was marked by cuts in subsidy and increased reliance on reconditioning to meet the housing needs of the poor who were priced out of council housing. Against this background the Greenwood Act with its more generous subsidy for slum clearance rehousing of larger households offered a greater prospect of providing new council housing for poorer households than had earlier legislation.

Between 1932 and 1939 dwellings built in slum clearance programmes rose from 2,400 to 74,000. In total 265,000 dwellings were completed. The abandonment of general needs building was however accompanied by reduction of size of dwellings on the grounds that this would bring prices within the means of the poorer households — and would restrain public expenditure. These smaller, low standard properties included an increasing proportion of utilitarian and ill-designed flats and were accompanied by the construction (for decanting) of estates on the edge of cities with high travel costs and poor location in terms of access to jobs, schools and community facilities. These negative developments and the cessation of general needs building detract from the achievements of the late 1930s. At a time when building costs were stable at their lowest point between the wars and when cost/income ratios would have favoured local authority building it was the private sector which was given the major role. The private sector responded and built at unprecedentedly high rates during 1934–9. However, this building did not benefit those who would have become local authority slum clearance tenants. Of the dwellings built by the private sector in this period 74% were for sale. Only 15% were for rental *and* had a rateable value (£13 or less) which put them in the 'working class' market (Bowley, 1945, p. 172).

The stock of council dwellings built in the slum clearance drive of the 1930s is generally regarded as inferior in comparison with dwellings built under earlier legislation. It was however superior to the 'reconditioned' private housing which was mostly demolished in later slum clearance programmes. By 1938 some 1.1 million council dwellings had been built. These represented 10% of the housing stock. Given the poor condition of the stock, the political rhetoric concerned with homes fit for heroes and the early targets for council house building (half a million dwellings in three years), what may seem remarkable is how little council housing had been built in 20 years. In general, however, government had been reluctant to build and to subsidise council housing. In the same period — up to 1938 — it was owner occupation that had expanded most dramatically. New building for owner occupation in the period accounted for 1.8 million dwellings. In addition 1.1 million properties had passed from private renting to owner occupation. New building by private landlords and other organisations accounted for 900,000 dwellings — not far short of the figure for local authorities. The declining importance of private renting was accelerated by sales to owner occupiers. And throughout that period legislation enabled the sale of council houses and a small but significant number of sales was completed. The conviction that there was a large and permanent role for council housing was not universally accepted. The impact of war and a change of government altered this situation considerably.

HOUSING POLICY SINCE 1939

The effect of wartime controls, damage and redeployment of resources was to cause a further deterioration in housing conditions and opportunities. By the time of the general election of 1945 a series of temporary and emergency steps had been taken to relieve this situation. In addition housing subsidies and arrangements for land acquisition had been extended.

The crucial decisions taken by the Labour government, after 1945, which distinguished its approach from that of 1919 and from the Conservative opposition, involved maintaining controls over private buildings and relying on local government to carry out the building programme. Party differences over the respective roles of public and private sectors were apparent, and have continued to affect policy development since 1945. By 1980 more explicit notions of privatisation, of a residual role for council housing and of direct individual encouragement of home ownership had developed from these earlier political positions.

Bevan as Minister of Health in 1945 justified a dependence on council housing in terms of the ability to plan and mobilise resources. However there was also an explicit social or distributional objective. Bevan stated:

> Before the war the housing problems of the middle-classes were, roughly, solved. The higher income groups had their houses; the lower income groups had not. Speculative builders, supported enthusiastically, and even voraciously, by money-lending organisations, solved the problem of the higher income groups in the matter of housing. We propose to start at the other end. We propose to start to solve, first, the housing difficulties of the lower income groups. In other words, we propose to lay the main emphasis of our programme upon building houses to let. That means that we shall ask Local Authorities to be the main instruments for the housing programme. (*Hansard*, 1945–6, vol. 414, col. 1222)

Bevan went on to comment on the disadvantages of allowing local authorities to build houses for only the lower income groups and private speculators to build houses for the higher income groups. He stated that as a result:

> You have castrated communities. You have colonies of low-income people, living in houses provided by the local authorities, and you have the higher income groups living in their own colonies. This segregation of the different income groups is a wholly evil thing, from a civilised point of view. It is condemned by anyone who has paid the slightest attention to civics and eugenics. It is a monstrous infliction upon the essential psychological and biological one-ness of the community. (*Hansard*, 1945–6, vol. 414, col. 1222)

As a consequence of segregation, public housing had a uniformity of design and had produced 'twilight villages'. Local authorities were now to be encouraged to build for higher income groups and make use of diversified designs linked to the different needs experienced at different stages of the life cycle. The principles of planning, priority for letting and diversification in local authority activity necessitated severe restrictions on building for sale. Building for private ownership was restricted by licence. Such licences were 'for the purposes of supplementing the main housing programme and not for diverting building labour and materials'. Where building for private ownership took place it was licensed by local authorities, was subject to be cut back in periods of stringency and a general instruction remained that such homes must go and be seen to go to persons in need. Although the government rejected municipalisation of property in the private rented sector, rent control was retained to complete the range of control over the housing stock.

At this stage in the reconstruction of a housing policy differences of approach were evident. When a Conservative commentator stated in 1946 that 'from the point of view of the country, it matters not one jot whether the houses are for sale or to let so long as houses are forthcoming' (*Hansard*, 1945–6, vol. 426, cols 791–2), his remarks had been prefaced by doubts at the over-reliance on local authorities which were not staffed, designed or organised to license or build. Individual Conservative members deplored the discouragement of owner occupation because of its impact on overall levels of construction. Government spokesmen replied that the question was one of social justice and not building technique and that local authority judgement was needed. These differences of emphasis became clearer and stronger as the housing programme progressed and as it was affected by other economic and social priorities.

By 1948, as local authority building completions increased private completions remained low and even declined. Local authority completions rose from 3,364 in 1945 to 190,368 in 1948, compared with 576 in 1920, 86,579 in 1922, 120,492 in 1928 and the previous high point 121,653 in 1939. This very rapid recovery was not sustained and economic crisis led to cuts in activity. Dwellings built between 1945 and 1951 were built to a standard in excess of that recommended by the Dudley Committee in 1944 (CHAC, 1944). In 1948 one quarter of the cost of postwar council houses was attributed to these improved size and amenity standards. The average area of a three bedroomed house in 1946–51 was 37% greater than in the period 1934–9. While the Labour government in 1951 promoted a reduction in 'circulation space', subsequent policy reduced living space and equipment. Between 1949 and 1953 the average floor space of three bedroomed dwellings had fallen by 13%. As a result dwellings built by local authorities in the 1950s were considerably smaller and less equipped, for example in kitchen storage space, than those built in the 1940s. Only after the publication of the Parker Morris report in 1961 (MHLG, 1961) did average dwelling size begin to increase.

After 1945 the Conservative party leadership had adopted the slogan 'a property-owning democracy' and their policy involved the promise 'to increase home owning as part of their plan to create a property-owning democracy: widening the scope for the private builder and lowering costs'. Private property was 'an equipoise to political power' and 'people find satisfaction and stability in the ownership of property, especially of their own homes and gardens'. Harris (1973) has interpreted the reformulation of policy within the Conservative party between 1945 and 1951 as an attempt to adopt proposals which appeared as a contrast and alternative to 'nationalisation' and 'public ownership'. In constructing such policies housing was of major importance, and on taking office in 1951 the Conservative government immediately committed itself to a shift in direction. It would be wrong to imply that this shift was doctrinaire to any greater extent than Labour's attachment to a particular approach. However, it is equally untenable to regard it as a natural evolution of policy, a reflection of changing circumstances, or the consequence of changing needs.

In 1951 Harold Macmillan, the Minister of Housing and Local Government in the new government, stated that:

> . . . there will always be a very large number of people in this country who are compelled to, or want to, live in rented houses; but there will also be, I hope, a growing number of people who both want to own their own houses and may be enabled by various means to do so. Since it is part of our philosophy that a wide distribution of property rather (than) its concentration makes for a sound community, we shall pursue this aim wherever it is appropriate and can be done with due regard to the interests of those who need to live in rented houses.
>
> I shall hope soon to give local authorities guidance in this matter, both in respect of the building of new houses for letting and for sale, and in respect of the sale of existing houses to the people. (*Hansard*, 1951, vol. 493, cols 846–7)

The Conservative government after 1951 achieved new building targets of 300,000 dwellings a year by raising subsidy levels under the Housing Act 1952, by setting higher targets for local authorities and by encouraging private building. Increased local authority building was also facilitated by the reduction in standards. This shift in policy, the relaxation of building licensing, its abolition in 1954, the return to a slum clearance policy in 1956–7 and the changes in

25

housing finance and rent control between 1954 and 1958 formed the basis of the Conservative review of policy and coloured attitudes towards housing policy until 1964. After 1955, in spite of increased slum clearance activity (29,000 in 1955; 71,000 in 1964), local authority new building declined.

At the same time as reducing local authority building for general needs the Housing Subsidies Act of 1956 encouraged multi-storey building. Subsidy levels were increased for blocks of flats even though the increased construction costs in high-rise building more than outweighed the savings in other costs. While the proportion of approved tenders which were in blocks of flats of five storeys or more averaged 6.9% annually from 1953 to 1959, it rose to 25.7% in 1966 and fell to 9.8% in 1970. As flats in very high blocks declined after 1970, dwellings in blocks of flats of less than five storeys rose from 27% in 1967 to 38% in 1970.

After 1953 both Labour and Conservative parties were increasingly concerned with the problem of deteriorating housing. In its revision of policy the government shifted emphasis towards slum clearance, conservation and rehabilitation. At the same time the intention was to encourage private ownership and to reduce the part played by the state in the housing market. One objective was to promote building for owner occupation as one of the best forms of saving and because 'of all forms of ownership, this is one of the most satisfying to the individual and the most beneficial to the nation' (MHLG, 1963). The expansion of owner occupation would enable local authorities to concentrate on slum clearance and would reduce their role and the burden of housing subsidies. In 1954 Harold Macmillan said: 'Local authorities and local authorities alone can clear and rehouse the slums, while the general housing need can be met, as it was to a great extent before the war, by private enterprise' (quoted in Samuel *et al.*, 1962).

This return to the prewar role of local authorities formed part of a more general 'market' philosophy in housing. The temporary and extraordinary shortages occasioned by war were now thought to be remedied. Problems were thought to arise because of mis-allocation of resources rather than absolute shortage. The market was seen as the best mechanism to re-allocate — local authority action was only needed to meet the peculiar circumstances of slum clearance. The combined effort of Rent Act and slum clearance policy was intended to arrest the deterioration of houses and ensure an improvement in the quality of the housing stock. Similar arguments urging 'realistic' or 'economic' rents in the public sector and the removal or reduction of subsidies were based on the assumption that better use of the stock would result. These arguments were held in spite of lack of evidence and in spite of the failure of the 1957 Rent Act to revive the private rented sector or remedy housing market problems (Cullingworth, 1963, 1965; Donnison, 1967).

The arguments were not solely based on economic assumptions. Views such as 'all subsidies should be regarded as a temporary but necessary evil . . . I do not believe that it can be socially or morally right for the rent of a house to be concealed to the extent that it now is' (Henry Brooke quoted in Samuel et al., 1962), or 'The council house system today is morally and socially damaging and I think we ought to do something about this nuisance during the life of this parliament' (Enoch Powell quoted in Samuel et al., 1962) read as simple, unqualified and provocative expressions of ideology designed to sustain and perpetuate a particular mythology.

At the General Election of 1964 some 86% of Labour election addresses referred to 'home ownership' compared with 57% of Liberal and only 33% of Conservative addresses (Butler and King, 1965, p. 143). The elections of 1959, 1964 and 1966 seem to offer some contrast with the view that the Conservative party was the party for owner occupation (Butler and King, 1966, p. 103). It is difficult to sustain a view that the parties' attitudes to owner occupation differed in principle. The difference lay rather in what steps were justifiable to achieve the objective and in the not unrelated aspect of attitudes to local authority housing and the private landlord. Labour's attitude to the authorities' role in housing was apparent from the outset — their 'primary job' was one of building houses to rent and some 50% of new building should be built for letting by local authorities. The balance between building for letting and for owner occupation was based on 'acute social need' and consideration of demand for purchase.

The Labour government attempted to reduce the impact of uncertainty about interest rates on housebuilding by revising the subsidy system. The Housing Act 1967 introduced a variable subsidy linked to the difference between loan charges incurred and charges under a 4% interest rate. The new subsidy system was backed up by a system of cost norms (the cost yardstick) based on building costs per bedspace. Subsidy would only be paid on costs which fell within these norms and no loan sanction would be given where tenders exceeded 110% of norms. As from January 1969 Parker Morris space and heating standards became mandatory. This led to some increase in dwelling standards. Although by 1967 almost 85% of council dwellings were being built to this standard the arrangements did not produce space standards comparable with those of 1945–51 and involved a new detailed cost control system. The revision of the cost yardstick and the operation of exceptions and flexibility around it brought central and local government into a new relationship which could lead to the adoption of 'bad' design to fit the yardstick. For central government, revision and administration of the yardstick were ways of regulating tender approvals and building rates.

The immediate effect of the new subsidy system was to raise the average basic subsidy from about £24 to about £67 per completed dwelling. By 1971 this figure had risen to £187 per dwelling as both construction costs (up to 1970) and interest rates rose. This increase was only sustained until 1967 although in 1970 it was still higher than at any stage between 1956 and 1964. Economic crisis led to reduced targets for building. The switch marked by the Housing Act 1969 involved a reduction in building for general needs and a reduction in redevelopment in favour of a strategy of voluntary private sector rehabilitation with more limited consequences for public expenditure.

It is in this period that major changes in tax relief subsidy to owner occupiers occurred. Merrett (1982) identifies the origins of tax relief for payments of interest associated with owner occupiers' house purchase but argues that before 1939 tax liability and therefore tax relief was limited to higher income groups. In addition, in the period up to 1963, the average owner occupier's Schedule A taxation offset any tax relief on interest repayments. Only with the abolition of Schedule A taxation of owner occupiers in 1963 and the increasing extension of tax liability down the income scale did the value of tax reliefs increase. These reliefs were extended in 1965 when capital gains from the taxpayer's sole or main residence were excluded from the new tax on capital gains and when in 1969 tax relief on interest paid on loans used for the acquisition or improvement of property was retained when other loan interest payment tax reliefs were abolished. These changes maintained or improved the fiscal advantages of the owner-occupier in a period when subsidies to council housing were to be radically changed and in the 1980s dramatically reduced.

As is outlined in the next chapter it is in the period after 1964 that council house sales emerged as a major aspect of policy. By 1980 what has become labelled 'privatisation' in housing had become a dominant element in policy and any hesitations connected with local autonomy and local needs had been displaced. The Conservative party's policy towards council housing after 1964 was informed by concern to avoid subsidising those not in need and proposals to sell council houses at current market values and avoid a situation in which local authorities were building more houses than was justified by the number of families in genuine housing need. Elsewhere it was argued that the prime threat to the development of a Conservative society was in 'the extension of state monopoly landlordism' (MacGregor, 1965) and proposals to give council tenants the right to buy their houses were presented as a way of breaking up 'huge municipal domains' (Howe, 1965).

On the Conservatives' return to office in 1970 one of the first actions of the government was to remove the restrictions on council house sales which had been introduced in 1968. The policy of council house sales now formed part of a new package designed to reduce the distorting effect of public intervention on the housing market. Rent levels and house prices were to be determined by the forces of supply and demand save where local scarcities unreasonably inflated rents. Protection of those unable to afford market prices was to be offered through rent rebate and allowance schemes. The principal vehicles for these policies were the Housing Finance Acts of 1972 and the 'fair rents policy' they embodied. What was involved was a 'return to the market'. It was argued that the main obstacle to achieving the aim of a 'decent house for every family at a price within their means, a fairer choice between owning a home and renting one, and fairness between one citizen and another in giving and receiving help towards housing costs' (DOE, 1971) was the existing structure of housing finance and especially of subsidies for public sector housing. If rents in the public and private sectors were allowed to rise to their 'natural' level (but not a level inflated by scarcity) better use of the housing stock would result. The fair rents policy of the 1970s was in this way a simple extension of the realistic rents policies of ten years before. It represented a strategy to introduce market forces throughout the housing system rather than to engineer tenure change in order to increase the share of the market sector.

The Housing Finance Act of 1972 removed local authority discretion in setting rents and granting rebates. In England and Wales council rents were linked to the 'fair rents' introduced for private tenancies by the Rent Act 1965. With the increase in rents a new mandatory national system of rent rebates for council tenants was introduced. The legislation of 1972 completed the partial abandonment of fixed unit subsidies which had been established in 1923 and continued until 1967. Whereas the Act of 1967 had only introduced a deficit subsidy in respect of new building, the Act of 1972 referred to the Housing Revenue Account as a whole. The Conservative government in 1970 initially emphasised the benefits of free enterprise and sought to limit the role of the state in all areas of policy. However, after a period of 12 to 18 months many of these policies were revised and the philosophy of non-intervention was reconsidered. In this reconsideration 'the changes that were eventually made in housing policy were neither as wide ranging nor as fundamental as elsewhere' (Lansley and Fiegehen, 1974, p. 140).

The essential features of the 'fair rents', free market strategy continued to operate in spite of major contradictions. The enthusiasm of Labour controlled local authorities for municipalisation had led to an increase in acquisition of private houses. The Minister expressed opposition to this if it was 'simply in order to bring them into public ownership' (*Hansard*, 1974, vol. 868, cols 1213–6). However the contradictions went much deeper. Rather than freeing the market and releasing the natural forces of demand and supply an increase in house prices and rise in interest rates had led to a slump in private building. Not only were fewer tenants coming forward to buy their existing houses but fewer households of all types were willing and able to buy. The effective demand for house purchase had declined and local authority housing waiting lists had lengthened alarmingly. In 1974 it was reported that 30,000 newly built houses remained unsold compared with a norm of some 10,000. The number of house completions in 1973 was 294,000 — the lowest figure since 1959.

Among the earliest actions of the minority Labour government elected in 1974 were a series of measures which abandoned the Conservatives' 'fair rents', free market approach. The freezing of rents, promise to repeal the Housing Finance Act, taking development land into public ownership, providing additional funds for municipalisation, building for sale by local authorities and municipal house building in general, formed the major elements of a very different housing strategy. Consistent with this, advice on the sale of houses in the new towns and by local authorities was changed. The Labour government's actions were not restricted to the public sector. Exchequer loans to building societies were designed to prevent interest rates from rising and, along with increasing lending by local authorities for house purchase and a new low-start mortgage scheme, were intended to sustain and increase effective demand for private house purchase.

All of these actions could be represented as logical and necessary steps to increase building output. Also, they reflected and were affected by the general economic situation which did limit local programmes. The continued support for owner occupation and for the measures embodied in the Housing Act 1974 demonstrate a considerable consensus between the parties. However, the particular components of the whole strategy and the emphasis within it reflected long-established views about policy and contrasted with fundamental elements in the Conservative government's policy between 1970 and 1974 and in the Conservative party's manifestos at both of the general elections of 1974. There were also important differences over the expansion of council housing. One simple example illustrates this. Local authorities in the first year of the Labour government bought over 9,000 new houses from private developers (*Hansard*, 1975, vol. 884, col. 2081). In addition to this, municipalisation of older houses represented an important extension of the public sector. The contrast with Conservative policies was marked. Conservative spokesmen argued that when no other buyer existed there may be an argument for local authority purchase, but 'there is no compelling reason why the houses should remain Government-owned thereafter', and that tenants should be enabled to purchase the houses (*Hansard*, 1974, vol. 872, cols 805–6). The general effect of these early policy measures was a significant increase in public sector housing starts, in municipalisation and in subsidy to the public sector.

In the general election of October 1974 housing policies were prominently displayed. The Conservative spokesperson on the environment, Margaret Thatcher, promised 9½% mortgage interest rates, the abolition of rates and a Bill to enforce the sale of council houses. In the midst of talk about 'coalition' these promises were stated to be non-negotiable. Legislation was to be passed to give council house tenants of three or more years standing the right to buy at one-third less than market value, with a five year pre-emption clause. No reservations referring to rights of appeal, to dwelling type, area or needs were included. The package of housing promises was denounced by Labour politicians as an attempt to buy votes and as 'midsummer madness' which would add 5p in the pound to the income tax. At a time when newly built houses were not being bought there was no reason to believe that council tenants would buy, even with a considerable reduction in price. Furthermore, such purchase would decrease rather than increase the demand for new houses.

31

The period 1974 to 1979 saw an erosion of priority for housing. In that period however public expenditure on housing grew by some 7%. With continuing restrictions on rent increases, rising interest rates and front loading of costs the fastest growing element within this expenditure was subsidy. Although housing expenditure retained its priority the pattern of expenditure within housing, especially if tax reliefs are taken into account, was haphazard and regressive. The Secretary of State for the Environment referred to it as a dog's breakfast (quoted in Harloe, 1978) and set up a major review of housing finance. But before this group reported, housing expenditure had been cut in the budget of 1975, concentrated in 'stress' areas (1976) and subjected to increasing control through annual allocations of loan sanction for capital expenditure. Expenditure cuts in December 1976 were connected with borrowing from the International Monetary Fund. These cuts were accompanied by cuts in planned expenditure and were a product of broader economic management rather than any review of housing policy. A stricter system of public expenditure control linked to cash limits provided a changed environment for local housing expenditure. The Housing Investment Programme system introduced following the publication of the consultative paper *Housing Policy* (DOE, 1977) was, from the outset, more concerned with control than improved planning.

While housing finance dominated debate and legislation in this period there were other developments. A considerable shift away from slum clearance and towards improvement was encouraged through area based schemes — General Improvement Areas (1969) and Housing Action Areas (1974) — which involved some municipalisation. The Housing (Homeless Persons) Act 1977 and to a lesser extent the Rent (Agriculture) Act 1976 laid statutory responsibilities on local authorities affecting one of their major remaining areas of discretion — allocation policies. The Inner Urban Areas Act 1978 provided for a special allocation of funds for inner city areas.

All of these changes had repercussions on the public sector. They were not accompanied by a significant review of any other areas of policy. A limit on the size of mortgage eligible for tax relief and a limitation of tax relief to one home were introduced in 1975. But at the same time new policies were developed to encourage owner occupation (savings bonus and loan scheme, equity sharing, improvement for sale, local authority building for sale). The government's Housing Policy Review is widely regarded as a conservative document indicating that by 1977 Labour's capitulation to owner occupation and acceptance of a limited, residual role for council housing was complete. The Green Paper *Housing Policy* declared that 'for most people, owning one's house is a basic and natural desire'. A consensus had developed in which the major political parties competed to be regarded as the party of owner occupation and in which there was little priority or policy for council housing.

Although the housing policy consensus established by 1976 is widely acknowledged, it is evident that the Conservative government elected in 1979 changed the approach towards council housing from one of residual neglect and lack of interest to one of aggressive restructuring. The success of the Conservative party electorally has been widely associated with the main plank of their housing policy — the introduction of a statutory right to buy for council tenants.

The policies pursued by the Conservative government in respect both of public expenditure, taxation and housing legislation involved considerable changes. No other programme was to be so heavily cut and the House of Commons Environment Committee considered that the 'Government's medium term strategy of reducing public expenditure thus relies principally on the achievement of the planned reduction in housing expenditure' (House of Commons Environment Committee, 1980). Housing was to decline from a major to a minor programme and immediate cuts in investment programmes resulted in a sharp decline in council house building programmes. The major elements of policy towards council housing supported this emphasis. Sharp, real, increases in rents enabled a reduction of Exchequer subsidy and increased the attractiveness of council house purchase. The majority of local authorities by 1983–4 were no longer in receipt of Exchequer subsidy and in many areas rents and income-related subsidies were more than covering the costs of providing council housing. In 1981–2, 74 local housing authorities transferred a total of some £18 million to their General Rate Fund. The sale of council houses formed by far the largest single element in the government's programme of disposal of assets.

The achieved reductions in Exchequer and Rate Fund subsidies to council housing were not accompanied by any parallel review of subsidies to owner occupiers. As a result the subsidies received by owner occupiers in process of purchase began to pull away from those received by tenants. In 1978–9 Exchequer subsidies plus rate fund contributions for council tenants in England totalled some £1386 million while option mortgage plus mortgage tax relief subsidy for owner occupiers was some £1299 million. By 1981–2 these figures were £896 million and £1495 million respectively. Average subsidy per council dwelling in 1981–2 was some £241 (including rebates) and £183 (excluding rebates) while the average subsidy from tax relief on mortgage interest and option mortgages was £285.

COUNCIL HOUSING IN THE 1980s

Council housing in the 1980s is no longer a new or insignificant phenomenon. Over 60 years of investment by local authorities have radically changed the face of British towns and cities. Municipal enterprise has produced a variety of dwelling types. Even in the early years of council development, experimental dwellings involving non-traditional building techniques and different estate and planning layouts meant that the public sector was by no means uniform. Some dwellings were built to higher standards under more generous subsidy schemes (the Wheatley and Bevan Acts) while others are associated with lower standards or prefabricated building methods (especially slum clearance building both before and after the Second War War). While the government-encouraged fashion for high rise building in the 1960s is regarded by some as 'delegitimising' council housing (Dunleavy, 1981) and damaging its public support and appeal, there are other elements in diversity which also played a part. Early unmodernised purpose built dwellings, slum dwellings acquired for clearance, conversion or improvement but used (perhaps after limited patching) pending such treatment, various prefabricated and nontraditional dwellings with design faults, dwellings in isolated locations or on stigmatised estates are all features of council housing which have affected its public image and popularity (Coleman, 1985; Cooney, 1974). It is variety and differentiation which marks council housing rather than uniform unpopularity. The bulk of council dwellings have been built to a high standard, are popular with tenants and consist of traditionally built houses with gardens. The dominant reality of council housing has not been that of the ghetto for the poor and the newcomer.

The period since 1914 has been marked by three major trends in housing tenure: the decline of private renting; the growth of owner occupation; and the growth of council housing. Table 2.1 indicates the major components in the changing structure of the housing stock in Britain. New building for private rental has been negligible since 1938 but even in the inter-war years was outweighed by sales into owner occupation. These transfers from private renting to owner occupation continued in the post-war period and losses to private

Table 2.1: Components of change of housing stock by tenure — England and Wales, 1914–81 (millions)

	Owner occupied	Local authorities and new towns	Private landlords and miscellaneous	Total
1914–38				
New building	+ 1.8	+ 1.1	+ 0.9	+ 3.8
Purchasers(+) or sales(−)	+ 1.1	*	− 1.1	0
Demolitions and changes of use	*	*	− 0.3	− 0.3
Net change	+ 2.9	+ 1.1	− 0.5	+ 3.5
1938–60				
New building	+ 1.3	+ 2.3	+ 0.1	+ 3.7
Purchases(+) or sales(−)	+ 1.5	+ 0.2[4]	− 1.7	0
Demolitions and changes in use[1]	− 0.1	*	− 0.4	− 0.5
Net change	+ 2.7	+ 2.5	− 2.0	+ 3.2
1960–75				
New building[2]	+ 2.6	+ 1.6	+ 0.3	+ 4.5
Purchases(+) or sales(−)	+ 1.1	+ 0.1	− 1.2	0
Demolitions and changes of use	− 0.2	− 0.1[5]	− 0.8	− 1.1
Net change	+ 3.5	+ 1.6	− 1.7	+ 3.4
1975–81[3]				
Net change	+ 1.2	+ 0.2	− 0.4	+ 1.1

Notes: * = negligible
[1] Includes 0.2 million destroyed by air attack
[2] Includes conversions
[3] Estimates
[4] Mainly requisitioned during the war and subsequently purchased
[5] Mainly pre-fabs
Source: Cmnd 6851 *Housing Policy*, Technical Volume, Part I, p. 39 and estimates for and estimates from figures in Hansard, vol. 5, no. 108, 21.5.81, col. 120, Department of Environment, Housing and Construction statistics.

renting as a result of demolitions and changes of use were a major additional element in 1960–75. New building and transfers between tenants have contributed most significantly to the growth of owner occupation. Only in 1938–60 (and especially in 1945–51) was new building principally in the public sector. As a result the numerical growth of council housing in that period was the highest absolutely and in comparison with the growth of home ownership.

The growth of council housing almost offset the decline of private renting in both 1960–75 and 1975–81. However Table 2.1 indicates that in the early 1970s high rates of council house sales and of slum clearance involved a substantial net decline of rented housing. By 1979 rented housing was again in decline — more as a result of low rates of building and of council house sales than of either slum clearance or losses to private renting.

In its period of early growth council housing consisted generally of high quality purpose built modern family housing. It did generally represent a superior housing stock and privileged housing situation. But by 1980 such uniformity and superiority had seriously changed. The earliest purpose built houses were over 50 years old, dwellings built in different periods and to different designs were of widely different quality. While houses built under the Wheatley Act and those built to the higher standards of 1945–51 proved of lasting quality, those built in the slum clearance drives of the 1930s and 1950s–60s, and especially prefabricated and system built dwellings often proved to have short lives and evidenced design and other faults at an early stage. Quarry Hill flats in Leeds, Ronan Point in Newham, the Piggeries in Liverpool and a variety of deck access and high rise flats have become notorious as modern slum houses built by local authorities. In different ways Airey, Orlit and Unity and other prefabricated dwellings have developed structural faults, and problems of dampness and infestation have been commonly associated with post-war dwellings. The difficult to let housing phenomenon which emerged in the 1970s was only partly associated with design and physical faults but reflected variability within the council housing stock and differential demand for it. Dwellings differ in terms of location, access to jobs, schools and other facilities, size, space standards, privacy, play space, reputation, popularity, floor height. Various design aspects make them more or less suitable for children, the elderly or any particular client group. In this sense the stock is not uniform and analysis is increasingly concerned with evidence of social polarisation within the council stock, and the tendency for those with least bargaining power to obtain the worst housing in the sector (English, 1979; Simpson, 1981; Phillips, 1985; Henderson and Karn, 1987).

The numbers and role of council dwellings vary considerably between districts. Some local authorities are very large landlords. In 1977, for example, Birmingham and Manchester each had over 100,000 dwellings and only Solihull of the metropolitan districts had fewer than 10,000 in its ownership. In contrast some three quarters of all non-metropolitan districts in both England and Wales had fewer than 10,000 dwellings, Teesdale with 1,292 dwellings, Stevenage (1,906) and Christchurch (2,093) had the fewest dwellings — fewer than many housing associations. Any analysis of the variations in the size and characteristics of the public housing stock and of correlates with these variations highlights the lack of any single universal relationship. Neither housing need, political control nor local financial resources can be seen to determine variations. Throughout the period of provision of council housing local authorities have exercised discretion in various ways and as a response to various pressures including the nature of their inherited housing stocks.

The size of the local authority's dwelling stock is not a simple reflection of its population size. There is a clear geographical pattern in which council housing is particularly important in the industrial conurbations of the North and West Midlands with a few additional places — Hull, Nottingham and Norwich — having unusually large public sectors. In contrast, authorities with very few council houses include coastal resorts and relatively wealthy commuter areas surrounding conurbations. The situation in London is more complex although council housing tends to be more important in Inner London boroughs. The nature of the public housing stock also varies between authorities. The London boroughs have the highest proportion of flats and of single bedroomed dwellings. The non-metropolitan districts tend to have fewer flats and fewer one bedroomed dwellings.

Moreover, in the 1980s not all council housing is purpose built. Large sections have been acquired from the private sector and some have been modernised to high standards. But some remain unmodernised and of low quality. Local authorities in some areas have become slum landlords and are responsible for letting the least desirable parts of the housing stock — including some purpose built as well as some acquired dwellings. Public images of council housing in this situation are not just affected by 'snobbery' and 'status' but by objective material judgements of the quality of housing. Dunleavy (1981) refers to the delegitimation of council housing arising from the high rise building of the 1960s and 1970s. The breaking of the equation that council housing equals high quality desirable housing involves other physical and design factors. Nevertheless the association of owner occupation with a house with a garden is in contrast with the association of council housing with flats or maisonettes. Such contrasts are more marked in certain localities depending upon the history of council building and design form. Other factors affecting attitudes to council housing are universal. The privileged financial situation of owner occupation and the recognition that council rents are always rising are important elements in attitudes to tenure.

Although council housing has been seen as a way of improving the housing conditions of working-class households a common criticism in the past was that the poorest households continued to live in the worst housing in the privately rented sector. Generally the view of the inter-war period is that while Exchequer subsidy encouraged local authorities to build it was not sufficient, in view of attitudes to rate subsidies, to bring rents within reach of those on the lowest incomes. The widely accepted conclusion is that the 'market for local authority houses was largely confined to a limited range of income groups, that is, in practice, the better off families, the small clerks, the artisans, the better off semi-skilled workers with small families who benefited most directly from the subsidies were the relatively small group of about half a million families who were among the best-off' (Bowley, 1945, p. 130). Local authority activity did result in lower value houses being built and in building for households who otherwise could not obtain modern dwellings of equivalent standard. But the ability to channel these dwellings to the poorest households was limited by rent levels, the absence of differential rent schemes and the dictates of good housing management practice which necessitated eviction if rent arrears accumulated. In order to avoid this, minimum income requirements were not uncommon in tenant selection — although this could not apply in slum clearance. The switch to slum clearance did not enable such exclusiveness and selectiveness and increased the prospect of council housing reaching the poorest households (aided by subsidy, falling building costs and reduced dwelling standards).

By 1939 legislation encouraged the development of rent rebate schemes and simplified rent fixing arrangements by requiring local authorities to pool all their housing income and expenditure into a single Housing Revenue Account. Thus irrespective of the Act under which individual dwellings were built and subsidised, all dwellings were included in a single account. It was only necessary to balance this account rather than each of a series of accounts associated with dwellings built under different Acts. This consolidation provided greater opportunity to devise differential rent schemes but by 1938 only 112 local authorities were operating rebate schemes. But in view of low and largely undifferentiated working-class incomes the failure to channel housing to the worst off cannot be attributed to a failure to develop rebate schemes. The problems rested in the level of subsidy available rather than its distribution. Exchequer subsidies were not sufficient to bring down the rents and the wage levels of tenants were not so varied for there to be a large enough group not 'needing' subsidy so that subsidy could be concentrated. The problem in the inter-war period remained one of general poverty. A gap continued to exist between the cost of housing and the wages of the mass of tenants and prospective tenants. Exchequer subsidies had partially narrowed the gap, but insufficiently. Some of these factors have continued to apply since 1939. The levels of subsidy have not consistently held rents at a level the poorest could afford but with the development of rent rebates and the effects of historic costing and rent pooling this has become less marked. Residential qualifications and management practice have been argued to have excluded certain vulnerable sections of the community or to have channelled them into the worst dwellings. Bearing these points in mind, however, it is clear that the proportion of lower income households who are council tenants had increased rapidly. As the private rented sector declined so local authority housing came to be the major source of housing for the poor.

If council housing has developed a more complicated image which varies from locality to locality it has also changed its financial and social base. It is no longer a heavily subsidised or privileged sector. As council housing has aged or matured so the structure of debt has matured and opportunities for cross subsidisation have become more important. As funding has taken this into account and as income maintenance arrangements and rent rebates have developed, council housing has been less exclusively for the affluent employed sections of the working class and those able to pay high rents. Indeed, as private renting has declined so council housing has taken on its role as the source of housing for the marginalised poor. In this, however, council housing has not developed a different style of management and one of the important features of collective provision has been an authoritarian, bureaucratic and paternalistic style often based on private sector practice. These features and the limited rights of council tenants have formed the basis of criticism that while council dwellings were generally of a high standard the quality of service in terms of rights, choice, representation and influence was remarkably low. While legal remedies for the grievances of private tenants accompanied rent control and especially rent regulation in the 1960s council tenants had no such remedies until the limited measures in the tenants' charter under the Housing Act 1980. The quality of service in terms of aid and advice, repairs and maintenance, and community facilities was generally very poor for council tenants. If council housing is regarded as a flow of services, rather than just a physical entity the 'delegitimation' of council housing is endemic.

The high rise building phase also reflects the influence and interest of private sector builders in council housing. Council housing has been largely built by the private sector. It has been privatised in its production throughout its history. And this privatisation has affected its costs and determined aspects of technology. In this sense council housing has never been separate from the private market and its form and function have been largely determined by market processes. Since its inception there have always been pressures to eliminate direct state intervention in its production, distribution and use. It would be wrong to associate privatisation exclusively with the Thatcher administrations since 1979 or to imply a dramatic breach in attitudes and policies in the early 1980s. Nevertheless in the 1980s privatisation became more prominent and part of a more general, thorough philosophy.

CONCLUSIONS

The 60 years of the growth of council housing have been even more notably the years of growth of owner occupation. Home ownership has become the dominant and normal tenure, has developed as an industry with major interests relying on it, has achieved a status which leaves it too powerful for political 'interference' and is suggested by some to have contributed to real changes in political and class attitudes in society. Its growth has represented a social revolution and a significant restructuring of private enterprise and capital. During this period of restructuring — of the withdrawal of rentier landlordism and its replacement by individual ownership backed by the home ownership industry, municipal activity has played a critical role in maintaining production and standards and in managing a transition and compensating for the dislocation and disruption associated with such a transition. But through the period of transition few have seen what was happening in this way. Some were concerned with temporary dislocations, some with re-establishing the traditional norm, some with building socialism, some with building barriers against socialism, some with social and environmental engineering and so on. Crises associated with war have created real shortages and problems which have been generally acknowledged. But even in these periods the consensus over how to proceed has been limited. The growth of council housing has always been accompanied by an orchestra of opponents and denigrators and of claims that the free market could do better. While such views are difficult to support in the face of historical evidence they have been consistently stated. It may be argued that they have had greatest weight in periods when the threat of civil disorder or the power of organised labour were weakest, when unemployment is highest, when housing problems are less severe and when the private market ideology is most strongly represented in parliament. The periods of residual policy when support for council housing was lowest or when the role of council housing was most limited (say to slum clearance) do broadly coincide with such a perspective. An adequate explanation requires more detailed discussion and more space than is warranted here. Nevertheless, it is possible to argue such underlying factors operated with additional ones in the 1970s and 1980s to predispose governments to a more substantial attack on council housing than had occurred previously. By the 1970s owner occupation was the majority tenure but could no longer expand at its established rate through new building and transfers from the much diminished private rented sector. For the first time support for the expansion of both home ownership and council housing were in conflict. The political ideology of radical and Thatcherite Conservatism and the pressures from its economic policy makers coincided to produce a more concerted and *in that sense* a new attack on council housing. Proposals for the privatisation of council housing formed part of a wider attempt to reduce public expenditure through the sale of assets and to facilitate the provision of services through the private rather than the public sector. At the same time the encouragement of home ownership continued to be a major feature of policy and was extended through a variety of special schemes including building for sale, sales of land, improvement for sale, homesteading, mortgage guarantees and shared ownership.

3

The Political Debate

Council housing has represented at various stages the product of working-class political demands and at others the minimal and temporary interventions associated with other pressures. It has been affected by a dominating concern to encourage the private sector and, in more recent years, owner occupation in particular. Periods of high subsidy and support for council house building and council tenants have been short-lived and policies to organise council housing according to market (realistic or fair) rents or to diminish the role of council housing have been dominant. Periods of residual policy have been more common than those in which council housing has been given a major role in housing policy.

The position of council housing in the 1980s reflects all of these factors. The major characteristics of the sector are not a product of the current phase of policy or even its immediate precursor. Differentiation within the stock, political and social attitudes, regional and local differences and the function of the sector are all products of a longer history. In view of the long periods of residual policy towards council housing the growth of the sector to account for 1 in 3 of all dwellings in the United Kingdom may seem remarkable. However there are a number of elements in this. Firstly, the impact of war, the decline of private renting and the importance of slum clearance and improvement policies has boosted the role of council housing. Secondly, with the decline of private renting and the absence of tests of means for continuing occupation of council housing, the sector has continually 'recruited' households at stages in the family and earnings cycle when they could not obtain adequate accommodation in the private sector. But it has not shed many of these households when their circumstances change. Unlike public housing in the USA the sector has catered for a relatively wide social mix even though it has applied criteria of need in allocating dwellings. Thirdly, the council sector throughout its history has accumulated dwellings through new building and acquisition.

Policies of privatisation in council housing have taken various forms. Policy developments in respect of direct labour organisations, urban renewal and housing management all involve elements of privatisation. Trends in rents and decisions about rent structures may also involve a move towards market pricing. However, none of these developments has been at the forefront. Rather it has been the sale of council housing and in particular a transfer from state ownership to that of private individuals which has dominated. Throughout the growth of council housing governments have encouraged the expansion of individual ownership through various mechanisms, and individual ownership has grown more dramatically than council housing. There have been continual demands for council houses to be sold. The most important nineteenth-century housing legislation required that council-built dwellings in redevelopment areas should be sold within ten years of completion. In the inter-war year powers to sell dwellings with Ministerial consent were present and were used, although on a small scale. For example by 1939 Birmingham had sold 3604 dwellings (City of Birmingham, 1939). Sales had to be carried out at the best price obtainable. It was not until the 1960s that council house sales became a major issue in political debate and housing policy action; not until the 1970s that policies to override local discretion were contemplated; and not until the 1980s that legislation providing tenants with a right to buy was placed on the statute book. Since 1945 the debate on council house sales has been largely conducted along party political lines. Although it has become a more prominent debate in recent years the difference of view is long established. The Conservative Party has consistently pressed for sales and has gradually moved to support for a 'Right to Buy' and subsequently to other methods of privatising council dwellings. The Labour Party, from a refusal to contemplate any council house sales (in 1945/51), came to accept the general stance of the Conservative Party until that party adopted the policy of a right to buy. Following its election failure in 1983, it changed even that position. Nevertheless in the period of apparent consensus there was a distinct difference in the tone of advice on the policy and occasionally a clear breach of real consensus and a real difference towards direct investment in council housing.

DISCRETIONARY POLICIES 1951-80

During the Second World War restrictions on the sale of rented property were accompanied by a refusal to grant consent to the sale of council houses. This refusal was maintained by the Labour Government after 1945 on the grounds that 'in present circumstances it is considered that as many houses as possible should be kept available for letting by local authorities' (*Hansard*, 1947-8, vol. 445, col. 1167), and that 'where public money and public facilities have been found to provide houses for letting to those in the greatest need, I do not consider that those houses should now be sold to others merely because they have the money to buy them' (*Hansard*, 1947-8, vol. 445, col. 1167); or 'it is contrary to the Government's policy to agree at the present time to the sale of council houses in view of the importance of ensuring that as many houses as possible are available for letting to persons most in need of them' (*Hansard*, 1948-9, vol. 468, col. 186).

Conservative promptings that council house sales should be permitted were justified on various grounds from 'there are hundreds of local authority tenants who would like to buy the house in which they live', to the potential reduction in rates and taxes or the relief of local authorities' and the state's local indebtedness (*Hansard*, 1945-6, vol. 427, col. 1423; 1947-8, vol. 445, col. 1167; 1950-1, vol. 489, col. 2132; 1950, vol. 478, col. 264). The Government continued to refer to keeping as many houses as possible available for letting to those in need. In 1951 the Minister for Local Government and Planning added that 'this means selling public property to private people, and on the whole I think that is objectionable and would arouse resentment from those on waiting lists for housing' (*Hansard*, 1950-1, vol. 489, col. 2132). The expanded role of local authorities in housing and controls on private building involved council housing in catering for a wider section of society. Consistent with Bevan's objection in 1945 to segregated, twilight villages, municipal housing ceased to be restricted to 'the working classes'. Such restrictions were disregarded for some years prior to their removal in the Housing Act 1949 (Nevitt, 1968).

In sharp contrast to the position of the Labour Party, by 1951 the Conservative Party was committed to the relaxation of licensing and the encouragement of policies for sales. The newly elected Conservative government in 1952 issued a general consent which enabled local authorities to carry out sales and notify the Minister only on completion. This general consent was not welcomed by the Labour opposition but was justified by the government on grounds wider than those of housing need or housing policy. Harold Macmillan, the Minister of Housing and Local Government in the new government, stated: '. . . we wish to see the widest possible distribution of property. We think that, of all forms of property suitable for such distribution house property is one of the best' (*Hansard*, 1951, vol. 494, cols 2227–354). This statement bears similarities to many made subsequently by Conservative spokesmen and differs in its attitude towards property and ownership and towards need, groups in need and the appropriate ways of dealing with need from those made by Labour spokesmen at the time.

The general consent issued in 1952 remained unchanged until 1960. The Housing Act 1952 had removed the requirement that the local authority, in selling houses, had to obtain the best price, provided powers for it to limit the resale price for a period of five years and to reserve the right of pre-emption in the event of any proposal to resell or lease within five years. Sale prices for houses completed before 1949 were to be not less than twenty times the net rent and for others not less than the all-in cost of the dwelling. The general consent generally required the local authority to exercise these powers in respect of pricing, pre-emption and resale in a way laid down by the Minister.

The impact of the general consent of 1952 was limited and the issue was defused by the lack of response to the policy. In March 1953 Macmillan stated that 'owing to the time taken by legal and other formalities the number of actual sales completed is at present negligible' (*Hansard*, 1953, vol. 513, col. 642). In October 1954 it was reported that about 2,440 council houses had been sold, and in May 1956 5,825 such houses. This rate of progress was slower than many desired. Although in 1953 60% of local authorities were estimated to be willing to offer houses for sale and 20% were undecided, the slow progress with sales caused some advocates of a policy of council house sales to find fault with local authorities. The request in 1955 that the Minister take steps to ensure that 'most local authority house tenants are granted the rights, with proper safeguards for the councils concerned, to purchase the house which they occupy' (*Hansard*, 1953, vol. 522, cols 191–2) heralded many similar requests. So did the view that 'it is unfortunate that in many cases people living in certain local authority areas have not the opportunities which are often given to people living in joint areas' (*Hansard*, 1953, vol. 522, cols 191–2). However, the ministerial view that local authorities should decide remained dominant.

It appears to have become accepted that the slow rate of progress with council house sales had explanations other than local authority intransigence. Figures for sales were regularly reported. Ministers did not consider it necessary to issue a further Circular encouraging local authorities to sell council houses and denied that there was confusion on the issue. Indeed by 1958 some 31% of local authorities in England and Wales had sold dwellings. It was apparent that demand was limited. Ministers suggested that 'the increasing number of houses being built by private enterprise and sold reduces the number of people who wish to buy council houses' (*Hansard*, 1955–6, vol. 544, col. 204). They also explained that 'many more local authorities have approved the policy of selling council houses, but there has been no demand for purchase' (*Hansard*, 1958, vol. 591, col. 997). However through the 1950s the Conservative Party moved from a prime concern with building targets to one based on a market philosophy. The Housing Act 1961 was designed to channel finance to local authorities with the greatest problems. A new general consent for council house sales in 1960 was designed to prevent sales at unreasonably low prices and bring pricing arrangements into line with those for compensation.

Although interest in council house sales appears to have been boosted by the new Circular, effective demand does not appear to have been boosted. The general consent for the sale of postwar houses set prices at not less than the all-in cost and just as this was not likely to lead to substantial profit on resale, so it was not an attractive purchase prospect. In addition some local authorities and development corporations did not offer dwellings for sale, or they introduced additional restrictions. This element of local autonomy was a consistent feature of policies for the sale of council houses until 1980. Until then the promotion of council house sales had never been the *primary* purpose of housing policy.

Some 16,000 council houses were sold between 1957 and 1964. This level of sales was not of great importance compared with the growth of municipal housing or the expansion of owner occupation. However, preoccupation with building output, with encouraging private contributions to this, with the problems of the private landlord and concern with council house sales formed a policy which contrasted with that before 1951 or after 1964. The policy did not just reflect interest in owner occupation but rather a commitment to the private sector in preference to further extensions of municipal activity.

Nevertheless at the general election of 1964 it was Labour which emphasised housing issues and home ownership. To this extent the consensus over the primacy of encouraging owner occupation was already established and the difference in policy between the parties lay over mechanisms and the role of local authorities in housing. Labour had adopted new increased building targets and identified a larger role for local authorities in house building. Some 50 per cent of new building should be by local authorities for letting. That Labour did not choose to withdraw or revise the general consent on sales issued in 1960 may be regarded as further evidence of policy consensus. Labour was actively in favour of sales in the new towns in order to achieve objectives of social and economic balance. It was also providing leasehold reform giving leaseholders the right to purchase freeholds or extend leases by 50 years. These and other considerations made it undesirable to prohibit council house sales.

In addition, in 1965 the volume of council house sales was insufficient to threaten the government's housing programme. The number of sales was not sufficient to merit actions which would further reduce local autonomy at a time when this reduction was a conventional complaint. This may have been further influenced by the composition of local authorities, especially in urban areas where housing need was felt to be most acute. Labour control of these authorities was radically changed, however, between 1966 and 1969. At the same time the number of sales completed shot up and the balance between the various factors under consideration changed.

At no stage did the Labour government other than reluctantly and passively accept local authorities' wish to sell council houses. This reluctance was evident in requests that local authorities in exercising their power to sell, 'should have regard to the value of the capital asset of which they are disposing' (*Hansard*, 1965, vol. 715, col. 39). By 1967 the reluctance was becoming more marked. The Minister stated that in general 'local authorities ought not to sell their houses where there is still an unsatisfied demand for houses to let at moderate rents and where they intend to continue a substantial programme of building houses to let' (*Hansard*, 1967, vol. 740, col. 1336). The encouragement of home ownership was desirable but was 'primarily a matter for the private sector to deal with' (*Hansard*, 1967, vol. 740, col. 1336).

The wish to avoid a complete ban on sales and to adopt a flexible approach was difficult to achieve. Newly won Conservative majorities in many cities had led to changes in policy which directly contradicted the Minister's stated principle. The main examples

47

were in Birmingham and London. It was suggested that 'during the long years of Socialist control in the City of Birmingham, the building of hew houses for sale has reduced to a mere trickle and that it is necessary now to restore a proper balance'. In these circumstances and in view of the 'widespread desire for extra home ownership' a policy of council house sales was 'right and proper' (*Hansard*, 1967, vol. 743, col. 203). Evidently this was not consistent with government policy, concern with households on the waiting lists or concern over a serious housing shortage in the city.

A new Circular introduced in 1967 was a response to the substantial development of sales in certain areas. It unequivocally expressed opposition to substantial sales in areas with a pressing social need for rented housing. Nevertheless the Circular renewed the general consent. The terms were changed and for the first time required sale prices to be based on market valuations. Because of problems of making valuations and restrictions on resale authorities could reduce values by up to 20% below vacant possession market value provided no loss on the sale was incurred.

Neither these new pricing arrangements nor the views expressed in the Circular restricted the local enthusiasm for sales and it was at this stage that Labour MPs began to press the Minister to prevent or limit council house sales. The Minister replied in terms similar to those used previously. In June 1967 he stated that 'I deprecate the sale of council houses if the sale of them affects the waiting lists and reduces the stock of available houses' (*Hansard*, 1967, vol. 748, col. 1397). Such a view was bound to draw Conservative comment. Mr Rippon predictably stated 'if the Council is satisfied that there is a legitimate demand for council houses to be purchased' the Minister should not 'thwart the electoral will' (*Hansard*, 1967, vol. 748, col. 1397). This line of argument was less likely to influence a decision than the likelihood of 'any substantial erosion of the housing stock in areas where there is still a long waiting list for accommodation at reasonable rents' (*Hansard*, 1967, vol. 755, col. 214). Consequently, the Minister reported in November 1967 that he had 'asked the G.L.C., Birmingham and the other major towns which are embarking on this policy for monthly reports on the progress which is made' (*Hansard*, 1967, vol. 755, col. 214). Although it was expected that there would be fewer sales in 1967 than there had been in 1966, the level of sales had reached a point incompatible with the stated position of the Government. The level had also reached a point where it was attracting adverse comment within the Labour Party.

In 1967 the Labour Party Conference debated, for the first time, the issue of the sale of council houses:

> This Conference views with concern the selling of council houses by local authorities, and sees the hardship this will bring upon municipal tenants who are unable to purchase the accommodation in which they live and upon those who are on waiting lists. It calls upon the Labour Government urgently to review its policy on this question with special regard to the sale of council houses by Tory controlled authorities in many areas where there is still an unsatisfied demand. (Labour Party, 1967, p. 139)

Some impression of attitudes in the Labour Party is provided by the record of the debate. The issue was not felt to be one of whether people should own their homes but 'whether houses paid for out of public funds should at any time be sold for private gain, and to the detriment of families in the greatest need'. Whatever shortages in houses for sale existed, the selling of any council houses where there was unsatisfied need for renting would be 'socially immoral'. Attitudes towards need and the role of rented accommodation in meeting need were dominant. Reluctance to sell public assets was not unrelated to consideration of need. If a local authority 'is compelled in the interests of fair play and justice to work out a scheme which is in point of fact a rationing of their houses, then surely it must be wrong to allow this gathering of homes to be depleted by those that can afford to buy them'. Similarly, it was argued that 'the large stock of municipal houses . . . represents the major instrument through which our community can give housing priorities to those in need'. These views crystallised into objections to the renewal of consent for sales, and objections to the use of any municipally owned land for building for sale.

Replying, the Minister of Housing and Local Government maintained that it was desirable to retain the general consent both because it was wrong to interfere with local authorities and because there were cases where sales were justified. However, he went on to say 'it would not surprise me if a lot of local authorities were praying for the Minister to . . . get them off the hook for what in many cases is an embarrassing electoral commitment'.

The concern which led to the issue of a new Circular limiting sales in the major conurbations does not appear to have been based on an objection in principle. The consistently repeated view was that the policy of council house sales was not an intelligent method of encouraging owner occupation. The policy was financially and socially unwise if pursued unchecked. The mass sale of council houses would seriously affect the ability of local authorities to meet needs as this depended on a regular supply of relets, as well as on new construction. It is in the context of these debates that the issue of a new Circular imposing a limit on the proportion of municipal stock to be sold annually in the major conurbations must be considered. Circular 42/68 represented the closest that any government has come, since 1952, to withdrawing any general consent for the sale of council houses, and not at the same time renewing that consent. In 1968 the general consent was renewed and a quota system introduced. The Parliamentary Report of the 1968 Labour Party Conference included a lengthy statement on the renewal of the general consent for council house sales. The conference condemned the sale of council houses 'which reduces the number of houses available for lettings'. This was accepted by the Minister who stated that sales were either not replaced (in which case there was a loss to the general housing stock for renting) or were replaced at a much higher cost (Labour Party, 1968).

The stance of the Conservative Party remained sharply different. At the Conservative Party Conference of 1967 the housing debate gave some prominence to support for council house sales. Summing up the debate, Sir Keith Joseph stated that the generally agreed policy regarding the sale of council houses had been a success but 'we must not regard it as the limit of our ambitions for altering local authority housing' (Conservative Party, 1967). At the Conservative Party Conferences of 1968 and 1969 the issue was again prominent and was directly referred to in the motion for debate. Opposition centred on the 'Government's doctrinaire attitude in obstructing the sale of council houses to tenants' and to 'Circular' dictation. The government's 'mean and spiteful' decision had frustrated tenants and a policy for which there was a 'clear mandate' in the Greater London Area (Conservative Party, 1968).

The view of the new Conservative government in 1970 was very different and the restrictions on sales introduced in 1968 were removed in line with a pledge in the 1970 election manifesto that 'we will encourage local authorities to sell council houses to those of their tenants who wish to buy them' (Conservative Party, 1970a). This decision to remove restrictions on sales in the conurbations and revert to the terms of the 1967 Circular was designed, the Minister said, 'to encourage the spread of home ownership and to increase the opportunities for tenants of council houses to own the houses in

50

which they live'. He believed 'that those people in bad housing conditions and on housing waiting lists will benefit more from what is being done as a result of this Circular than by waiting for existing tenants to vacate their homes'. Sales would release resources and so help people still on the housing list (*Hansard*, 1970, vol. 803, cols 1340–1).

This encouragement of sales backed by study of successful sales methods was felt to be compatible with 'vigorous action to meet the needs of those who are homeless or inadequately housed' (*Hansard*, 1970, vol. 803, col. 155) with the interests of those on the waiting list and with opposition to local authorities' building for sale. Dedication to the proposition of a property-owning democracy was being tested by the promotion of council house sales rather than by any other action. In a period of house price inflation the issue of council house sales retained an independent, perhaps symbolic status. Conservative members urged further steps and compulsions and considered that 'it is healthy and right that a man should own the house in which he lives and that any means which brings this about can only be good' (*Hansard*, 1970, vol. 807, col. 413).

The Conservative Party Conference in 1970 complimented the government on its 'prompt action in removing unnecessary restrictions on the sale of council houses' (Conservative Party, 1970b). In 1968 the Party Conference had been urged to prepare plans for council house sales so that they were 'all lined up' for the return of a Conservative government (Conservative Party, 1968). Whether or not this advice had been followed, many local authorities in areas previously subject to restrictions responded quickly to their new freedom.

The Conservative Party in opposition had strengthened its commitment to market processes. But in relation to council house sales the enthusiasm also reflected a dislike of the prospect of a nation of council dwellers and had become an end in itself. Consistent with this, much of the earlier caution over both purchase prices and restrictions were put aside. Increasing reference was made to the 'Right to Buy' and decreasing reference to safeguards for the local authority. In addition, local authority representatives were demanding an increased discount for purchasers. At the 1971 Conservative Party Conference, the Minister for Housing and Construction announced his willingness for Birmingham as well as Manchester to sell at a 30% discount instead of 20% and stated: 'I hope that others will follow suit' (Conservative Party, 1971, p. 92). Commenting on allegations that Labour councils, which had replaced Conservative control, were breaking faith with tenants when reversing sales policies the Minister replied that the electoral process was a better method of prevention than his interference with local government. However, he also stated: 'I have a little list of Tory authorities which refuse to sell council houses', and hoped that this list would be shorter in the next year. The whole tenor of debate had changed considerably from that of the 1950s and early 1960s. It was to change further with disappointment at progress with this and other housing policies after the initial interest of 1970–2 which included a growth in the number of council houses sold from under 7,000 in 1970 to nearly 46,000 in 1972. The decline from this peak after 1972 inevitably aroused comment within the Conservative Party.

At the Party Conference in 1972 it was urged that councils which refused to sell to their existing tenants should be compelled to sell at current prices, with an appropriate allowance for the years of tenancy and a restriction of, say, three or five years, before resale was allowed. It was argued that this would still enable authorities to pursue vigorously 'that part of the housing need which is properly their responsibility – that is, concentration on slum clearance and housing of the elderly' (Conservative Party, 1972, pp. 67–70). Whether or not this assessment was accurate and whether or not this argument was widely accepted in the Conservative Party, it appears that a new justification for council house sales was being put forward. In addition to the general encouragement of owner occupation, the dislike of municipal activity, the wish to restrict the role of public agencies, the rights of tenants and electoral calculations there was now the desire to cushion the private market against increased demand emanating from local authority tenants who wished to become owner occupiers. Demands that local authorities be obliged to permit tenants to purchase their houses were not trimmed by unwillingness to breach local autonomy.

At the Conservative Party Conference of 1972, the Secretary of State for the Environment claimed that the provisions of the new rent rebate scheme and the opportunity of purchasing homes at a 20% discount on the market price were greatly to the benefit of council tenants. He deplored:

> . . . those Tory councils which, from what I believe is normally bad advice of their officials, do not offer the prospect of owner-occupation to the tenants. I deplore also those Socialist councils which, out of political doctrine, wish to keep council house tenants as tenants and do not wish them to own their own houses.

He went on to claim 'we are beginning to succeed' and pointed to 'good news' in figures which showed that in the first half of 1972 nine times as many council houses had been sold as in the same period of 1970. This, however, was 'nowhere near enough' and Labour councils should be confronted with tenants 'deploring the manner in which they have been deprived of this very basic right' (Conservative Party, 1972, pp. 67–70).

If the number of council house sales was to be a measure of success in housing policy it was likely that consideration would be given to methods of boosting figures. The general consent was extended to Scotland and departmental Circulars were increasingly admonitory. Permission to increase the discount on purchase price was extended and the Housing (Amendment) Act, 1973 enabled the Minister to authorise or require local authorities to control resale for a period of over five years. This last provision was intended to remove objections which were based on the fear that purchasers would 'make a quick profit' after buying houses. It is probable that, despite these changes, the general rise in house prices had taken the value of dwellings beyond a level which many remaining tenants wishing to buy could afford or were willing to pay. The figures for council house sales were also, no doubt, being held down by the unwillingness of many local authorities to incorporate sales policies into their housing programmes. Criticism of such local authorities, both Labour and Conservative controlled, has already been noted. This criticism was regularly linked with suggestions that Government should make it obligatory for local authorities to facilitate tenant purchase. By 1973 it was clear that any traditional reluctance to interfere with local autonomy, within either the Ministry or the Conservative Party, was wearing thin. The Party Conference was told that the sale of council houses with discount together with the Housing Finance Act could form a basis for election victory.

The Conservative Party election manifesto of February 1974 included a commitment that 'subject to the right of appeal to the local authority on clearly specified grounds, we shall ensure that, in the future, established council tenants are able, as of right, to buy on reasonable terms the house or flat in which they live' (Conservative Party, 1974). Although the manifesto did not state on what grounds appeals would be made, it is clear that the intention was to limit the autonomy of local authorities. It was stated that the number of new home owners would have been still larger had certain councils not opposed the sale of council houses to those council tenants who were willing and able to buy them with the help offered by the government. Frustration, or concern at the failure to maintain sales at a high level, was apparently widely felt within the Conservative Party and merited a considerable change in the approach to local government. By 1973, the number of sales was falling in spite of government policy. This cannot be attributed simply to local authority obstruction. Indeed, the fall was marked in new towns where there was no discretion in implementing policy.

The newly elected Labour Government in 1974 did not adopt the policy of a right to buy but nor did it rescind the general consent to council house sales. The Conservatives in the general election of October 1974 reiterated the promise of legislation to provide council tenants of three or more years standing the right to buy at one-third less than market value, with a five year pre-emption clause. The Labour Government contented itself that it had in March 1974 reissued the general consent with a stern refutation of its predecessor's advice but with no change in the terms to be followed. The government's complacency in this was, no doubt, affected by the dominance of Labour groups in the large urban authorities. However as local electoral fortunes changed Conservative councils began to implement policies within the terms of the general consent but yielding increasing numbers of sales. By 1977 sales were higher than those which had led to the quota system nine years before. In 1978 they more than doubled to the third highest figure ever. Only in March 1979 did the government intervene to restrain this development with a revised general consent preventing sales of empty houses and restricting sales to sitting tenants to those of two years standing.

The Conservative manifesto of 1979 referred to housing under the heading 'Helping the Family' and devoted one and a half pages to it — more than to social security or education or health and welfare or the elderly and disabled. The issues referred to under housing were principally about ownership and the sale of council houses and no reference at all was made to investment in new building or improvement or to homelessness or housing need (Conservative Party, 1979).

The new Conservative government itself was in no doubt about the electoral appeal of its housing policies and in the Debate on the Queen's Speech in 1979 the Prime Minister stated:

Thousands of people in council houses and new towns came out to support us for the first time because they wanted a chance to buy their own homes. We will give to every council tenant the right to purchase his own home at a substantial discount on the market price and with 100% mortgages for those who need them. This will be a giant stride towards making a reality of Anthony Eden's dream of a property-owning democracy. It will do something else — it will give to more of our people the prospect of handing something on to their children and grandchildren which owner occupation provides. (*Hansard*, 1979, vol. 967, cols 79–80)

The government had revoked Labour's short lived Circular, restoring and extending that of 1970 — by increasing discounts. That this Circular was successful is evident in the continued high rate of sales in 1979 and in sales in 1980 (in spite of changes in local control which did not favour the policy). But the innovation in 1979 was the pursuit of legislative action to enforce the right to buy which had been a Conservative commitment since 1974. Any hesitation about local autonomy, or housing need, or the terms of sales, had been overcome and the drafting of the Housing Act 1980 represented a determined attempt to ensure that neither the aspirations of those tenants wishing to buy nor those of the Conservative Party could be frustrated by local opposition.

THE 'RIGHT TO BUY'

By 1980 the debate about the principle of selling council houses was completely changed by the introduction of new legislation providing council tenants with a Right to Buy. It is appropriate to examine this developing legislation in some detail rather than to focus upon the political debate. It is this legislation which signalled the beginning of the new and more extensive phase of privatisation. The new mechanism to achieve privatisation in housing was Chapter I of the Housing Act 1980. This involved major changes in policy and practice towards council house sales. The principal elements and innovations were as follows:

(i) a statutory right to buy replacing local discretion and applying to the bulk of secure tenants with three years' tenancy and to all council properties (with the exception of some dwellings for the elderly or disabled and some other lesser categories);

(ii) a statutory procedure for sale laid down to limit local variation over implementation of the right to buy;

(iii)   very strong powers for the Secretary of State to intervene in local administration of the scheme;

(iv)   a price for sale to be determined on the basis of valuation less fixed rates of discount linked to the number of years of tenancy (in any council or other relevant dwelling); the discounts were those introduced in the general consent of 1979 and rose from 33% (for three years' tenancy) by 1% for each additional year of tenancy up to a maximum of 50%; procedures in relation to valuation, appeal against valuation, cost floors and maximum discounts generally regarded to be very favourable to the potential purchaser rather than the landlord authority;

(v)   discounts to apply even where no pre-emption clause or other restriction existed — save in designated rural areas (where a locality condition or pre-emption clause could be adopted) no pre-emption powers existed; the only disincentive to early resale related to repayment of discount (reduced by 20% of the total for every complete year of residence) if resale occurred within five years;

(vi)   the legal right to a mortgage and the powers of the Secretary of State to determine procedures (for example multiples of income and age limits for mortgage qualification) to govern local implementation;

(vii)   initial freezing of valuations and the existence of a deferred purchase scheme under which the right to buy at the appropriate current price would be kept open for up to two years (upon payment of £100);

(viii)   the continuation alongside the Right to Buy of a discretionary scheme providing local authorities with powers to include properties and persons not embraced by the Right to Buy in their own scheme.

All of these features could be expected to reduce local variation in the operation of policy. Consistent with its policy commitments the government, both in drafting legislation and associated regulations, and in its actions in connection with this policy, has sought to limit local policy obstruction in order to minimise and reduce the numbers of properties and persons excluded from the policy and to adopt an approach which would maximise the opportunities to buy. Other contemporary policies and notably policies towards rents and subsidies have reinforced this policy by increasing the relative advantages associated with purchase.

These and other aspects of the Housing Act 1980 are generally regarded as providing very wide and detailed powers to the Secretary of State to influence local action and to maximise incentives to purchase. Since the implementation of the Act these powers have been consistently used in this way. As is indicated later in this book the nature of central monitoring and intervention have significant implications for central-local relations. The Act does represent a thoroughly centralist compulsory approach to policy implementation.

The sections of the Housing Act 1980 providing the Right to Buy came into operation on 3 October 1980 — less than two months after the Act's final parliamentary stages. The printed version of the Act was not available until very shortly before the commencement date. Although local authorities knew the broad outline of the legislation, some detailed amendments — including those governing the sale of dwellings built for the elderly — were not clear to all those with responsibility for implementation until after the Act was available in printed form.

Chapter 9 of this book details the active role of central government in publicising and implementing the policy and aspects of central-local relations and resistance over the Right to Buy. The determination of Ministers to ensure that local authorities did not delay or divert demand to buy led to unusual monitoring, scrutiny and conflict. The experience however suggested that the Housing Act 1980 was insufficient. By 1983 further legislation was being planned and the general consent governing discretionary sales was amended in July in anticipation. The Housing and Building Control Act 1984 was principally concerned with the Right to Buy. Arden and Cross (1984) argued that given the innovatory nature of the Right to Buy, it had to be anticipated that, even at the time it was passing into law, a technical amendment Act would be required. The general direction of the Act of 1984 was to increase the extent and effect of the Right to Buy and to close loopholes in the original legislation. Part I of the Act comprised 38 of the Act's 66 Sections. And of the 12 Schedules, seven were concerned with Part I. Part I was concerned with the disposal of public sector dwelling houses and the rights of secure tenants.

The Right to Buy was no longer to be restricted to tenants of properties the freehold of which was owned by the landlord. Some 50,000 secure tenants of public leasehold property became entitled to buy leases (as long as this was of 21 years or more for houses and 50 years or more for flats). More dwellings for the disabled were brought within the Right to Buy and there was a general extension to tenants of county councils. The residential qualification for exercise of the Right to Buy was reduced from three years to two, with the minimum discount reduced by 1% to reflect this reduction (33% to 32%). This change brought some 250,000 additional secure tenants within the right to buy. The maximum discount was increased from 50% to 60%. Children succeeding to their parents' tenancies became entitled to discounts as of right rather than under discretion. The definition of periods to be taken into account when determining residential qualification and discount was harmonised and expanded, in particular by inclusion of periods of occupation with a wider range of public or quasi-public landlord. The circumstances in which a discount would have to be repaid were reduced and the procedure which the landlord would have to follow during the exercise of a right to buy were tightened up, to allow less room for delay. Corresponding tenants' obligations were relaxed, allowing greater freedom and time before there was any risk of cancellation of the transaction. The Secretary of State's powers of intervention were considerably enlarged, and a power to grant assistance to those having difficulty exercising the right to buy, including by way of legal advice, assistance and representation were added.

One major innovation was the creation of a 'right to a shared ownership lease' arising when a tenant sought a mortgage from the landlord or the Housing Corporation, and was not entitled to a mortgage amounting to the whole of the purchase price (plus specified related costs). The shared ownership lease would start at a 50% slice of the equity, with a right to buy further shares, and a right to mortgage for initial and subsequent purchases. Subsequent slices of equity would be at 'later' values. Other new rights for public sector occupants (or those who buy from the public sector) included a service charge protection similar to that enjoyed by tenants in blocks of flats, relating to leases and freeholds of houses on estates where continuing services are to be provided. Tenants of charitable housing associations not within the Right to Buy were, following government defeats in the House of Lords, brought within a scheme providing a right to transferable discounts — a sum equivalent to the discount to which they would have been entitled had they been within the Right to Buy — to be used to purchase a different property in the private sector. The Housing and Building Control Act 1984 generally involved a strengthening of the position of central government relative to a local government. It was at least in part a response to concerns about delays and loopholes.

The Housing Defects Act of 1984 can be seen as an unanticipated but necessary offshoot of the sale of council houses. The Act originated because some council house purchasers had bought properties which they were unable to sell. Problems had emerged with dwellings built with precast and reinforced concrete and particularly Airey houses. As a result building societies were reluctant to provide mortgages in respect of these dwellings. Consequently purchasers under the Right to Buy or more probably under earlier general consents, found it impossible to sell or move house. Rather than regard this as a reasonable commercial risk the new legislation enabled the Secretary of State to designate classes of buildings which he regarded as defective by reason of design or construction and which, as a result of these defects having become generally known, had their value substantially reduced. Such dwellings became eligible for assistance where the dwelling had been sold by a public sector authority before a specified cut-off date (usually the date on which designation came into operation) and had not been resold on or after the cut-off date. The assistance involved could be a grant to meet the costs of work needed to 'reinstate' the dwelling or repurchase. The Act in effect protects purchasers of designated defective dwellings against loss. At the same time it pre-empts expenditure and obliges local authorities to take action on sold dwellings in such a class. In the Housing Investment Programmes for 1985–6 and 1986–7 local authorities were permitted to increase expenditure in relation to these obligations but these increases were widely regarded as inadequate. Where reinstatement costs were incurred it can also be argued that councils were forced to incur costs in a piecemeal fashion and on properties where defects made them difficult to sell but did not make them difficult to let or live in. The policy disturbed priorities in a manner rarely connected with concern about living conditions. The Housing Defects Act of 1984 emerged as a classic example of one form of intervention requiring further intervention. The unusual aspect is that in this case the intervention was seen as reducing the role of the state. The consequences of action as with other aspects of this policy were to increase the complexity and detail of legislation and the role of detailed regulation in housing.

While the Housing Act 1985 consolidated legislation on the Right to Buy it was the Housing and Planning Act 1986 which provided the next extension to it. In introducing the Bill, John Patten, the Minister for Housing, Urban Affairs and Construction, stated:

The Bill has one underlying theme – the need to create the conditions in which available resources, private and public, human and financial, are released and mobilised to improve the conditions in which our people live, especially to help improve housing conditions and to tackle problems in the inner cities. I intend to consider housing, inner cities and then planning.

The Bill marks one more stage in the development of the Government's housing policies. We can claim major practical achievements for our housing policies since 1979, but perhaps even more important, we have won the argument about housing in the long term. Quite simply, the intellectual landscape of housing policy has changed, and the centre ground has shifted. Nothing could illustrate that more vividly than the gradual change in the attitude of the Labour Party to our policy of council house sales. That policy has been so successful that we have irreversibly altered the perceptions of tenants of the choices and opportunities which should be open to them . . .

Nobody would deny that public sector housing faces major problems. There is a legacy of bad stock, ageing stock, bad design and poor workmanship. Much good work is being done by housing managers in local government, but too much of it is still remote from tenants and insensitive to their needs. In some authority areas, such basic tasks of property management as keeping down rent arrears and arranging that houses are not left empty are sadly neglected . . .

Money alone is not the answer. Resources were poured into public sector housing in the 1960s and the early 1970s, and look at the result. Too often, the result has been vast, impersonal estates – the concrete desolation in which few people would today choose to live. The problem in public sector housing does not lie with money alone. Of course there is a continuing role for public sector housing, but in the rest of this century and the next century it will be different. It will be smaller and more specialised. The old bureaucratic and paternalistic monopoly which has characterised public sector housing for too long must go.

The keynote is not doctrinaire privatisation, but diversification and an end to bureaucractic control. (*Hansard*, 1986, vol. 91, cols 153–4)

The 1986 Act increased the discounts available on flats under the Right to Buy and increased the protection against high service charges in the early years after purchase of flats. The discount on

Figure 3.1: Discount entitlement under the Housing Acts, 1980–6

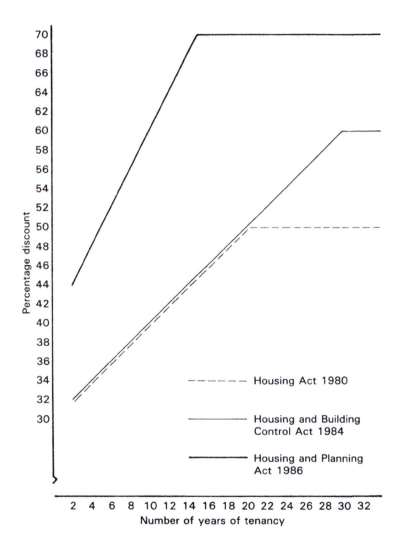

houses remained at 32% (for eligible secure tenants with the minimum of two years' tenancy) plus 1% for each additional complete year up to a maximum of 60%. But for flats the discount started at 44% (for the minimum two years) and rose 2% for each additional complete year up to a maximum of 70%. The implications

61

of this are that tenants of flats qualified for a 50% discount after only five years secure tenancy. After ten years they qualified for a 60% discount and after 15 years for 70%. The gap between their discount entitlement and that of tenants of houses is particularly striking at this 15 year stage (Figure 3.1). The Minister acknowledged that 'sales of flats in the big blocks in our major cities have so far been relatively few' and the Bill was designed to encourage further sales through higher discounts and regulation of service charges and the introduction of a right to a loan in respect of service charges (*Hansard*, 1986, vol. 91, col. 155).

The advantageous position of tenant purchasers was further increased by reducing the period during which discount must be repaid on resale from five years to three. The argument for this change was stated in terms of encouraging labour mobility. The most striking feature of the Housing and Planning Act however is in the shifting emphasis away from the Right to Buy. Perhaps reflecting the changing intellectual landscape and the more pervasive philosophy of privatisation, this Act contrasts with its predecessor of 1984. Whereas 38 of the 66 sections of that Act and seven of its twelve schedules were concerned with the Right to Buy, only five of the 59 sections and none of the 12 schedules of the 1986 Act were so concerned. Even in Part I of the Act concerned with housing, the Right to Buy formed only five of 24 sections and none of the five schedules. The most striking shift within this housing framework was in other provisions relating to public sector housing and to assured tenancies. These provisions enabled local authorities to delegate the management of particular estates; to provide tenants with home loss payments where the local authority has obtained possession in order to redevelop an estate; to provide an additional ground for possession where local authorities wish to dispose of properties under approved redevelopment schemes. The emphasis for demunicipalising had shifted from sales to individual owner occupiers and towards creating a variety of different arrangements for ownership and control. Alongside the Right to Buy and public sector landlordism with more encouragement for training and management innovation there was a concern to draw in private sector resources and break up council housing. The Act required consultation before disposal to a private sector landlord and required councils dispossessing tenants to provide suitable alternative accommodation. It also provided that former secure tenants and their qualifying successors should have their right to buy preserved. The Secretary of State's approval or regulation was required in all these circumstances and represented the ultimate rights. Urban Housing Renewal Unit (UHRU) resources were available to encourage private funds in regenerating or redeveloping areas.

CONCLUSIONS

The Housing and Planning Act 1986 includes safeguards to prevent the effects of the new policy encouraging disposal of council estates from eroding the rights introduced under the Right to Buy and the tenants' charter. However, the new policy is potentially in conflict with previous policies and this and the process of extending the Right to Buy has transformed the simple conception of council house sales into a remarkably complicated and rule bound package. Dismantling public sector housing has proved more complicated in practice than in principle. This reflects the wide variety of properties and circumstances involved and the decisions and resolutions required at various stages of various people. And the complex system has not prevented the emergence of major anomalies. Elsewhere in this book the anomalies associated with the wide regional and local variations in valuations and house prices are discussed. The value of the right to buy varies enormously and not only in relation to length of tenancy. Different rules apply for those in houses than for those in flats. When it is borne in mind that some flats are highly desirable, perhaps low rise house conversions, the anomalies associated with this are more obvious. The prospect of substantial disposals of property leads to further complications with households in the same circumstances having different rights as a result of accidents of their history, legislative changes, local political decisions and ministerial approvals.

The period since 1979 has generally been one of increasing legislative and financial support for selling council dwellings. It has also seen decreasing opposition. The Labour Party's preference for discretionary policies and commitment to repealing the Right to Buy became less strident. In its election manifesto of June 1983 Labour policy had been to end enforced council house sales, empower public landlords to repurchase homes sold under the Conservatives on first resale and ensure that future voluntary agreed sales will be at market value. Following the general election of 1983 Labour opposition to the Right to Buy gave way to acceptance, to an emphasis on investment and the extension of housing rights. By the time of the Housing and Planning Bill 1986 the opposition was supporting amendments tabled in committee to increase discounts beyond the level suggested by government. While doubts and disagreements existed within the Labour Party, the political and electoral judgements left the party joining a Conservative led consensus about the sale of council houses.

4

Welfare Housing for Marginal Groups?

By the early 1980s it was clear that something was happening to British council housing. As illustrated in the previous chapter the most obvious development was its contraction in both absolute and relative terms. This numerical decline was, however, combined with other observable processes. It was increasingly catering for specific groups within the working class such as single parent families and the homeless. And there was a general shift towards market determined opportunities and costs in terms of rising rents and the sale of parts of the existing public rental stock. There was an increasing emphasis on means tested benefits and a poor law ethos was evident in developing attitudes towards council housing. Whilst such attitudes were by no means new they were now more explicit. Homes were now only fit for heroes if they were owner occupied.

These and other factors have combined to inform the view that council housing is becoming a *residual* service and this has been a dominant theme in recent literature concerned with housing trends in Britain (Harloe, 1978 and 1981; Murie and Forrest, 1980; Malpass and Murie, 1982 and 1987; Ball, 1982; English, 1982a and b; Clapham and Maclennan, 1983; Murie, 1983). Whilst there has, however, been a common view of trends the precise social implications of a residualised public housing sector have remained somewhat unclear. Moreover, some of this literature has been rather narrowly concerned with council tenants and council housing and has understated other longer term changes in the British housing market (in particular the decline of private renting) and in the social and economic structure.

TOWARDS POOR LAW HOUSING

Recent literature and commentaries on council housing offer a considerable contrast between the present status of council housing and the picture of council housing between the wars or in the postwar period as providing a privileged or preferential housing status. The stereotypical image of the oversubsidised council tenant living in a desirable dwelling has been replaced by a new stereotype of a disadvantaged group living in less desirable properties, high rise flats, low quality and difficult to let dwellings. Council housing was being transformed from housing for the working classes to housing for the poor. The relatively privileged sections of the working class were now being drawn into home ownership either through the private market or through the sale of publicly owned dwellings. A new hierarchy was developing with council housing now assuming the role of private landlordism. It was tempting to draw parallels between the developing role of council housing in Britain and the historic role of social renting in countries such as the USA and Australia. As Pugh (1980) has observed:

> British public housing has taken its characteristic from its origins as a *working class* housing policy . . . In Australia, public housing is only part of working class housing with other parts in separate home ownership policies. In the United States, public housing has developed as housing for the poor, not generally for the working classes. (p. 168)

The view that council housing was for those unable to participate fully in the mainstream of social consumption was explicit in the statements of the newly elected Conservative government in 1979. In May 1979 Michael Heseltine, the Secretary of State, outlined some of the intentions of the government's housing policy:

> In terms of housing policy, our priority of putting people first must mean more home ownership . . . We certainly intend to ensure that local authorities are able to build homes for those in the greatest need – and I have in mind especially the elderly in need for sheltered accommodation and the handicapped. (*Hansard*, 1979, vol. 967, col. 407)

The general tone of the Conservative administration's housing policy was that *some* people *need* council housing but most people *want* owner occupation. Of course, such a view has not been restricted to the Conservative Party but it has been used to justify a massive reorientation of resources towards sustaining and extending the owner occupied sector. This has further structured preferences in favour of home ownership and fuelled a further round of social surveys that show (unsurprisingly) that a majority of households aspire to owner occupation. As the Minister for Housing and Construction stated in 1984: 'The policy which the Government have followed has responded to the needs and aspirations of the people, while continuing to make substantial provision for public sector housing'. (*Hansard*, 1984, vol. 68, col. 911) Revealed preferences are presented as spontaneous, natural expressions of desire — not as Kemeny would argue the consequences of 'political tenure strategies' which favour the development of one form of tenure at the expense of the others (Kemeny 1981).

FROM WORKING TO NONWORKING-CLASS HOUSING

The view that council housing accommodates increasingly a disadvantaged residuum is indicated by a number of statistical comparisons and trends. Among the evidence frequently quoted in this context is that which shows that a rising proportion of semi-skilled and unskilled workers, of those on low incomes and of those on supplementary benefit, are council tenants. Table 4.1 indicates that as private renting declined there was a steady trend through the 1970s for those dependent on supplementary benefits to become council tenants. And this is not a trend determined by the dominance of the elderly in both categories. Rather it is equally true for the elderly, the unemployed, the sick or disabled and single parent families on supplementary benefit (Table 4.2). The marginal decline in the proportion of benefit recipients who are council tenants since 1982 is hardly surprising given the numerical contraction of the tenure. Moreover, the increasing numbers of home owners in the various benefit categories underline the fact that poverty is not confined to council housing. Nevertheless, it is in the public sector that disadvantaged groups are concentrated. Whilst the percentage increases in supplementary benefit recipients within home ownership have been dramatic, in numerical terms they continue to represent a small proportion of all home owners. Between 1979 and 1984 the owner occupied stock grew from 11.6 million to almost 14 million dwellings. In 1979 just under 4% of home owners were in

Table 4.1: Supplementary Benefit recipients — tenure, 1967–84

Year	Number (OOO)	Proportion of recipients in each tenure (percentages across)		
		Owner occupiers	LA tenants	Tenants of private landlords
1967	2154	17	45	38
1968	2223	17	47	36
1969	2296	17	49	34
1970	2329	17	51	32
1971	2471	17	53	30
1972	2475	17	55	28
1973	2292	17	56	27
1974	2268	17	58	25
1975	2261	17	57	25
1976	2328	18	58	24
1977	2432	19	59	22
1978	2420	18	60	21
1979	2342	19	61	20
1980	2462	19	61	19
1981	2869	19	61	19
1982	3208	19	62	18
1983	3191	21	61	18
1984	3389	21	61	17

Note: There have been changes in methods of estimation and slight variations in figures given for particular years.
Source: DHSS, *Social Security Statistics*, HMSO, London.

Table 4.2: Supplementary Benefit recipients by tenure in 1972 and 1984

Tenure	All recipients	Supple-mentary pensioners	Unemployed	Sick and disabled	Single parent families
1972					
Number (thousands)	2482	1796	269	183	164
	%	%	%	%	%
Owner occupiers	17	18	14	14	7
LA tenants	55	53	53	60	63
Tenants of private landlords	29	29	33	26	30
1984					
Number (thousands)	3389	1550	1069	151	425
	%	%	%	%	%
Owner occupiers	21	22	22	22	14
LA tenants	61	61	55	65	75
Tenants of private landlords	17	16	23	13	12

Source: DHSS, *Social Security Statistics*, HMSO, London.

receipt of supplementary benefit. The comparable figure for 1984 was 5%. In comparison, in the same period council housing shrank from 6.8 million to just over six million dwellings. Over the five-year span the proportion of council tenants who were on supplementary benefit rose from 21% to 34% (DHSS, annual). And if rent rebates are also taken into account it emerges that 63% of council tenants were receiving some form of means-tested assistance by 1986–7 (*Hansard*, 1987, vol. 108, cols 346–8).

The General Household Survey provides trend data on the association between socio-economic groups and tenure for the period 1971 to 1984 (OPCS, 1972–86. These data cover a period in which private renting has declined from providing for 16% of all households to 12% while home ownership grew from 49% to 59%. Local authority renting grew from 31% to 34% in 1981 and declined to 29% in 1984. It is the socio-economic groups which were most highly represented in private renting at the beginning of the period where changing housing tenure is most apparent. Thus while there has been little change in the distribution of professionals, employers and managers between tenures other groups have experienced a change. The pattern of change — and the data must be treated with some caution — implies a polarisation. The intermediate non-manual category is less represented in private renting, has not increased its representation in the public sector and has increasingly become a category of owner occupiers. In contrast the majority of semi skilled and unskilled workers have remained in the rental tenures. The more uncertain picture for junior non-manual and skilled manual workers does not diminish this polarisation. In 1984 88% of professional workers were owner occupiers and only 1% were public sector tenants. At the other extreme only 36% of unskilled workers were owner occupiers and over half were in council housing.

Most striking of all is the rising proportion of households in council housing with economically inactive heads. Demographic shifts towards a more elderly population are producing this effect across the population as a whole but it is particularly evident in the public sector. Between 1979 and 1984 the proportion of households with heads aged 65 or over rose from 33% to 37%. And households with single elderly members rose from 20% to 25%. Overall, the proportion of households with economically inactive heads rose from 41% to 53%. If those unemployed but seeking work are added, the proportion of non-working heads rises to nearly two thirds of council tenancies. Further detail on unemployment is provided by the Labour Force Survey (OPCS, 1986). For example, among young married household heads aged below 25 the proportion of council tenants out of work was 39%. The comparable figure for owner occupiers was 5%. Similarly, among married male council tenants of working age who were not seeking work 60% gave long-term sickness or disability as their main reason. Other studies have reported similar findings. White (1983) found that two-thirds of the long-term unemployed were in council housing. The combined effects of an ageing tenant population, low levels of new building, selective disposal through sales and the impact of economic recession is rapidly transforming council housing from working-class to nonworking-class housing.

In examining longer term trends, Hamnett (1984) has recently carried out a comparison of the 1961, 1971 and 1981 Censuses to demonstrate the development of socio-tenurial polarisation. In doing so he points to important problems of comparability:

> Although the classification of the population into the now familiar 17 standard socio-economic groups has remained essentially unchanged since the 1961 census, the classification of different occupations into the various SEGs was changed in both the 1970 and 1980 Classification of Occupations. Whilst the changes in 1970 were not large enough to significantly affect the comparability of the 1961 and 1971 census results, the 1980 changes posed more of a problem. What appears to have happened is that a number of occupations previously classified under SEG4 (professional) have been down-graded into SEG5 (intermediate non-manual). Similarly, a number of occupations previously classified under SEG6 (junior non-manual) have been reclassified in SEG7, 10 and 15 (semi-skilled and personal service workers). (p. 395)

And there is a further problem:

> . . . the increase in the proportion of economically inactive households from 1961–81 was so large that it significantly reduces the proportion accounted for by all the other SEGs in the council tenure and all but the professional and managerial group in the owner-occupied tenure. This distortion is magnified by the very considerable changes which took place in the sizes of the different economically active groups over the period. Whereas the number of households headed by a professional, managerial or other non-manual householder increased by 50 per cent and 15

per cent respectively over the twenty year period, the number of households headed by skilled, semi-skilled and unskilled manual workers decreased by seven, three and 24 per cent respectively. In the circumstances, the direct comparative analysis of tenure by SEG for all households (including the economically inactive) is rendered rather problematic. (p. 396)

Hamnett is nevertheless able to conclude that: '. . . the semi-skilled and the unskilled have become increasingly concentrated in the council sector relative to the other SEGs' (p. 397). More generally he asserts that the continued selective impact of privatisation will reduce the public housing sector '. . . to an increasingly residual role housing the oldest and the poorest in the worst property' (p. 404). Further evidence supports this general picture. Thus while in 1963, 26% of households in the bottom three income deciles were council tenants, in 1985 this has risen to 57% (see Table 4.3). And over the five-year period 1980–5 a comparison of the income structures of owners and council tenants reveals an increasing income polarisation between the tenures. In 1980 32% of public sector tenants were in the top five income deciles. By 1985 this had fallen to 23%. And other statistics are no less significant in their implications of a growing social division. For example, in 1984 70% of council tenants had no formal education qualifications, 41% had no telephone and 66% had no car. The comparable figures for mortgaged owners were 28%, 7% and 13% respectively (OPCS, 1986).

Table 4.3: Household income distribution: owner occupiers and local authority tenants, 1980 and 1985

Base decile group	Owner occupiers		LA tenants	
	1980 %	1985 %	1980 %	1985 %
1	4	1	17	24
2	7	5	15	19
3	8	8	12	14
4	8	9	11	11
5	9	10	12	9
6	10	11	9	8
7	12	13	8	6
8	13	14	6	5
9	14	14	5	3
10	15	15	4	1

Note: Because of rounding columns may not total 100.
Source: Derived from Department of Employment, *Family Expenditure Survey*, 1980 and 1985.

RACE AND GENDER

Discussion has so far focused on income and social class divisions in housing. Indeed this has been the dominant preoccupation in analyses of the progressively residual status of council housing. Arguably, however, there are other dimensions which are emerging as of equal if not greater importance in understanding the transformation in the public housing sector. In some areas council housing is serving an increasingly black population and there is some evidence of a progressive feminisation. Some estates have high concentrations of single parent families and the ageing of the council tenant population has meant an inevitable increase in single elderly female tenants. Between 1978 and 1984 there was a 6% increase in female headed households bringing the overall proportion to 36%. According to the General Household Survey (OPCS, 1984) 50% of divorced or separated females are council tenants. This compares to 37% of divorced and separated males. And among certain ethnic minority groups the likelihood of being a single parent tenant is considerably higher. A survey carried out by the Policy Studies Institute in 1984 (Brown, 1984) provides the most up-to-date evidence on the connections between ethnicity and tenure. As regards single parenthood the PSI study found that 55% of white lone parents were council tenants. Among households of West Indian origin, however, the percentage rose to 74%.

As regards more general associations between tenure and race the PSI study confirmed the high level of home ownership among Asian households (although an increasing number are now entering council housing). Indeed, with the exception of household heads in professional or managerial employment the level of home ownership is higher among Asian than white households. Whereas only 40% of white heads of households in semi-skilled manual employment were owner occupiers in the PSI survey, this was true for 70% of Asians. Such crude comparisons conceal, however, a polarisation of housing conditions within owner occupation between ethnic groups. Studies such as that by Karn et al. (1985) have brought out the qualitatively different nature of owner occupation among ethnic minorities in cities such as Birmingham and Liverpool. This is also evident in the PSI study where typically Asian and West Indian households own older, smaller, low value properties with inferior amenity provision, in poor condition and in poor localities. This polarisation between black and white is, however, more evident in the council sector. Black council tenants tend to be in the less desirable parts of the stock and in older, smaller properties. They are more likely to be in flats and the flats are more frequently on the upper floors:

> Only one in ten black tenants has a detached or semi-detached house, compared with more than one in three white tenants, while over a third of black tenants live in flats with entrances above ground floor level, twice the proportion found among whites. (Brown, 1984, p. 307)

This disparity in dwelling types between blacks and whites has increased over the last decade due to a combination of processes. Blacks have made up a higher proportion of new tenants — and new tenants are more likely to be allocated flats rather than houses. A number of studies have elaborated on the factors behind the unequal treatment of black applicants (Simpson, 1981; Phillips, 1985; Henderson and Karn, 1987).

Asian and West Indian households are geographically concentrated in London and the West Midlands conurbation. And there are marked concentrations in inner urban areas. The coincidence of high numbers of black households and high numbers of council flats in the inner cities does not, however, offer a simple explanation for the disparities in dwelling types occupied by different ethnic groups. Whereas within the white population there is a marked polarisation between inner and outer urban areas this is not the case for West Indian households. In inner London, Birmingham and Manchester 55% of whites live in flats. In the rest of London, the West Midlands Metropolitan County and Greater Manchester the proportion in flats falls to 18%. The comparable figures for the West Indian population, however, are 39% and 31% respectively.

RESIDUALISATION — OF WHAT, OF WHOM AND WHERE?

The weight of the statistical evidence combined with a longstanding bi-partisan encouragement of home ownership have contributed to a wide acceptance of a changed role for council housing. These underlying trends were well established by the late 1970s but they have been accelerated by policy developments and socio-economic changes in the 1980s. In 1978 Harloe speculated on pressures which would lead to a reduction in 'the further development of the public sector to a residual role' (Harloe, 1978, p. 14) and went on to describe a future public housing sector which would be seen as an

'. . . ambulance service concentrating its efforts on the remaining areas of housing stress and dealing with the variety of "special needs" such as the poor, the homeless, one-parent families, battered wives and blacks' (p. 17). More recently, Malpass and Murie (1982) refer to residualisation as:

> . . . the process whereby public housing moves towards a position in which it provides only a 'safety net' for those who for reasons of poverty, age or infirmity cannot obtain suitable accommodation in the private sector. It almost certainly involves lowering the status and increasing the stigma attached to public housing. (p. 174)

There is also reference to changes in the stock of dwellings. Ageing of the purpose built stock, acquisition of sub-standard dwellings, identification of design faults, the unpopularity of certain dwelling types such as high rise flats and the sale of more popular dwellings have been seen as reducing the quality of the stock.

These changes have coincided with another and arguably more thorough phase of residual policy — in which investment and subsidy for council housing have been reduced and increasingly associated with provision for special needs. There have been other periods of residual policy (Merrett, 1982) but the importance of the present phase is its coincidence with the consequences of longer term and wider trends in the housing market. Residualisation, therefore, rarely refers to a *single* feature of council housing. Rather it emphasises process and a direction of policy change which involves a number of dimensions. Most of the debate, however, is within and about housing, state policy in housing and specific housing processes and this emphasis does encourage examination of certain limited propositions. We have drawn out five which emphasise different elements in residualisation:

(i) *The size of the public housing sector*. It may be implied that the size of the public sector has implications for the nature of the service (Clapham and Maclennan, 1983, pp. 9–10). Thus it is implied that a decline in the size of the public sector is *per se* evidence of residualisation or conversely that a sector which houses over one in four households cannot be residual or comparable in role to the US or Australian public housing sectors which cater for well below 10 per cent of households. But this kind of proposition, however it is mobilised, does not stand up to closer examination. A small public sector prior to and in the period immediately after 1919 was not residual but is generally assumed to have catered for relatively affluent sections of the population. And a large sector could be more uniformly used by the poor, be of lower quality or involve fewer rights for tenants.

(ii) *The quality of the stock.* Some discussion concentrates on the nature of the quality of the housing stock and would emphasise social and physical obsolescence in council housing as the key factor in residualisation. Reference to absolute standards must be complemented by reference to relative standards. Even if council housing was uniformly of relatively low physical standard, other factors could offset this. However, in a situation of considerable variability in the standards both of council housing and of dwellings in tenures with which it could be compared issues of residualisation in terms of quality alone would not be tenure specific.

(iii) *The characteristics of tenants.* Implications that the characteristics of who uses the service are the major elements in residualisation are equally open to question. A one-class service could be a service in which users had considerable power and could receive a high quality of housing accommodation. Equally a situation of 'social mix' is not incompatible with low quality service. 'Mix' in terms of age or income or family type may also be a product of life cycle changes and does not imply that entry is possible for a mix of households or that choice is involved. In this context, however, mix in terms of social class is more indicative of the social role of council housing. This is particularly significant in discussion around those marginalised in the labour market and is developed below.

(iv) *The nature of policy.* Much of the housing literature refers to a residualisation solely in terms of policy (Malpass, 1983). However periods of residual or minimal intervention through council housing operate against a background of housing developed in other policy periods and in a changing environment where the subsequent effects of policy may differ from those intended. Thus residualisation as a process referring to policy alone does not embrace changes in the service provided.

(v) *Means testing.* Is residualisation associated with the extent and nature of means testing, the selectivity of subsidy and the methods of payment for services? While this will reflect policy aspects and the characteristics of tenants (and is therefore assumed under other headings) it is also of limited meaning without being set in the context of other measures of the quality of service or of changes in employment, income and occupation.

Each of these propositions, by emphasising particular aspects of change in council housing, is in conflict with a view of residualisation as a trend and process involving a variety of dimensions. In addition, however, these dimensions are essentially aspects of housing itself. But what is happening to council housing is the product of wider processes of economic and social change — and indeed of changes in other tenures as well as council housing. It is in relation to this wider context that *residualisation* begins to summarise an important convergence of changes.

It is important to distinguish between a static notion of a residual service and residualisation as a dynamic process concerned with the direction of development. The social policy literature tends to emphasise aspects such as the (minimal) level of state intervention, concern with temporary and emergency situations and the dominance of market-relationships in distribution. Reference is also made to issues of stigma and a link can be made to literature concerned with dependency and the relationship between parties in an exchange. In this perspective a feature of redistributive services is that they are given and received as a right of citizenship and serve an integrative function which is not damaging to the identify of the recipient (see, for example, Wilensky and Lebeaux, 1965; Pinker, 1971; Titmuss, 1973, 1974; Mishra, 1981). In contrast receipt of services may 'spoil' identity and involve stigmatisation. This may be an intention of policy (as with the poor law), a consequence of implementation and the prejudices of administrators, or a product of dependency. But it is a characteristic of residual services. Mishra (1981) refers to residual services in relation to a continuum at the other end of which are structural (totally need-based) social policies. Residual on this continuum equates with *laissez faire* approaches and refers to an ideal-type notion of totally market-based distribution. Discussion of changes in council housing, however, is not concerned with establishing that council housing has become a residual service, but rather with the direction of development.

In this context the social policy literature offers some other perspectives which are relevant. The references made to stigma and exchange relationships imply that analysis of the direction of policy change should refer to the terms on which services are received, to the style of management, and to issues of social reputation. It should not be concerned solely with the formal structure of policy and its stated goals. In a similar way analysis of the social division of welfare involves not just the pattern of direct provision of a particular service but of fiscal and occupational welfare and of the pattern of benefit from services. Thus it is not just the visible public service delivery which should be examined but the development of fiscal and occupational welfare and the economic and political forces of which they are the consequence. Titmuss (1976) emphasises the division of labour and sectional, group or class aims and the translation of aims ostensibly set for society as a whole into sectional aims 'invariably rewarding the most favoured in proportion to the distribution of power and occupational success'. The framework for analysis of changes in welfare and in the social division of welfare is a broader understanding of social and industrial change and of the implications of these changes in a complex society marked by inequalities in political and economic power. Field (1981) has pursued this aspect by referring to the different 'welfare states' associated with tax allowances, company fringe benefits and inherited wealth. More recently, Harrison (1986) has taken up similar issues and argued that urban theorists have tended to work with stereotypical images of the welfare state, with crude public and private distinctions and have neglected a social division of welfare which is more complex and relates to the social division of labour. And recent work on the structure of housing assistance has highlighted the significance of occupational benefits (Salt, 1985; Forrest and Murie, 1987).

The role of 'urban managers' has also been a prominent aspect of debates on the delivery of housing services. The early literature in this area emphasised a certain degree of autonomy in the social control and allocative functions of, for example, housing officials, building society managers and social workers. Discussion, however, moved from emphasising the independent social control functions of managers to a view that it was not the managers themselves who determined the nature of services and their delivery but constraints deriving from the nature of the state and the structure of the economy. In other words although managers allocate scarce resources they do not themselves create scarcity. While those who distribute resources occupy an important position in the urban structure, these institutions are located within a system which heavily constrains and determines the nature, size and distribution of the social surplus. In this respect it has been argued that rather than state social services having a major influence on the development of society their development will reflect changes in the economic structure and the needs of the dominant class (see, for example, Pahl, 1975; Means, 1977; Williams, 1982). One of the implications of this is that to explain what is happening to a particular service it is necessary to have some conception of the broader pattern of economic change and its impact on different classes.

Essentially, however, this approach takes us beyond examination of the service itself and the relationship existing in its delivery and involves reference to the changing social environment and the relationship between these changes and the service concerned. In other words we must link housing market change with segmentation and differentiation in the labour market, the expansion of the residuum or surplus population, the social division of welfare and processes of social and spatial polarisation.

MARGINALISATION AND RESIDUALISATION

The relationship between council housing and a group variously described as 'the surplus population' (Friend and Metcalf, 1981), 'the stagnant reserve army' (Bryne and Parson, 1983) or 'the excluded' (Sipila, 1985) is crucial in understanding the changing structural position of state housing. Whilst *residualisation* describes the direction of change, *marginalisation* explains why such developments have been possible. The marginal poor, those with least political and economic muscle, have always been in the worst housing. What is new is the close association between this group and state housing. When council housing was of higher quality and status it served a skilled working class with the poorest sections of society concentrated in the privately rented sector. Good quality council housing was a product of both political struggle and strategic necessity. The residualisation of the state housing sector is a product of the diminished necessity for living labour and the exclusion of a substantial minority from the labour market. That minority, representative of spent or surplus labour power, is disproportionately accommodated by the state housing sector, whilst the employed majority is increasingly in owner occupation.

Council house sales and disinvestment from council housing sits then within a more general restructuring of the welfare state. Collective housing provision is being progressively peripheralised and the dominant mode of state-subsidised individualised provision is becoming more segmented and stratified. The rapid growth of unemployment and underemployment and the consequent weakening of certain sections of organised labour has facilitated a renegotiation of welfare provision. The political constraints preventing a reduction in the 'burden' of collective provision have been reduced. And there are dimensions to council housing which explain why the restructuring in this area of welfare provision has been more radical and extensive. Council housing, unlike comprehensive education or the National Health Service, has always been a minority provision for the working classes and its erosion has no obvious, immediate impact on the services available to others. The political and ideological support for council housing has been steadily diminishing since the early 1950s and public support for council housing is limited (Taylor-Gooby, 1982; 1983). For a government preoccupied with public expenditure issues, council housing has provided an easy target.

One element in this is that the management of council housing has remained insulated from political demands and has not reflected consumer demand. Political demands have been for more and better housing — from 'homes fit for heroes' through to the mass housing of the 1960s. Political responses have been about building and investment. The concern to provide more houses was not complemented by a parallel concern for management and maintenance. Households who valued the dwelling they had obtained did not necessarily value the other attributes of public landlordism. What is involved in these developments, however, is not a privatisation of welfare in terms of disengagement by the state. Rather it is a polarisation of forms of provision. At one extreme, and typically associated with council housing, we have the development of state dependent communities where marginalised groups subsist increasingly on a range of stigmatised and pressurised subsidies. At the other are the highly mobile, high earners extracting the maximum benefit from mortgage interest tax relief, capital gains exemptions and other tax concessions (Forrest and Murie, 1987). What is common and what cuts across tenures is a reassertion of the connections between housing opportunities, housing conditions and earning power.

The appropriate concepts for discussion of residualisation derive from a broader literature concerned with political power, and socio-spatial divisions. An understanding of residualisation in relation to public housing provision involves more than an appreciation of housing market changes. Among other things it involves analysis of the ways in which various processes interact to change the supply, distribution and other characteristics of council housing. It involves an understanding of the uneven impact of economic change, the general reorientation in state intervention and the political marginalisation and the powerlessness of some in relation to the formal channels of political influence. And it involves reference to the increasing dominance of market relationships within a housing system characterised by haphazard and regressive subsidies and by differential mobility and capacity to accumulate wealth. Moreover, there are significant spatial dimensions to this process captured crudely but not completely erroneously in references to North-South divisions, and inner-outer city polarisation.

Taking a broader view of these socio-spatial relationships locates the restructuring of housing provision in the context of the restructuring of the economy. And it moves the discussion into that dangerous area referred to by Saunders (1981) as 'the problem of the receding locus of power' (p. 135). In other words, is it possible to construct a satisfactory explanation for developments in council housing without reference to changes in the international economy and international labour markets? In this book we are offering a partial explanation of part of the social world. It is essential, nevertheless, to link the privatisation of Britain's public housing stock with certain other social processes in order to see residualisation as both historically and spatially specific. It is unnecessary to delve into world systems theory to illustrate the connections between current housing policy, privatisation, fiscal reorientation and the weakening of organised labour. Patterns of housing provision reflect and act upon the enormous variations in growth and decline within and between regions and cities. The decaying council estates in the inner city and the urban periphery are high rise monuments to that uneven development. As Smith (1984) has observed: 'Uneven development is social inequality blazoned into the geographical landscape and it is simultaneously the exploitation of that geographical unevenness for certain socially determined ends' (p. 155).

At root therefore we are concerned with contemporary forms of the reproduction of inequality. Rather than examining parts of the housing market and features of services we need to approach these issues through an understanding of the creation and transformation of residual and marginal groups. If particular parts of the housing market are increasingly providing for these groups that in itself has implications for the service and its development. It is against this background that changes in the nature of state intervention and the relationship between state housing and wider economic processes can be assessed. The context for discussion of residualisation involves issues of economic, political and social power. As Miliband (1974) has stated:

> The tendency is to speak of the poor as the old; or as members of fatherless families; or as the chronic sick and the disabled; or as the unemployed and their families; or as the low paid. But old age, membership of fatherless families, sickness and disablement, and even unemployment are not as such necessarily synonymous with poverty. Some people in these categories are not poor at all: to be an old, ailing and an idle *rentier* may not be agreeable, but neither need it mean poverty. Nor even are some members of the middle classes who happen to be low paid 'in poverty', since they may command a variety of private resources which enable them to live in reasonable comfort. (p. 184)

A focus on the marginal poor rather than special needs emphasises the shift from manufacturing to service employment and changes which have marginalised some groups in relation to the labour market. Progressive deskilling, structural and cyclical unemployment do not affect all groups equally. Those in unskilled manual work and the personal service sector are most harshly affected (Showler and Sinfield, 1980). Permanent non-employment rather than temporary unemployment has the effect of politically and economically marginalising substantial sections of the population.
As Miliband (1974) argues:

> The poor are an integral part of the working class: but many of them constitute its inactive part, and are self-excluded from the defence organisations which organised labour has brought into being, and which have helped to improve its bargaining position. (pp. 181–8)

Old age, chronic sickness and disablement are not conducive to autonomous, sustained and effective pressure and low paid adult wage earners include many in industries with a large number of small enterprises with a contracting and ageing labour force and an above average proportion of low paid women workers. The economic and political powerlessness of the marginalised poor is both a factor in their becoming and remaining as tenants and in the quality and terms of service they receive.

CONCLUSIONS

We have explored some of the broader processes affecting the role and status of council housing. Neither the size of the sector, the quality of the stock, the characteristics of tenants nor the specific features of policy are in themselves determining or necessary factors in the residualisation of council housing. Whilst accepting the legitimate use of 'residual' as an indication of general trends we have stressed its limitations as an explanatory device. For explanation we have to look to *marginality* as the pivotal concept.

Those on the social and economic margins are characterised by powerlessness as much as any other characteristic. It is in relation to these considerations that the strengthening of the relationship between unemployment, low wages, supplementary benefit recipients, unskilled and semi-skilled work and public housing is significant. And changes in the management style of council housing, its size, quality of stock or level of subsidy are symptoms or consequences of the powerlessness of those using the service to resist reductions in standards or to achieve high standards. The marginalised poor have always tended to be in the worst housing in each tenure and to have greatest difficulty in negotiating access to and through the housing market. What is new in the present situation is the level of concentration in the public sector especially as the private rented sector declines and in a period in which the 'residuum' is increasing in size as a consequence of economic and employment changes. At the same time public policy decisions in connection with new investment, rents, subsidies and council house sales are reinforcing the service-specific disadvantages associated with the consequences of broader social and economic changes.

There is little economic pressure to maintain and improve services. In terms of housing needs the social costs of industrial restructuring fall increasingly on the public sector. To minimise the financial implications of this there is considerable logic in minimising the costs associated with direct housing provision. Increased rents and means testing, council house sales, reductions in public expenditure and subsidy in that part of the housing market are logical reactions to a situation where those affected are unable to respond to increases in cost with wage demands or political action. Furthermore the extent to which tenants have a common interest in opposing increasing rents and demanding an improved quality of service is potentially undermined by opportunities for the more affluent to avoid or escape the impact of these developments through exercising their right to buy. Government policy for the housing needs of the 'productive' labour force are promoted through owner occupation rather than policies towards council housing. With continuing high unemployment and technological change these differences will become more marked. Stigmatisation associated with dependency is likely to be exacerbated by these developments and by any tendency for managers, policy makers and a wider range of agencies to adopt authoritarian (poor law) policies for the undeserving underclass. The very status of tenant in an increasingly consumer and credit-oriented society is likely to add to the disadvantages of the marginal poor. Access to credit and accumulation of wealth are significant attributes of home ownership. While not all home owners benefit or benefit equally there is a consumer power associated with individual home ownership which is denied to non-owners and which exacerbates the economic and political powerlessness which contribute to housing status.

The marginal poor are not exclusively in council housing but they are numerically and spatially concentrated in that tenure. That relationship will, however, vary between localities and may well change over a relatively short period. Socio-tenurial relationships will, for example, change dramatically if government policies begin to transfer substantial sections of public housing into private or quasi-public hands.

It is important to stress, however, that neither council house sales nor the housing policies of the Thatcher administrations provide adequate explanations for the deteriorating housing opportunities and housing positions of those on the social and economic margins. Whatever housing policies had been pursued over the last ten years or so, the decline of private renting, the uneven impact of recession and transformations in the labour market would still have had a major impact. The shape and tone of the Conservative government's housing policies have accentuated and accelerated the trends referred to earlier, but these developments were underway long before 1979. Moreover, similar processes can be observed in other European countries (Burton *et al.*, 1986). As governments reorient their fiscal priorities towards areas of greater strategic importance, social housing in its various forms comes under attack and scrutiny. Whether it is rising homelessness in Amsterdam or London, the deteriorating position of migrant workers in France or West Germany, inner city deprivation or peripheral urban isolation, explanations are rooted in the relationship between political powerlessness, economic marginality and social undesirability.

There are, of course, limits to how far housing policy can compensate for deep-seated changes in the labour market and in patterns of social inequality. Unfortunately, recent policy priorities and evolving patterns of provision have tended to exacerbate rather than ameliorate the housing position of the marginal poor in Britain.

These sorts of considerations go beyond a particular focus on council housing and relate to the overall transformation of tenure relations. Residualisation is not tenure specific but it is in the council housing sector where these residualising forces find their most concentrated expression. It is in the council sector where we find the greatest spatial concentration of those sub-groups within the working class which are suffering the most profound effects of chronic unemployment and the reduction of welfare benefits. Also, in a culture of market dominance these groups and sectors excluded from market-determined, individualised consumption are, by definition, residual.

But it would be highly misleading to isolate council housing from a more general restructuring of social relations in the housing sphere. Residualisation is part and parcel of the general reorientation in state intervention towards the facilitation of market processes and away from direct provision. This process of commodification (Murie and Forrest, 1980; Forrest and Williams, 1984) or recommodification (Harloe, 1981) of housing combined with other economic and demographic changes has an impact upon all tenures. And these processes were established well before the current phase in policy. Within the general context of economic decline and cutbacks in public expenditure we have an increasing dependence on private housing provision and a growth of single person households, single parent families, the unemployed and the elderly. The sociology of housing is now more complex (perhaps it always was) with more unconventional household structures, more complicated housing histories and a growing recognition that a higher level of home ownership generates new problems requiring new forms of state intervention.

It is not processes within housing such as the relative sizes of the tenures or housing quality which are producing a residual council sector. It is the product of broader social and economic processes. The key processes include the increasing dominance of the market which economically marginalises certain groups within housing and other areas of consumption; the political marginalisation of a new underclass which is effectively excluded from formal channels of political expression, and thus has little bargaining power; the uneven spatial impact of the economic recession. Council housing tends to be concentrated in those areas most adversely affected by the current economic recession. Industrial decline and the restructuring of the British economy is reflected in different but related forms of marginalisation: economic, political and spatial. The residualisation of council housing is part of that process. The particular relationship between marginalisation and council housing will, however, vary between localities. In this way it would be wrong to expect uniformity in the pattern of residualisation. Underlying social and economic processes combine with the specific nature of local housing markets to produce different forms of residualisation. This conception of housing market change is elaborated later in this book.

5

Financial and Electoral Aspects of Housing Privatisation

Commentaries on British housing policy since the mid-1970s, and especially since the election of the Conservative government in 1979, have tended to emphasise two prominent features: reductions in public expenditure and more pervasive support for the growth of home ownership. Both academic and policy debates have been preoccupied with fiscal crisis and fiscal austerity. Ministers have frequently referred to 'what the country can afford' as the background to public policy and public expenditure decisions (Murie, 1985). While there have been significant changes in the pattern of public expenditure, it would be misleading to attribute changes in housing policy as logical and inevitable outcomes of fiscal constraint. An overemphasis on expenditure cuts directs attention from some of the other shifts which have occurred in housing policy. Rather than representing what has happened in terms of reductions in public expenditure it is more appropriate to set the reshaping of housing policy against a broader fiscal background which highlights a reorientation rather than an overall reduction in expenditure in the housing sphere.

In this chapter the broader context for the operation of the mass sales policy of 1980–6 is outlined. In particular the importance of capital receipts is emphasised. It is argued that the scale of capital receipts has emerged as an important element in the policy — considerably larger than anticipated. The fiscal opportunity created by sales has been an added bonus for a policy with strong political and ideological support. Indeed, council house sales have represented a happy coincidence of ideological, electoral and financial imperatives. Some of the evidence concerning the electoral impact of the policy is considered later in the chapter.

THE HOUSING POLICY CONTEXT

The principal features of housing policy in Britain in the period after 1979 are crucial to the policy of selling council housing. Sales have not occurred in isolation or against a background of high investment or increased supply. Whilst the government's actions in housing were preoccupied with the expansion of home ownership, the overall shape of housing policy had to coincide with taxation and public expenditure priorities. A plethora of new housing policies as well as a continuation of existing measures to assist owner occupation was involved. But this is more accurately seen as a shift in the nature, direction and methods of intervention rather than a simple withdrawal from or abandonment by the state of housing.

The whole policy package has reflected a view that there is a limited continuing role for social housing. This role is largely concerned with meeting the needs of a residual population who cannot fend for themselves in the owner occupied market and cannot obtain adequate housing in the privately rented sector. This tendency to see public housing as only *necessary* for the elderly, the poor and certain groups with special needs is apparent. It is fully consistent with a view that public resources should be channelled towards those in 'real need'. What has been anomalous in the 1980s is that policies to encourage private ownership channelled more resources towards those with higher incomes, more wealth and better housing.

In simple terms, public expenditure on housing has experienced a series of cuts both prior to and since the election of the Conservative government in 1979. The severity of the cuts has relegated the housing programme from a major to a minor one. As set out in the annual Public Expenditure Survey Committee (PESC) White Paper (HM Treasury, 1987), spending was to fall in real terms from £6.6 billion in 1979–80 to a planned £2.1 billion in 1985–6 (at 1983–4 prices). This represented a reduction of 68%. Housing's share of total public spending was to fall from 7% in the mid-1970s to an anticipated 2% in 1987–8. The housing programme was to bear the lion's share of public expenditure cutbacks and in 1980 the Select Committee on the Environment noted that planned housing cutbacks accounted for 75% or more of all public spending reductions (House of Commons Environment Committee, 1980).

The result, in terms of investment and subsidy, can be briefly summarised. Public sector dwelling starts and completions have fallen dramatically. Council house building has declined to its lowest peacetime level since 1925; the availability of council housing to rent has declined for the first time in peace time since 1919; exchequer subsidies benefiting council tenants in general have been drastically cut and council rents have risen substantially. The reduction in general assistance subsidy for council housing and in housing capital expenditure generally has been achieved partly by switching housing subsidy expenditure into the social security budget. As rents have risen, so the costs of means tested assistance with housing costs have increased. The cash cost of rent rebate and supplementary benefit equivalent assistance to local authority and new town tenants in Great Britain was £630 million in 1979–80. In 1986–7 the estimated figure was £2,418 million. This rate of expenditure increase was much greater than that for social security benefits generally (which increased by a multiple of just over two in the same period) (*Hansard*, 1987, vol. 108, cols 346–8). Taken in conjunction with the increasing proportion of supplementary benefit recipients who are council tenants, this amounts to a significant switch in method of subsidy and does not involve as substantial a *reduction* as appears from examination of housing expenditure.

Crucial to all these assessments is the inclusion or exclusion of items as public expenditure on housing. There are two significant categories which do not appear in the housing public expenditure programme. Firstly, there are items counted as public spending but incorporated in other programmes, of which the most important, Housing Benefit, appears in the Social Security programme. Secondly, there are items which are not defined as public spending at all, of which the most important include tax foregone as a result of mortgage interest relief, exemptions from capital gains tax of capital gains made on sales of main residence, and discounts to purchasers of council housing.

Moreover, the structure of tax relief and other subsidies to home owners has not been reviewed. The cost of mortgage interest relief increased by almost five times in real terms between 1963–4 and 1983–4. In 1985–6 official estimates put the cost of mortgage interest relief at £4,500 million. This is considerably greater than the cost of the total public expenditure housing programme (£2,834 million) and compares with total capital expenditure (net of capital receipts) of £1,669 million. The value of exemption from capital gains tax was tentatively estimated at a further £2,500 million. And discounts for council house sales under the 'Right to Buy' involved a new set of subsidies (with a new set of inequities). Discounts or receipts foregone averaged some £1,000 million per annum between 1980 and 1986. The limit on mortgages qualifying for tax relief was raised in 1983 at a cost of some £60 million in revenue foregone. Expressed in these ways, it would seem that either there has been little systematic application of notions of what the country can afford, or the view is that the country can afford substantial support for home owners but not for housing investment or other housing subsidies.

The other important dimension to this is the regressive nature of tax expenditures associated with owner occupation. Only some 55% of owner occupiers have mortgages and benefit from tax relief on mortgage interest. Those who do not benefit include elderly and low income outright owners. The regressive nature of mortgage interest tax relief is increased because tax relief is also given at above the basic rate of income tax. In 1985–6 some 690,000 tax payers with mortgages and with total incomes below £4,000 p.a. benefited on average from £360 tax relief. At the other extreme those with incomes over £30,000 benefited to the tune of an average £1,300 (*Hansard*, 1987, vol. 109, cols 411–12). The regressive nature of tax relief on mortgage interest is further complicated by equity withdrawal and its application to low priority housing expenditures or expenditures other than for buying or improving a dwelling (see, for example, Kemeny and Thomas, 1984). In 1987 the government changed the arrangements for assistance with mortgage interest payments through Supplementary Benefits by restricting such help during the first three months of claims for certain categories (at a saving of £23 million). This further differentiated between the support available to lower and higher income households. The average annual value of mortgage interest tax relief in 1985–6 was £560, compared with the average Exchequer subsidy for council dwellings of £105 (£345 if dwelling of local authorities not receiving subsidy are excluded). Rate fund subsidies per council dwelling amounted to an additional £167 per dwelling.

There is, of course, considerable debate as to whether these tax expenditure items should be counted as subsidies to home ownership and hence as public spending even though they are essentially income foregone rather than moneys paid out (see, for example, Ermisch 1984). Such debates, however, often proceed as if the exercise was merely technical, resting on accounting conventions. Balance sheets may not be politically constructed but they certainly have political implications.

In contrast to the story of the finance of home ownership, changes to the system of assistance with housing costs for tenants with the lowest incomes had to be made at nil extra cost. The new housing benefit system introduced in 1983 involved a loss of benefit for some and a perpetuation of key benefit problems. Additional administrative difficulties left this scheme with the appearance of the government's worst managed piece of 'reform'. Since its introduction the income levels on which housing benefit is paid have been substantially reduced and government has consistently attempted to reduce the cost of the scheme.

If the items referred to above are included in the public expenditure calculus then the impact of public expenditure and taxation decisions affecting housing is somewhat different from the official picture. As Table 5.1 shows, in 1986–87 £2.8 billion will be spent on the housing programme, and almost £3.5 billion on Housing Benefit. In addition, mortgage interest tax relief will cost some £4.5 billion and capital gains tax exemption some £3 billion. Public spending on mortgage tax relief was about a third of the level of spending on the housing programme in 1979–80, but in 1986–7 it is expected to exceed it substantially. Reductions in rates of interest and in the rate of taxation reduce the tax expenditure bill but these are offset by the continuing rise in house prices.

Table 5.1 indicates that even if we confine our analysis to include Housing Benefit, mortgage interest tax relief and the conventional housing programme, the total of expenditure, after remaining fairly constant in *cash terms*, rose sharply after 1982–3. What we have seen is a major transfer of resources from those programmes conventionally included in the housing programme (mainly subsidies to public sector housing and new capital investment) towards other expenditure (Housing Benefit and support to home owners). In Government's own terms this must count as a major failure in public expenditure policy. On the other hand the nature of the transfer, from the public sector to the support of home ownership, from investment to subsidy, and from the subsidisation of the production of public housing to the subsidisation of individual consumption reflects other priorities which have tended to override expenditure considerations.

In addition, within the official housing programme not all expenditure is on council housing. In the period of reduced expenditure since 1979 a striking feature has been that both the voluntary sector (housing associations) and home owners have obtained an increased share of this expenditure. In 1979–80 the housing association sector accounted for some 15% of net capital spending; by 1982–3 this had risen to 48% and it was expected to remain near that level subsequently. Figures for new completions (Table 5.2) indicate the

Table 5.1: An alternative housing programme (£ million cash)

	1979/80	1980/1	1981/2	1982/3	1983/4	1984/5	1985/6	1986/7	1987/8
Public sector[1] housing expenditure									
Gross capital expenditure	3,152	2,928	2,564	3,313	4,010	3,973	3,440	3,440	3,661
Net capital expenditure (i.e. gross expenditure less value of capital receipts from the housing programme)	2,680	2,328	1,518	1,436	2,054	2,169	1,669	1,554	1,959
Planned housing programme (capital and revenue)	4,522	4,464	3,131	2,695	3,140	3,250	2,834	2,815	3,204
'Other' housing programmes									
Housing Benefit	932[2]	1,039[2]	1,395[2]	1,663[2]	2,517	2,833	3,126	3,454	3,518
Tax relief on mortgage interest[5]	1,639	2,188	2,292	2,456	2,767[3]	3,500	4,500[4]	4,500[4]	
Exemption from capital gains tax[5]			2,800	3,000	2,500	2,500	2,500	3,000	

Notes:
(1) Local authorities, new towns, Housing Corporation and home loan scheme.
(2) Estimated figures. Payments of housing costs to supplementary benefit applicants not included in Housing Benefit for 1979–83.
(3) Excludes £55 million (Mortgage Interest Relief at Source).
(4) *Hansard*, 30.1.87, Cols 411–12.
(5) Public Expenditure White Papers indicate that estimates to these items are subject to large margins of error and are affected by changes in the operation of this tax.
Source: Annual Public Expenditure White Papers 1979/80 to 1986/7; *Hansard*, vol. 49 (25.11.83).

Table 5.2: New public sector dwellings for rent completed — England, 1979–87

	Local authorities	Number of dwellings New Towns (incl. rehabs)	Housing associations
1979–80	70,000	7,000	16,700
1980–1	65,400	7,700	19,700
1981–2	39,700	7,800	14,800
1982–3	27,200	2,100	9,700
1983–4	28,000	1,100	14,000
1984–5	26,700	1,600	13,400[1]
1985–6	20,800	600	12,100[1]
1986–7	16,071	384	9,781

Note: (1) Estimate based on *Housing and Construction Statistics*, HMSO.
Sources: Cmnd 9428, Cm. 56 and *Housing and Construction Statistics* Part 1, no. 29.

relative success of the voluntary sector in maintaining its capital programme.

It should also be borne in mind that by 1985–6 housing associations' sales of dwellings under low cost home ownership schemes (5,300) exceeded those for local authorities (4,500). New town activity in this area was greater than either of these (5,600).

For home owners the significant development has been the six-fold increase in improvement grant expenditure between 1979–80 and 1983–4. In 1983–4 improvement and thermal insulation grants, most of which are paid to home owners, accounted for some 28% of local authority gross capital expenditure. Expenditure on home improvement grants fell from £911 million (250,000 grants) in 1983–4 to £735 million (195,000 grants) in 1984–5 and was expected to level out at around £440 million (125,000 grants) thereafter. This was still more than double the level of expenditure of 1981–2 (HM Treasury, 1987).

FISCAL OPPORTUNISM

The picture of fluctuations in *gross* capital expenditure understates what has been achieved. The results of the 'Right to Buy' for council tenants and other measures have been to produce an enormous increase in the level of capital receipts especially for local authorities. These rose four-fold between 1970–80 and 1982–3 and have remained remarkably steady since then. As a result the level of *net expenditure* (gross expenditure less capital receipts) by local authorities has been reduced much more significantly than has gross expenditure. In cash terms, new net capital expenditure by local authorities in 1982–3 was only about 29% of its 1979–80 level. Although gross spending increased during 1983–5, the continuing high level of capital receipts reduced the rate of increase of net spending which even in 1984–5 only reached 73% of its 1979–80 level in cash terms. The estimated out-turn for 1986–7 only represented 48% of the 1979–80 figure in cash terms. The government has used the level of capital receipts to permit the reduction of net new investment on a dramatic scale. In 1982–3 net capital expenditure by local authorities (£744 million) barely exceeded the net level of funding of housing associations by the Housing Corporation (£680 million).

As was stressed in Chapter 1 capital receipts associated with the housing programme have been more substantial than those from any other programme despite the publicity which some sales (such as British Telecom) have received. Table 5.3 shows the annual level of total receipts from the housing programme and compares these with receipts from the government's wider privatisation programme. Housing capital receipts between 1979–80 and 1985–6 totalled £9,527 million. Other privatisation activities generated £7,732 million. In each year up to 1984–5 the housing programme yielded more capital receipts than all the other acts of privatisation together.

Table 5.3: Capital receipts from housing and other privatisation (£ million), 1979–86

	Housing programme	Other
1979–80	472	370
1980–1	603	405
1981–2	1,045	493
1982–3	1,877	488
1983–4	1,955	1,142
1984–5	1,804	2,132
1985–6	1,771	2,702

Sources: Cm 56, Cmnd 9702.

Housing capital receipts grew rapidly to 1982–3 and remained relatively steady until 1987–8 when they increased (Table 5.4). Local authority receipts form by far the largest part of all receipts and with the growth of council house sales initial receipts from these

Table 5.4: Capital receipts from the housing programme (£ million cash)

	1979–80	1980–1	1981–2	1982–3	1983–4	1984–5	1985–6	1986–7[1]	1987–8[2]
Local authorities	448	568	976	1,739	1,761	1,628	1,600	1,670	2,315[3]
Housing corporation	4	13	29	75	110	87	101	115	68
New towns	20	19	38	63	84	88	68	98	50
Central government	–	4	2	0	0	1	2	3	3
Total	472	603	1,045	1,877	1,955	1,804	1,771	1,886	1,702
Gross capital expenditure	3,152	2,933	2,564	3,313	4,010	3,973	3,440	3,440	3,661
Net capital expenditure	2,680	2,330	1,518	1,436	2,054	2,169	1,669	1,554	1,959

Notes: (1) Estimated out-turn.
(2) Plans.
(3) Figures given in the Chancellor of the Exchequer's autumn statement, November 1987. The previous estimate in Cm 56 was £1,581 million.
Source: Cm 56, Cmnd 9702.

Table 5.5: Sources of local authority housing capital receipts (£ million cash)

	1978-9 £m	%	1979-80 £m	%	1980-1 £m	%	1981-2 £m	%	1982-3 £m	%	1983-4 £m	%	1984-5 £m	%
Sales of land and other assets	24	5	38	8	96	17	99	10	135	8	103	6	105	7
Initial receipts from sales of dwellings	138	28	122	27	186	33	532	55	1,017	58	970	54	830	57
Repayments of sums outstanding on sales of dwellings	40	8	43	10	53	9	89	9	282	16	445	25	315	22
Repayment of loans by private persons	293	58	241	54	216	38	240	25	287	17	246	14	185	13
Repayment of loans by housing associations	7	1	4	1	16	3	15	3	18	1	25	1	30	2
Total	501	100	448	100	568	100	976	100	1,739	100	1,789	100	1,465	100

Source: Cmnd 9143 II and 9428 II and *Hansard*, vol. 49, 23.11.83, cols 212-13.

Table 5.6: Local authority capital receipts

	1981-2	1982-3	1983-4	1984-5	1985-6	1986-7 provisional	1987-8 forecast
Sales (thousands)	128.2	181.2	122	91.4	83.5	90	80
Average market price (£ thousand)	16.9	16.9	18.5	21.6	23.7	27	29.4
Discount %	42	42	42	44	46	46	47
Private finance ratio %	41	57	70	72	80	80	80

Source: Cm 56.

sales have supplemented repayment of loans as the major element (Table 5.5). In the peak years for receipts (1983–4 and 1987–8) sales were actually lower than in 1982–3. Evidently the value of receipts does not fluctuate in line with sales. Table 5.6 illustrates that two other factors are crucial. Firstly, the ratio of private finance increased from 41% in 1981–2 (it had been 30% in 1979 and rose to 80% in 1985–6) to 70% in 1983–4. Secondly, the increase in average market price after 1982–3 has had an important impact on receipts. These two factors rather than discount levels have had an important impact. They will continue to have an important impact in the future. In 1986–7 half the number of sales will yield equivalent cash receipts to those in 1982–3 and 1983–4. In 1987-8 a new peak is associated with a relatively low rate of sales.

Council house sales in the period 1979–84 were more than double those in the previous 40 years combined and have exceeded those completed in the whole history of council housing. Neither sales nor capital receipts are a totally new phenomenon. The main difference in recent times however is in the relationship of the volume of capital receipts to capital expenditure. The local authority housing capital programme has become substantially self-financing. Proceeds from the sale of housing assets have been set against the public sector borrowing requirement which has been considerably smaller as a result.

A number of arguments could be advanced over whether capital receipts 'should' be reinvested in housing. Without entering into such a debate at length it is apparent that the housing sector's demands on 'new' funds have been more substantially cut than is compatible with the level of gross capital expenditure. Housing capital receipts in recent years have protected the housing programme from even more severe cuts. At the same time they have prevented housing coming into sharper conflict with other expenditure programmes.

Receipts on this scale are of importance in the whole public expenditure calculus. They are not matters of housing policy alone and the interest of the Treasury and economic policy considerations are important. Council house sales offered a politically acceptable mechanism of relieving fiscal problems in a period when central government expenditure associated with economic recession was rising. In a situation in which central rather than local government spending has been out of control a 'raid' on local assets has reduced the borrowing requirements of local authorities and helped to achieve monetary and public expenditure policy objectives. The raid has been achieved firstly by introducing a mandatory policy under which purchases are very attractive and sales and receipts are high. Secondly, it has been achieved by restricting the use of capital receipts by individual authorities and so ensuring that the total volume of receipts did reduce the PSBR. The mechanism under which this has occurred can be outlined briefly. Prior to 1981 reinvestment of capital receipts was only possible to the extent explicitly allowed through loan sanction. Loan sanction provided under the Housing Investment Programme system took capital receipts into account in determining the total level of investment possible but they were not referred to in determining allocations to individual authorities. The choice for local authority Treasurers was between writing off housing debt and thereby reducing Housing Revenue Account (HRA) loan charges or letting receipts accumulate, and crediting the interest to the HRA. In either case a lower level of borrowing would be required to finance local authority activities and the PSBR would be reduced.

Under the new arrangements introduced in 1981–2 (following the Local Government Planning and Land Act 1980), local authorities were able to augment their block allocations for capital spending by drawing on capital receipts obtained during the year and any accumulated unspent receipts. But this facility was limited by central government in two ways. Firstly, there were restrictions on the proportion of receipts which could be drawn upon in this way. Secondly, it was taken into account in decisions on housing investment — resulting in lower HIP allocations. The initial 50% level by which HIPs could be augmented from housing capital receipts meant that if local authorities used the facility to the maximum there would still be substantial unused receipts which held PSBR down. Government has subsequently reduced this 50% in stages (to 20% in 1987) and it seems probable that the facility will be removed altogether under new arrangements. The effect of these increased restrictions is to further ensure that capital receipts can be offset against new restricted levels of expenditure rather than simply flow out again in higher levels of spending. It ensures that the bulk of any higher than anticipated receipts do not result automatically in higher spending. It enables the Chancellor to control the use of such receipts — to reduce borrowing or to use them for other purposes rather than being channelled to housing or other local authority services.

Furthermore it should be acknowledged that not all local authorities have chosen to use the facility to augment their HIP expenditure. In some years there has been an underspend because of this. In other years the sum of individual local decisions has resulted in spending above that anticipated by central government and further restrictions have been introduced (Leather and Murie, 1986; Malpass and Murie, 1987).

For local authorities the picture was more complicated. Firstly, the dwellings concerned represented a flow of service as well as a realisable asset. Even if full asset values could have been realised, the situation would have been complicated. The unique nature of housing assets affects the capacity to replace them through reinvestment — at best it is similar dwellings in similar locations which could be provided. But a second factor highlighted the different positions of local and central government over the issue. Discounts and controls on investment of capital receipts helped central government to achieve its fiscal objectives but introduced elements which would normally be resisted by local authorities. These were selling at below market value, failing to represent the ratepayers' collective financial interest in the disposal of assets and restricting autonomy in decisions over the use of receipts.

It is important to recognise that neither the initial volume of receipts nor the maintenance of the level of receipts in face of declining sales was anticipated. The volume of capital receipts was difficult to calculate at the outset. Not only was the number of sales uncertain but so were discount levels and sale prices. Furthermore the proportion of the capital value of sales yielding an immediate capital receipt was unpredictable. With the introduction of higher discounts and of the 'Right to Buy' a higher rate of sale could be anticipated. However, apart from a forecast of 62,500 sales made in April 1980 the only semi-official statement of expectations was the figure of 120,000 incorporated in the Housing Investment Programme allocations for 1981–2.

The Environment Committee in 1981 (House of Commons Environment Committee, 1981) drew on these estimates and took the view that the highest level of sales which could be safely assumed between 1981–2 and 1983–4 was 100,000 a year although considerable fluctuation between years was possible. In the light of these calculations the level of sales actually achieved has been high. Three other factors have also had an impact on the level of sales and capital receipts. In 1979 the average discount on sales was 27%. Under the 'Right to Buy' it rose to 42% (1981 to 1984). Higher discounts under the new legislation of 1984 increased this to 46% (1985 to 1987). The consistency of discount levels is mainly explained by family cycle effects and the remarkable consistency in age and length of tenancy of purchasers. It is the other two factors to which unexpectedly high levels of receipts can be attributed. Estimates of the level of receipts are crucially dependent on the split between cash or private funding which deliver immediate capital receipts and local authority mortgages which yield a slow trickle of capital receipts. Both the Department of the Environment and the Environment Committee made assumptions based on the operation of previous discretionary policies. At the end of 1979, and in 1980 prior to the 'Right to Buy', initial payments represented 30% or less of capital value. This was broadly in line with past experience. With the right to a mortgage increasing access to council mortgages and with the building societies showing reluctance to commit themselves or earmark funds, there seemed few grounds on which to expect private funding to become more important. In practice, however, private finance and initial payments have represented an inordinately higher proportion of capital value (Table 5.6). These figures combined with the high rate of sale explain the unexpected 'windfall' gains associated with sales. They also partly explain why rapidly falling sales did not result in dramatically falling receipts. This latter aspect however is even more dependent on what happened to capital values. Put simply, while the average market value of dwellings sold remained relatively stable in the early years of sales (£16,900 in 1981–2 and 1982–3) when numbers of sales were highest, the valuation of council dwellings then moved upwards in line with the trend in house prices. The average market price of sold dwellings rose to £18,500 in 1983–4, £21,600 in 1984–5 and to £23,700 in 1985–6 (Table 5.6). The provisional figure for 1986–7 was £27,000. Thus as the number of sales has fallen the capital value of each sale has risen, discounts have not substantially risen to erode this (in percentage terms) but private finance has increased to deliver a larger share of the capital value as an immediate repayment. Moreover, the earlier sales with council mortgages continue to yield a steady flow of repayments over a longer period thus helping to sustain the level of capital receipts as sales decline.

This combination of factors has consistently meant that the programme has exceeded expectations in terms of the delivery of capital receipts. The flow of funds into and out of building societies and the changing attitude of these societies to meeting mortgage demand rather than rationing mortgages has been crucial. Public expenditure White Papers in the 1980s have consistently underestimated capital receipts. The mid-year revisions of housing capital expenditure have consistently involved upward revisions of capital receipts. A fiscal bonus has added to the attraction of the policy and the role of the housing programme as a source of 'revenue' rather than a drain through spending has been greater than anticipated. The clearest example of this process is the most recent one. The Public Expenditure White Paper of 1987 estimated that local authority housing capital receipts would be £1,581 million. The Chancellor's autumn statement in 1987 showed public spending undershooting the planning total by about £1 billion and showed unexpectedly high housing capital receipts (£2,315) to be an important factor in this. This 'windfall' gain was associated partly with a higher level of sales but more importantly with rising house prices and values. It enabled the Chancellor to increase housing spending — but not to the full extent possible. In effect, net housing expenditure was cut by 20% compared with the previous forecast and housing capital receipts enabled the Chancellor to adjust other programmes where real rather than illusory increases were made. The scale of unanticipated capital receipts in relation to these adjustments demonstrates that housing was a key element in spending plans and adjustment of plans.

At present it seems likely that capital receipts from the sale of council houses will remain steady in cash terms unless there are new measures to stimulate them. Interest in purchase by tenants has shown a steady decline despite more generous incentives. Many tenants who remain in the public sector may be too old or too young to consider buying, may be occupying an unattractive dwelling or may simply be too poor, unemployed or insecurely employed. Family cycle factors will maintain sales for some years although housing stock factors are likely to be an increasingly important limiting factor. Faced with this any government wishing to maintain or increase housing capital receipts would need to consider other ways of selling the council stock. Emergent government policy suggests a shift from incentives for individuals to purchase towards a greater emphasis on the wholesale transfer of local authority estates to private or quasi-public organisations.

THE ELECTORAL IMPACT OF COUNCIL HOUSE SALES

In all of these changes government's attitude to council housing occupies a prominent position. Not only has its historical development represented a major and very visible ideological irritation for the Conservative Party but its management and allocation has been one of the major areas in which locally elected councils could exert influence on the local social and economic structure. With the extension of home ownership high on the political agenda (with its symbolic value as the extension of citizenship rights) the disposal of council houses has been in the forefront of a broader ideological crusade. These ideological considerations have, however, progressively been complemented by fiscal imperatives. And these fiscal imperatives have neatly meshed with the perceived electoral advantages gained in the promotion of council house sales. For the Conservative Party such advantage had immediate and longer term aspects. The apparent popularity of the policy would appeal, at least, to the instrumental working-class vote (Marshall *et al.* 1985). And home owners, it was believed, would be more likely to form a longer term allegiance to the Conservative Party. The position of the Labour Party was necessarily more pragmatic.

Labour's conversion to council house sales was influenced in part by the evident electoral popularity of the policy — or at least the clear electoral unpopularity of opposition to sales. This popularity had long been accepted and promoted by the Conservative Party. Moreover, whilst those who advocated sales appeared to offer a clear and uncomplicated package of rights and benefits, opposing arguments seemed abstract, complex and predominantly negative in content. To suggest that a substantial number of sales occurring in the context of substantial disinvestment in public housing was liable to have an impact on transfers, exchanges and initial access, or that the benefits on offer were highly uneven or possibly illusory, was a difficult message to convey. Whilst it seemed to demand self-sacrifice on the part of those tenants who wished to buy, little of immediate benefit was apparently on offer to those tenants in the least attractive parts of the public housing sector. This is evidenced by the overwhelming support for the policy even among those tenants who are unlikely to benefit. Although various surveys (see Chapter 6) show that the vast majority of remaining tenants are unlikely to buy their existing dwellings, some 60% of tenants questioned in 1986 expressed unqualified support for the 'Right to Buy' (Jowell, Witherspoon and Brook, 1986). This does, however, suggest that to read off the electoral impact of opposition from the apparent support for sales would be to overstate the case. Party positions on selling council houses could well have influenced those tenants who fully intended to exercise their 'Right to Buy'. But for the majority of tenants who continue to show no interest in purchase the impact on voting behaviour must be more ambiguous and the issue of sales less central to their material interests. And local examples demonstrate that support or opposition to council house sales is clearly a contingent factor in political success or failure. The pioneering and unambiguous support for council house sales within Birmingham's Conservative group had little local political impact in the 1960s (Murie, 1975). Equally, the majority Labour group in Norwich, campaigning on an explicitly anti-sales platform in 1979, strengthened its political position (see Forrest and Murie, 1986a, and Chapter 9).

The electoral impact of council house sales is enmeshed in a wider sociological and psephological debate around the relationship between tenure and class and the coalescence of processes of tenure and class transformation. At the heart of the debate is a longstanding claim that increased levels of home ownership among the working classes is a central factor in the decline of the Labour Party. Put crudely, the 'privatised' working class are more likely to vote Conservative. The literature on this topic displays a considerable dispute between those who argue for the continuing importance of class as the basis of British party politics — occupational class and voters' image of their class being major determinants of voting behaviour — and those who argue for a substantial weakening of the ties between classes and parties. In the latter school there is a further split between those who see class cleavages replaced by volatility or pragmatic voting behaviour and those who see a new basis for electoral divisions. It is in relation to the latter that housing tenure has been identified as an important dimension of voting and as a key element in consumption sector cleavages which cross cut occupational class. Analyses of a 1983 electoral survey show that within occupational classes, the greater the dependence on forms of collective consumption provided by the state the greater the likelihood of voting Labour. Thus manual workers in council-owned homes, without a private car, and reliant on state health, education and social services gave Labour a lead over Conservative of 36 points, but among controllers of labour with three or more consumption items provided by the market, the Conservative lead was 64 points, and among comparable non-manual workers it was 41 points (Dunleavy and Husbands, 1985; Johnston, 1987). Johnston's analysis of 1983 voting shows that while the usual relationship between occupational class and voting held (the petty bourgeoisie and salariat strongly pro-Conservative and anti-Labour, the working class the strongest Labour supporters) so did that relating to housing tenure.

Owner occupiers preferred Conservative to Labour by a ratio of about 3:1, whereas council tenants preferred Labour by about 2.5:1. Owner-occupiers were 50% more likely to vote Alliance than were council tenants; the latter were more likely to abstain. Members of the third tenure category (mainly renters from private landlords) were much closer to the owner-occupiers than to the council tenants in their relative preferences for Conservative and Labour; like the council tenants, however, they were less pro-Alliance and more likely to abstain.

Very substantial within-class variations exist according to housing tenure. Within the salariat and the routine non-manual classes, for example, whereas the Conservative:Labour ratio among owner occupiers was almost 4:1, Labour was preferred (by a 2:1 majority in the latter class) among council tenants. Even in the petty bourgeoisie support for Labour was almost as strong among the small number of council tenants as it was in the salariat, though the Conservatives retained a plurality of votes. For foremen and technicians, the ratios ware similar to those for the routine non-manual workers. In the working class Labour had a 3:1 lead over Conservative among council tenants, but a slightly smaller percentage of the vote than did Conservative among owner occupiers.

Johnston adds to this picture by including regional variations. He concludes:

> . . . that the evidence for significant spatial variations in voting behaviour within groups of voters defined by both occupational class and housing tenure is strongest for the working class category — manual workers other than foremen and technicians. Among the owner occupiers in that class, the propensity to vote Labour was significantly greater in the older industrial areas and regions than in the 'booming' areas of small town and agricultural south eastern England, by a ratio of as much as 4:1. (p. 118)

He suggests that:

> . . . where exchange values are high and rising, members of this class whose major item of consumption is obtained through the private sector tend to desert the party (Labour) which is closely associated with public sector housing provision . . . Where exchange values are low, however, Labour obtains significantly above average support from this group. (p. 119)

Among working-class council tenants the spatial variations are even more substantial. One explanation offered by Johnston is that:

> Those who live in the northern regions and the older industrial areas have been socialised in strongly pro-Labour milieux and most live in dominantly working class areas, especially the council estates. They provide few voters for the Conservative party and above average support for Labour. In the south east, the growing smaller towns and the agricultural areas the milieux are however very different. Prosperity is greater, life chances more buoyant, labour organisation relatively weak, local government dominated by Conservative, and class consciousness more difficult to sustain. As a consequence, support for Labour is significantly below average. (p. 119)

Preliminary results from current research conveys a similar message. Prior to the 1987 general election only 26% of households in Cheltenham in council housing areas expressed support for the Labour Party. In contrast, among owner occupiers in Consett only 6% supported the Conservative Party.

Johnston's conclusions from this kind of evidence are salutory for the whole debate:

> Most social theory, and certainly most social theory that informs voting studies, is compositional in form: it allocates people to categories (such as occupational class) and assumes that they will act as members of those categories. Such theory pays no regard to the role of context, to the milieux in which behaviour patterns are learned and enacted. Yet membership of a category is something whose meaning must be learned, almost certainly in the local environment, and variations in the nature of milieux can thereby influence how people learn about their compositional situations and how to act accordingly. Thus compositional theories must be complemented by contextual theories, people learn about what they are, and what that means, in environments which are locally as well as nationally structured . . .

> How people voted in 1983 in Great Britain reflected not only their occupational class and housing tenure, but also where they lived. Local context was apparently an important influence on how people interpreted being working class, in both major housing tenures. (pp. 120–1)

It may further be argued that where people lived and their housing history and experience of housing is an important influence on how people interpret being owner occupiers or being council tenants and on whether membership or changing membership of these categories has a short or long term impact on voting behaviour.

The evidence on voting behaviour in Britain is, however, far from conclusive and the changing relationship between tenure and class remains ambiguous. In this debate Heath, Jowell and Curtice (1985) in particular have taken issue with the view that there has been a major political realignment and that there is a new working class who are more inclined to vote Conservative. Moreover, as they point out, *associations* are not necessarily *causal* connections. They suggest that: '. . . in the case of housing it is quite plausible, and perfectly consistent with the data, to argue that social attitudes influence one's choice of housing rather than the other way round' (p. 49). To support this claim they show from their analysis that: '. . . purchasers of council houses were . . . more likely to have been Conservative voters in 1979 than were council tenants as a whole' (p. 49). Equally, however: '. . . purchasers were no more likely than other tenants in 1979 to defect to the Conservative or to abandon the Labour Party' (p. 49). In the 1983 election support for the Labour Party among Labour tenants and Labour purchasers (according to their voting behaviour in 1979) was roughly equal.

Thus, for Heath, Jowell and Curtice one's consumption location in the housing market does not cross cut occupational class position as regards political effects: 'Housing does not form the basis for a new cleavage in British politics but rather acts as a separate source for the maintenance of class cleavage' (p. 54). In this debate, it is important however to recognise that what the evidence purports to show (or not show) depends crucially on prior definitions of the class locations of particular groups. The housing tenure structure may be changing but so too is the class structure. Occupational class appears, therefore, to remain paramount in the shaping of political attitudes because whilst the level of home ownership has increased the size of the working class has declined. The proportion of the working class who are council tenants, in these terms, has remained relatively constant over the last 20 or so years. And on the same definitions the level of working-class home ownership has shown only a marginal increase. This might offer little comfort to a political party which sees its fortunes tied closely to the traditional working class but it does call into question the independent effect of housing tenure on political attitudes. This could, however, change if new and more extensive forms of privatisation in housing began to accelerate housing tenure change and outstrip the rate of change of the class structure. In other words independent housing effects could emerge if the proportion of council tenants in the working class (on the strict Heath *et al.* definition) did begin to fall, and if as a result of sales in the longer term communities began to change their character. Certainly there is some suggestion from the 1987 election results that privatisation policies in London were an important determinant of political fortunes but through changes in local class structures rather than through transformations of political consciousness. The nature of the London housing market and the scope for more extensive and immediate changes in the class character of local areas through the sale of vacant estates offers the possibility of more conscious forms of gerrymandering. But if inner London continues to gentrify, the assumption must be that some areas of outer London will become more proletarianised. The longer term political effects must therefore remain ambiguous.

NEW ISSUES

The policy of privatisation through council house sales did not emerge because of some financial calculation. Rather it was presented as a means of extending home ownership, redistributing wealth and reducing the power and control of the state. However, as the policy has developed since 1979 it has increasingly contributed to the relief of fiscal problems. Large capital receipts have helped government to meet its spending plans without raising taxation. Without such receipts either spending programmes would have had to be further cut or policies on taxation and borrowing revised. But the appeal and apparent success of the policy raises important issues about the future development of privatisation and the emergence of a crisis in housing supply and condition.

Dilemmas in relation to the future of privatisation are already emerging. The sale of council houses to sitting tenants has a declining appeal as tenants in the best position to buy and in the best properties complete their purchases. But what of the very large (by international standards) remaining state housing sector? And how can capital receipts generated by this asset be maintained? The emerging solution appears to involve alternative forms of privatisation. The Housing and Planning Act 1986 with its measures to facilitate estate sales can be seen in the context of concern to maintain capital receipts. Sales of estates or portfolios of properties to privately financed housing trusts and approved landlord bodies would generate capital receipts. But unlike sales to sitting tenants they do not obviously also meet the tenure or other housing aspirations of households.

The period since 1980 has seen the culmination of trends to privatisation. A long established political debate on the sale of council houses bore fruit in new mandatory legislation designed to ensure mass sales of council dwellings. At the same time other housing policies (and especially rising rents) increased the attractiveness of the Right to Buy. Finally the capital receipts generated by sales were considerably larger than anticipated and emerged as an important aspect of the policy. Maintaining the flow of capital receipts represented a real opportunity to government alongside maintaining the growth of owner occupation and was at the same time consistent with the development of other forms of privatisation.

The fiscal opportunity outlined in this chapter has been an opportunity for *central* government. Looked at from other perspectives, opportunities have been foregone. The release of funds through sales could have represented a *housing* opportunity — a chance to release funds 'tied up' in good housing and put them to work in order to improve the stock, or invest in new housing or acquisition to meet local housing needs. The fiscal opportunity has involved restricting local autonomy over decisions on how best to use resources. It has run counter to pleas for more rational financial management and more informed choices in decisions over the use of resources. The Audit Commission's criticisms of the system of capital controls (Audit Commission, 1985) relate to this. Also relevant are critiques of accounting conventions under which local authority investment is treated as public expenditure whether or not it involves use of capital receipts but which treat private investment in the same activities in a different manner. The switches in housing spending since 1979, the treatment and restriction on capital receipts represent a conscious encouragement of owner occupation and a use of the housing programme to meet other social, political and economic objectives rather than any attempt to enhance financial management and value for money in housing. In these ways they differ from acts of privatisation which have been strongly concerned with costs and value for money.

6

The Spatial and Social Pattern of Council House Sales

Until the mid-1960s the numbers of council houses sold by local authorities under their then discretionary powers fluctuated at fewer than 4,000 a year. There have been two phases in which the rate of sales has been considerably greater than in this pioneering phase. There was an explosion of sales in the years 1971–3. But by far the greatest increase has been in the period since 1977. The unprecedentedly high sales of 1980 were exceeded in 1981, and in 1982 this record level was almost doubled (see Table 6.1). Since 1982 sales have been in decline but remain nevertheless far in excess of levels achieved when local authorities were able to exercise discretion in this policy. These levels of sales were achieved against a background of declining new council building. As Figure 6.1 demonstrates the earlier phases of high council house sales coincided with relatively high rates of new building. Even in 1972 when new building in England and Wales fell below 80,000 the council sector was still growing. Figures referring to other additions to the local authority stock (acquisitions) and to other losses (eg slum clearance) show that by 1980 the council sector was in absolute decline. The major factors in this decline involve the relative levels of sales and of new completions. This decline has occurred alongside a continued decline in the number of dwellings rented from private landlords. The rented sector as a whole has been in decline since 1979 and was also in decline in 1972–3 (Forrest and Murie, 1984a; b).

'RIGHT TO BUY' PROGRESS

Chapter 1 of the Housing Act 1980 provided tenants with three or more years' secure tenancy with the 'Right to Buy' the dwelling

108

Figure 6.1: Local authority sales and completions — England and Wales, 1969–86

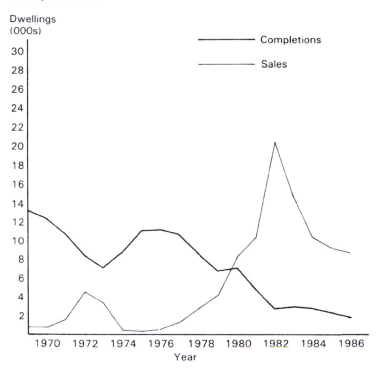

Source: *Housing and Construction Statistics*, HMSO.

they occupied. This section of the Act came into operation on 3 October 1980. Prior to this the Secretary of State for the Environment had extended the general consent covering the sale of council dwellings. This enabled local authorities to sell at their discretion on the same terms as they were required to subsequently. Tables 6.1 and 6.2 indicate that local authorities in 1977–80 chose to make substantial use of their discretion. The high sales figures for 1979–80 are partly attributable to the more favourable terms for sale allowed in the revised general consent but also reflect the pattern of local authority control and the publicity concerning sales.

Once the 'Right to Buy' (RTB) came into operation sales completed under other schemes declined to a small residual amount. By 1982, 90% of all sales were to sitting tenants under the 'Right

109

Table 6.1: Sales of dwellings by local authorities, 1960–86 — England and Wales

Year	All sales of dwellings
1960	2889
1961	3795
1962	4404
1963	3673
1964	3817
1965	3590
1966	4906
1967	4867
1968	9979
1969	8590
1970	6816
1971	17214
1972	45878
1973	34334
1974	4657
1975	2723
1976	5793
1977	13020
1978	30045
1979	41665
1980	81485
1981	102825
1982	201880
1983	145585
1984	103180
1985	92295
1986	88410

Source: *Housing and Construction Statistics*, HMSO.

to Buy'. It had become the dominant mechanism for selling council dwellings. Non RTB sales to sitting tenants and other sales of existing dwellings have declined through the period. Even sales of land and of dwellings built for sale have been relatively unimportant mechanisms for privatisation and the expansion of home ownership.

Analysis of quarterly figures on the RTB (Table 6.2) shows a levelling out of both claims to buy and completed sales. Claims exceeded 140,000 in each of the first two quarters following the introduction of RTB. Subsequently, the general pattern of declining claims only altered in 1986. Completions climbed steadily until the first quarter of 1982 (46,855). Since then they have been at much lower levels. This pattern of fluctuation is as expected but the rate of sales is considerably greater than some had anticipated (see Forrest and Murie, 1984b). The decline in early 1983 could be taken to indicate a falling off in demand after the initial impact of publicity and with the meeting of pent up demand associated with previous limitations on sale. Legislative changes in 1984 and 1986 increased discounts and the proportion of tenants covered by the RTB. Changes in rents, interest rates and the relative costs of renting and buying variously sustained the rate of sales and prevented a more rapid decline.

REGIONAL VARIATIONS

Council house sales have not proceeded at the same rate throughout the country. Table 6.3 shows that in the period 1979–85 some 12.5% of the council stock in England was sold under the various policies. But sales were considerably higher in the South East, East Midlands, Eastern and South West regions. Sales were lowest in London and the Northern regions. Table 6.4 also refers to all types of council house sales and shows that over 1 in 3 of all sales have been in the South East. In the period up to 1980–1 the South East had an even greater share of all sales. And in the period since 1982–3 its share had risen again. Only East Anglia shows a similar pattern of fluctuation. Other regions tended to have smaller shares before RTB sales developed and reverted back to a lower share as these sales declined. When RTB sales *alone* are considered the South East's share rose from 24% in 1981–2 and 1982–3 to 40% in 1984–5. Over this period all other regions except East Anglia and the South West had a declining share of RTB sales.

Non RTB sales to sitting tenants declined early in this period and levelled off at around 10,000 a year. The South East and East Anglia again had a relatively high share of these sales. The North West also had a relatively high share (14% compared with 11% of RTB sales). Sales of vacant dwellings are less significant numerically. The North West and West Midlands had relatively high shares of these sales while the South East and East Anglia remained well represented. Figures for non RTB sales are the results of local discretionary policies. The South East and East Anglia have high rates for both categories of sales. The housing markets and tenure structures of different regions are diverging with a tendency for a privatised Southern and Eastern market and with the North remaining municipalised. In general it appears that the highest sales are in those

111

Table 6.2: Council house sales and RTB progress — local authorities in England and Wales, 1979–85

Period		RTB claims received[1]	RTB accept-ances issued	RTB sales completed	Other sales to sitting tenants	Other sales of existing dwellings	Built for sale	All sales
1980	Q1				21430		150	25360
	Q2				15100	35	130	21595
	Q3				13785	1935	380	17410
	Q4	142000	100400	55	13785	1900	525	16205
1981	Q1	158500	109200	2540	10295	1010	110	13955
	Q2	60300	101900	9970	5755	1205	155	17080
	Q3	39000	46200	24045	4390	1070	165	29670
	Q4	21800	28800	36005	4055	935	210	41205
1982	Q1	50500	36900	46460	3415	1215	205	51295
	Q2	41800	45100	46360	2315	925	105	49700
	Q3	41200	37700	46855	2485	685	70	50095
	Q4	39100	40900	46210	2585	1005	105	49900
1983	Q1	44700	39900	41840	2140	960	100	38945
	Q2	40800	40300	32945	2025	3875*	100	38945
	Q3	28300	28300	27395	1465	855	70	29785
	Q4	21600	23900	25675	1995	1095	170	28935
1984	Q1	33200	28800	29480	2275	980	105	32840
	Q2	32800	30900	20950	2645	895	50	24540
	Q3	31100	28500	18760	1940	535	75	21310
	Q4	35900	38300	19655	2590	995	110	23350

1985	Q1	30000	27200	23375	2005	795	65	26630
	Q2	31400	30400	19720	1475	805	40	22200
	Q3	32100	30200	20000	1395	625	115	22330
	Q4	27800	29600	18475	1290	1030	120	21130
1986	Q1	34700	29300	18765	1450	1095	130	21635
	Q2	46200	42600	18220	1350	605	60	20450
	Q3	39700	39200	19005	1765	750	75	21860
	Q4	33800	36100	22705	1000	445	70	24455
1987	Q1	54700	42100	22130	1845	580	65	24800

Note: These refer to full ownership sales only.

* Including sales of some 3,000 dwellings on Cantril Farm Estate, Knowsley.

(1) No adjustment for withdrawals or applicants who have applied previously.

(2) Including sales for homesteading and under improvement for sales scheme.

Source: *Housing and Construction Statistics*: Part 2, no. 8, Part 2, no. 12.

Table 6.3: Regional distribution of council house sales, 1979–85
— England

DOE region	All sales	Sales as % stock
South East	140468	16.7
East	36844	15.5
South West	54305	15.0
East Midlands	63658	14.6
West Midlands	78379	12.5
North West (including Cumbria)	84234	11.1
North (excluding Cumbria)	46291	11.0
Yorkshire and Humberside	59290	9.7
Greater London	86954	9.6
Total	650414	12.5

Note: Stock is taken as stock of dwellings at 1.3.85 plus all sales.

regions where council housing is least common (Table 6.5). This picture of the pattern of sales suggests a regional polarisation of tenure which would be likely to be more marked at a local authority level but which also obscures variations within each region. The most striking example of this is that Scotland, which has the highest level of council housing in Great Britain (50%), had the lowest rate of sales.

Sales under the RTB in England up to the end of 1982 were proportionately highest in the East Midlands and lowest in Greater London. Some of the early variation in RTB completions was undoubtedly due to different administrative and political responses to new legislation. By the end of 1982, however, and with close central government scrutiny and progress chasing, major variations in sale completions were not so easily attributed to the different mechanics of policy. Some assessment of the demand for RTB purchase can be made from claims to buy made by tenants. While many claims will be withdrawn and even this can be affected by local policy the variation in claims is an indication of likely variation in completions. When claims made by the end of 1982 are expressed as a percentage of stock a considerable variation is evident. The range was from 14% in East Midlands to 7% in Greater London. The same calculation of claims as a percentage of stock made for claims up to 31 March 1982 showed less of a variation. At that date in Greater London claims represented 6% of stock while in the East

114

Table 6.4: All sales of council houses,[1] 1979–87 – England and Wales

	Council stock at December 1979 – thousand	All sales of council houses									
		1979	1980 (1st qtr)	1980–1	1981–2	1982–3	1983–4	1984–5	1985–6	1986–7 (1st %)	Total 1979–87
England & Wales	5565	41115	25360	66223	144503	201081	133917	101007	91081	69828	874115
England	5257	36918	21922	65283	132100	185580	126008	95312	85744	65491	814358
North	489 (9%)	735 (2%)	214	1097 (2%)	13890 (10%)	22200 (11%)	10372 (8%)	6516 (6%)	5904 (6%)	4321 (6%)	65249 (7%)
Yorkshire & Humberside	617 (11%)	1902 (5%)	1654	4899 (7%)	12510 (9%)	20370 (10%)	9564 (7%)	7168 (7%)	7115 (8%)	5211 (7%)	70393 (8%)
East Midlands	425 (8%)	4034 (10%)	1982	4896 (7%)	14590 (10%)	20210 (10%)	10564 (8%)	7196 (7%)	7040 (8%)	5801 (8%)	76313 (9%)
East Anglia	192 (3%)	2492 (6%)	1333	3122 (5%)	6010 (4%)	6310 (3%)	5136 (4%)	4885 (5%)	4340 (5%)	3349 (5%)	36977 (4%)
South East	1767 (32%)	16968 (41%)	9916	30147 (46%)	42950 (30%)	53880 (27%)	45741 (34%)	42064 (42%)	37012 (41%)	28529 (41%)	307207 (35%)
Greater London	853 (15%)	7993 (19%)	3465	12825 (19%)	13720 (9%)	20390 (10%)	15097 (11%)	14660 (15%)	14930 (16%)	10375 (15%)	113455 (13%)
Rest of South East	914 (16%)	8975 (22%)	6451	17322 (26%)	29230 (20%)	33490 (17%)	30644 (23%)	27404 (27%)	22082 (24%)	18154 (26%)	193752 (22%)
South West	369 (7%)	2343 (6%)	1272	4394 (7%)	12610 (9%)	14120 (7%)	10890 (8%)	8852 (9%)	7824 (9%)	5829 (8%)	68134 (8%)
West Midlands	647 (12%)	5806 (14%)	3782	8529 (13%)	12360 (9%)	23170 (12%)	16445 (12%)	10463 (10%)	8254 (9%)	6538 (9%)	95347 (11%)
North West	751 (13%)	2638 (6%)	1769	8199 (12%)	17180 (12%)	25310 (13%)	17296 (13%)	8168 (8%)	8255 (9%)	5913 (8%)	94728 (11%)
Wales	308 (6%)	4197 (10%)	3438	940 (1%)	12403 (9%)	15501 (8%)	7909 (6%)	5695 (6%)	5337 (6%)	4337 (6%)	59757 (7%)

Note: (1) Sales to sitting tenants and built for sale but excluding shared ownership.
Source: *Housing and Construction Statistics, 1969–79*, Table 97, and *Local Housing Statistics*, quarterly, HMSO.

Table 6.5: Regional distribution of council housing and rates of council house sales

	Local authority and new town dwellings as a % of all dwellings December 1979	Proportionately high sellers or low sellers
North	41.1	'Low'
Yorkshire and Humberside	33.1	'Low'
East Midlands	29.4	'High'
East Anglia	26.5	'High'
Greater London	31.0	'Low'
Rest of South East	24.3	'High'
South West	22.1	'Balanced'
West Midlands	33.9	'Low'
North West	30.7	'Low'
Wales	29.0	'High'
Scotland	54.0	'Low'

Source: *Housing and Construction Statistics*, 1969–79, p. 119.

Midlands and the South West they represented 11%. The other regions were North (excluding Cumbria) 10%; Eastern, South Eastern and North West 9%; and West Midlands and Yorkshire and Humberside 8% (Forrest and Murie, 1982). Thus in a nine-month period in which new claims were made by some 80,000 tenants (20% increase) there was a tendency for greater unevenness rather than for convergence. Looked at on the basis of completed sales or claims the pattern is one of considerably different impact at a regional level. The regional geography of council housing is being altered to increase regional contrasts in tenure structure.

LOCAL VARIATIONS

Variations in the sale of council houses are more marked between local authorities than between regions. Figure 6.2 presents the rate of sale for all local authorities in England. This reinforces the general North-South split in rate of sales. As well as heavy concentrations along the South coast and around London there is a belt of high sales running East-West from Hereford and Worcester to Norfolk. There are, however, other areas of relatively high sales in

Figure 6.2: The geography of council house sales in England, 1979–85

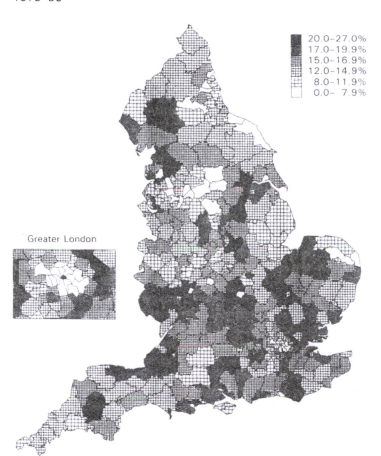

Note: Percentages refer to all completed sales as a percentage of the council housing stock in 1985 *plus* all completed sales.

Lancashire and Nottinghamshire. The most notable exception to the high rate of sales in the South are the inner London boroughs.

Table 6.6 provides a top and bottom league table for sales in the period 1979–85. The bottom of the league table has to be treated with some caution. It is these figures which are most affected by incomplete returns. However a broad pattern has remained

117

Table 6.6: Council house sales in England, 1979–85 — the highest and lowest sellers[1]

Local authority	% sales	Rank order
Highest sellers		
Knowsley	26.7	1
Corby	26.2	2
Havant	26.0	3
Fenland	24.8	4
Bracknell	24.7	5
Fareham	23.8	6
Crawley	23.7	7
Weymouth	23.4	8
Epping Forest	23.2	9
Gedling	23.1	10
Arun	23.0	11
South Herefordshire	22.3	12
Breckland	22.2	13
South Northants	21.8	14
West Devon	21.7	15
Eastleigh	21.7	16
City[2]	21.6	17
Rushcliffe	21.6	18
Wycombe	21.5	19
Surrey Heath	21.4	20
Kingswood	21.4	21
Spelthorne	21.3	22
Milton Keynes	21.2	23
Havering	21.2	24
Woking	21.1	25
Wealden	21.0	26
Rochester[2]	20.9	27
Basingstoke/Deane[2]	20.9	28
Huntingdon	20.7	29
South Bucks	20.7	30
Lowest sellers		
Rochdale	8.0	337
Brighton[2]	7.9	338
Northampton	7.8	339
Newham	7.6	340
Redditch	7.5	341
Kirklees[2]	7.4	343
Hammersmith/Fulham	7.1	343
Sandwell	6.6	344
Kingston-upon-Hull	6.6	345
Scarborough[2]	6.6	346
Blackburn	6.4	347
Leeds	6.3	348

Haringey	6.1	349
Kensington/Chelsea	5.8	350
Manchester[2]	5.6	351
Oldham	5.4	352
Salford	5.4	353
Greenwich	5.2	354
Brent[2]	4.8	355
Sheffield	4.8	356
Scilly Isles	4.5	357
Westminster[2]	4.3	358
Preston[2]	4.2	359
Lewisham[2]	4.0	360
Tower Hamlets[2]	2.4	361
Lambeth[2]	2.0	362
Southwark	1.9	363
Islington[2]	1.8	364
Camden	1.4	365
Hackney[2]	1.0	366

Notes: (1) Excludes GLC.
(2) Incomplete returns.

remarkably consistent over time and it is unlikely that complete returns would significantly affect rank order. What the league table demonstrates is the enormous variation in rate of sale. Three authorities had sold more than one in four of their properties between 1979 and 1985. Twelve authorities had sold fewer than one in 20. The general picture is of high sales among Southern, and particularly rural authorities, with low sales being associated with inner London boroughs and more Northern urban authorities. The most notable exception to this pattern is Knowsley. However this tops the rankings due to the disposal of a significant number of council properties to a private housing trust (the Stockbridge Village Trust) and in this sense is an exceptional case. Some other authorities are significantly affected by discretionary policies. Corby has sold a considerable number of dilapidated and void properties to individual purchasers. Wandsworth, Milton Keynes and Birmingham each sold exceptionally high numbers of vacant dwellings. None of the 30 top sellers are in the Northern or Yorkshire and Humberside regions and with the exception of Knowsley none are in the North West. In contrast twelve are in the South East and seven in the Eastern region. The only West Midlands top seller is rural South Herefordshire which has a very small council stock. In

119

London none of the high council housing inner boroughs are among the top sellers.

The bottom sellers present a contrasting picture. None (again) are in the Northern region. Almost half of the bottom 30 are London boroughs (nearly all inner London). Six of the bottom sellers are in the North West and five in Yorkshire and Humberside. The Eastern region has no low sellers and in the South West only the Isles of Scilly with a council housing stock of some 110 dwellings is a low seller. If Scottish authorities were added to this picture, none of them would enter the highest seller category. Even by June 1986 after a longer period of sales, more than a third of Scottish authorities would be amongst the lowest sellers (Table 6.6). The pattern within Scotland tends to conform to that found in England. The highest selling authorities tend to be in attractive, coastal and rural districts. Lowest sales are found in Glasgow and the declining industrial areas.

Analysis of the variation in rates of sale between local authorities within the same region indicates that the lowest selling regions are not all pulled down by authorities with very low rates of sale. The Northern region has neither any very low selling districts nor any very high sellers. Its relative uniformity is in striking contrast to Greater London which has the widest range of variation.

In a separate exercise (Dunn, Forrest and Murie, 1987) we have carried out a correlation and regression analysis to clarify the reasons for the pattern of local variation which exists. The correlation analysis shows as follows:

— that sales tend to be high in areas with high existing levels of owner occupation and/or low levels of public renting. Rather than sales 'evening up' tenure structures, they are tending to accentuate local variations;

— there is a strong positive relationship between the level of sales and the proportion of council tenants with children aged 5–15. A less strong positive association exists between sales and the percentage of tenants with children aged under five; and a weaker negative association with the percentage of pensioners. Local demographic differences affect the pattern of local variation in council house sales;

— sales tend to increase with the relative affluence of tenants and areas;

— sales tend to be high in areas where the council stock is houses, and low in areas where there are large percentages of flats, one bedroomed dwellings and pre-1939 stock;

— there is a strong positive association between sales in the period 1974–9 and sales 1979–85;

— local authorities under Conservative control are the highest sellers and Labour the lowest. However the variation in rate of sale is largest among Labour and lowest for Conservative controlled authorities.

Further regression analysis shows the level of council house sales is significantly positively related to the percentage of council house tenants with children aged 5–15, the level of sales in the period 1974–80, and to local political control by the Conservatives; and is significantly negatively related to the percentage of local authority stock which is flats and the local level of male unemployment. These five variables are all clearly significant, in statistical terms, and together account for 45% of the variation of council house sales between local authorities. For the whole time period the average selling price of council properties is not a significant influence on council house sales.

The pattern of change over time identified by the regression results also corresponds to the results from the correlation analysis. The tenant life cycle variable remains fairly constant over time, always significant and positive. The council stock variable is also fairly constant, and always negative and significant. Male unemployment is always statistically significant and negative with some evidence that the strength of this relationship is increasing over time.

SALES OF FLATS

One of the factors identified in patterns of local variation of sales is dwelling type. While flats comprise some 30% of the council stock they formed only 5% of sales in the period 1981–5. Sales of flats have been disproportionately low throughout the period although there has been some increase in the importance of flat sales since 1982 (partly attributable to sales of vacant dwellings). Those which have been sold often appear to have been converted, low-rise and often more attractive flatted properties. One of the difficulties in assessing this is that properties categorised as flats are enormously diverse. Flats do consist of unpopular deck access and medium rise purpose built estates as well as tower blocks. But they also include

121

converted, acquired properties in attractive, gentrified areas. This aspect is likely to influence the impact of higher discounts on flat sales. Assessment is further complicated because there tends to be an inverse relationship between popularity and the cost of buying. This is partly reflected in differences in valuation. For example, a flat in a tower block in Liverpool is liable to be valued at less than £10,000, whereas some acquired flats in attractive inner London locations have been valued at over £150,000. Discount entitlements will reduce purchase price in both cases. However, the maximum discount restrictions will still leave the purchase price of the London property some 40 times that of the Liverpool property. Moreover, in the case of higher priced areas, buying flats is still likely to increase housing costs. In the Liverpool case, however, a 100% mortgage on £3,000 will bring day-to-day housing costs well below the previous rent. The new legislation in 1986 is designed to encourage sales of flats. Higher discounts may persuade more sitting tenants in flats to buy. However, the available evidence suggests that dwelling type rather than price is the key factor for not considering buying. It may be that it will only prove possible to sell flats on a substantial scale by selling estates as a whole to private developers or trusts — and moving out tenants prior to sale.

THE SOCIAL PATTERN OF SALES

The apparently overwhelming desire for home ownership among households has been the principal political justification for the sale of council houses. Government policies have been presented as a response to natural preference and choice. A procession of surveys has shown the desire to purchase among a high proportion of public and private tenants and rising expectation of home ownership among newly formed households. Table 6.7 shows the results of various surveys of tenure preferences undertaken over the last 20 years. Taken at face value the message is clear. Tenure preferences diverge widely from current housing situations. If these preferences were transformed into actual housing circumstances Britain would have one of the highest levels of home ownership in Western Europe. There is however increasing recognition that expectations may have outstripped what is possible and that home ownership may not be the most appropriate or desirable tenure for households at particular stages of the family life cycle or in vulnerable economic circumstances. Interestingly, the most recent survey carried out by

Table 6.7: Tenure preferences

	1967 %	1975 %	1978 %	1983 %	1986 %
Owner occupation	66	69	72	77	77
Council housing	23	21	19	16	17
Private renting/housing associations	11	8	5	5	4
Don't know	—	3	3	2	3

Source: Building Societies Association, 1983; BMRB, 1986.

the British Market Research Bureau (BMRB) for the Building Societies Association shows that more households *expect* to be home owners in ten years' time that express a current desire to be in that tenure (BMRB, 1986). And this divergence of preferences and expectations is particularly evident among council tenants. Whereas 56% of current public sector tenants would most like to be in council housing in two years' time, only 44% expect to be in that tenure in ten years' time.

Tenure preferences are not formed in a vacuum but are heavily influenced by the pattern of subsidy, general housing policies and the individual judgements regarding financial expectations and changes in family circumstances. Nevertheless, there is wider recognition that expressed housing preference may be a reflection of constraint rather than choice for some households. For example, Boleat has referred to an unnatural demand for owner occupation in inner city areas deriving from a lack of available private rented accommodation for the young and transient (Boleat, 1982). Similarly, Jones (1982), in a useful review of the demand for home ownership, noted that for some households '. . . the act of house purchase derives more from dissatisfaction with the accommodation available in the local authority sector than from any desire for home ownership as a form of tenure' (p. 121).

Certainly ineligibility for council housing among certain groups, long waiting lists, the prospect of being allocated an unpopular flat or maisonette, the lack of private rented accommodation, rising rents and a general decline in investment in public housing are all factors which can fuel preferences for home ownership. Expressions of tenure preference therefore need to be carefully contextualised and should not be presented as evidence of something 'innate' or 'natural'. And as we pointed out earlier if such evidence is to be interpreted uncritically and used to buttress ideological predilection then there is little comfort for those who wish to encourage new forms of private renting as a way of providing greater housing choice. Only 4% of respondents in the BMRB survey said they would most like to be living in privately rented accommodation in two years' time.

Geographical unevenness in the desire for home ownership is also of interest. The expectation could be that the desire to purchase would be greatest in those areas with currently low levels of home ownership. But Scotland with the lowest level of home ownership also has the lowest level of preference for it. This suggests that far from being a natural or inevitable desire, preference to own is learned and culturally embedded and can be affected by a variety of policy and other changing social and economic circumstances.

Expressed preference for home ownership conflates preference for a collection of housing attributes such as space, quality, a house with a garden, the desire for a particular location as well as reflecting specific tax and subsidy advantages. In this sense the basic question is not whether people are becoming owners but whether their particular needs and aspirations are being satisfied. The two are not necessarily synonymous. As we show in a later chapter quite different motivations may be behind council house purchase in different areas of the country. And those tenants who purchased in the earlier phases of the policy, say in the early 1960s, may have done so under circumstances which contrast markedly with those tenants doing so today.

Having said that, there has been a striking consistency in the general profile of tenant purchasers and in the kinds of property they buy. The problem faced by government in translating the expressed desire for home ownership among council tenants into council house purchases has been that many potential purchasers want to buy someone else's property — not the one they have been allocated. A further problem for a government committed to a reduced role for public housing is that a large section of the tenant population regard themselves as too old or financially insecure for purchase to be a sensible option. The consequence has been that after seven years of a vigorous sales policy with ever-increasing discounts, rising rents and other incentives to buy, more than a quarter of households remain as council tenants.

Details of the characteristics of what has been sold and who buys have been provided in a variety of earlier studies and for various localities, and some reference is made to them in Chapter 8. In this section some of the more recent evidence from larger scale surveys is discussed.

The General Household Survey in 1982 provided data on owner occupied households in Great Britain who had bought their accommodation in the last six years and who had previously rented the accommodation from a local authority. This data is of limited value. It refers to fewer than 350 owners buying under different policies, and to current characteristics rather than characteristics when they bought. Nevertheless, the picture presented is consistent with other evidence. The youngest and particularly the oldest tenants are under-represented amongst purchasers as are the economically inactive and those living in flats and maisonettes.

A more substantial picture is obtained from the 5% sample of building society mortgage completions (Building Societies Association (BSA), 1986). Building societies have financed an increasing proportion of council house sales (55–60% in 1985 compared with about 33% in 1982). In the third quarter of 1985 the average age of sitting tenant purchasers was just over 43 compared with about 31 for all first time buyers. The age profile of council tenants is, however, even more skewed towards older households. Sitting tenant purchasers also have significantly lower incomes than first time buyers in general and the average price paid was only just over half that paid by all first time buyers. The BSA data also show that the age distribution of houses purchased by sitting tenants reflects more or less the age distribution of existing council houses. In view of this data it is not surprising that sitting tenant purchasers required smaller mortgage loans than first time buyers in general. In the third quarter of 1985 the average mortgage of sitting tenant purchasers was £11,974 compared with £20,327 for all first time buyers. The average loan for a sitting tenant purchaser was 95% of the average purchase price whereas it was 85% for all first time buyers.

Similar evidence emerges from the Labour Force Survey (Table 6.8). A comparison between all tenants and sitting tenant purchasers in 1984 reveals that those in semi-skilled and unskilled employment are under-represented among economically active purchasers. And whilst 75% of sitting tenant purchasers had heads of household in employment (at time of interview) this is true of only 35% of tenants as a whole. Consistent with other surveys both young and elderly tenants are significantly under-represented.

Data on a different group of council house purchasers — purchasers of vacant dwellings — are obtainable from a Department of the Environment Survey (Littlewood and Mason, 1984). These sales are not RTB sales or sales to sitting tenants but are included in many of the aggregate statistics on sales. Sales of vacant

125

Table 6.8: Characteristics of sitting tenant purchasers, potential purchasers, unlikely purchasers and all tenants. Great Britain, 1984 — heads of household

	All tenants	Sitting tenant[1] purchasers	Tenants who had considered buying in the last two years[3]	Tenants who had not considered buying in the last two years[3]
	%	%	%	%
Socio-economic group[2]				
Professional/employers and managers	6	13	7	5
Intermediate/junior non-manual	13	14	12	12
Skilled manual	43	51	50	40
Semi-skilled/unskilled manual	38	21	31	42
Employment status				
Employed	35	76	—	—
Seeking work	13	4	—	—
Others not in work	51	20	—	—
Age of head of household				
Under 30	11	3	12	12
30–44	19	31	66	35
45–59	21	41	66	35
60 or over	48	24	21	54

Notes: (1) Characteristics at time of interview.
(2) Figures for all tenants and sitting tenant purchasers exclude those whose last job was three or more years ago, those not seeking work and any people aged 65 or over; figures for tenants considering/not considering buying exclude only those economically inactive heads of household.
(3) 1983 and 1984 figures combined.
Source: *Labour Force Survey,* 1983–4; *General Household Survey,* 1984.

dwellings are discretionary and who takes advantage of them will depend on local policy and its implementation. The particular design and sample in the DoE Study may be affected by this but the results are broadly comparable with those of other studies (see Forrest, Lansley and Murie, 1984). The survey refers to 174 vacant dwelling sales, 40% of which were terraced houses and 27% purpose built flats/maisonettes; 38% consisted of five or more rooms. The largest group of properties was newly built: 25% were built before 1919, 15% 1919–44, 19% 1945–79 and 41% 1980–2. Unlike sitting tenant purchasers single people, childless couples and household heads under 30 are strongly represented amongst purchasers of vacant dwellings. Large adult households and elderly households are less well represented than amongst sitting tenant purchasers. In terms of age, household structure, social class, income and purchase price purchasers of vacant dwellings are more like first time buyers in general than sitting tenant purchasers. This is a similar conclusion to that drawn from research on shared ownership (Allen, 1982).

TO BUY OR NOT TO BUY?

As the sales policy has progressed and with the prospect of declining sales to individual purchasers so government statistical reports have become increasingly concerned with reasons for not purchasing. Indeed considerably more effort and money has been channelled into investigating the attitudes of non-purchasing households than into any systematic research into the housing policy consequences of council house sales. The style and method of some of this research has at times been more akin to product research than to broader social or economic analysis.

The reasons for government concerns with tenants' attitudes is demonstrated in Table 6.9. Evidence from different surveys over the last four years shows that the vast majority of tenants are unlikely to exercise their Right to Buy. The General Household Survey 1984 expressed the issue in the following terms:

> . . . with around 600,000 sales of council houses to sitting tenants in 1981 to 1984 a reduction in the proportion of remaining tenants expressing an interest in buying might have been expected. [The data] does not, however, show a significant decline in interest over this period (OPCS, 1984, p. 46).

However, it might have been expected that rising rents and the general climate of disinvestment in council housing would have generated an increase in the propensity of purchase. And as Table 6.9 shows, the additional incentives in the Housing and Building Control Act 1984 did not increase significantly the number of

127

Table 6.9: Likelihood of buying present home — council tenants — Great Britain, 1983, 1984 and 1986

	1983	1984	1986
Base	639	1761	563
	%	%	%
Very likely	8	5	7
Quite likely	7	7	8
Neither likely nor unlikely	5	—	4
Quite unlikely	8	4	14
Very unlikely	70	76	65
Not allowed to buy	—	6	—
Don't know	2	—	3

Source: British Market Research Bureau, 1983 and 1986, *Housing and Savings*, Technical Report and Tables; Jowell, R. and Airey, C., 1984, *British Social Attitudes — the 1984 Report*, Gower.

potential purchasers in 1986. At most the measures *maintained* the number of likely buyers.

The General Household Surveys (GHS) for the years 1981 to 1984 reveal a fairly consistent picture of the characteristics of those tenants who had or had not considered buying their dwellings (OPCS, 1983, 1984, 1985, 1986). In Table 6.8 combined data for 1983–4 show that the dominant purchasing group is still skilled manual workers in middle age. More detailed analyses from published and unpublished tables from this source illustrate other dimensions. Whilst, in 1984, 37% of tenant households had heads aged 65 or over, only 12% of potential purchasers fall into this category. Conversely 43% of likely purchasers are aged between 30 and 49 (1984 figures). And households with at least three adults, typically indicating a grown up family, have a higher propensity to purchase. Trend data do suggest that more elderly households are being drawn into the purchasing categories reflecting perhaps the impact of higher discounts and the general ageing of the population. There is however an inevitable ambiguity here in that purchases by apparently elderly households may in fact be *for* and *by* their sons and daughters.

Among the economically active those in non-manual and skilled manual occupations were nearly twice as likely as those in unskilled manual jobs to have considered buying their accommodation. Those in the higher socio-economic groups and those with higher incomes were more likely to have considered buying and to have taken more active steps to buy. Among those who had not considered buying the mean gross weekly income of the head of household was £68 in 1984. For tenants as a whole the comparable figure was £108 for economically active heads. It is also evident from local studies that a sharp division exists within the public tenant population between multiple earning households and those with one or no wage earners. For example, among purchaser households in Derwentside, an area with severe unemployment, almost 90% had at least two earners. And in a study in Aberdeen, Williams *et al.* (1986) found that 75% of purchasing households had at least two wage earners whereas 64% of non-buyers had either one or no wage earners (p. 277).

Evidence from the General Household Survey also shows that there was no clear association between tenants' interest in buying their accommodation and the length of time they had lived at their current address. Property type was a key differentiating factor. Tenants living in houses were some five times as likely to have considered buying as those living in flats or maisonettes. The General Household Survey also asked those who had not considered buying why they had not bought or were no longer considering buying. Those who had thought about it but had abandoned the idea and those who had never considered it cited financial reasons most frequently. Age was the other principal factor. Other reasons related to the unsuitability of the accommodation itself or to dissatisfaction with some aspect of the neighbourhood.

Problems associated with the accommodation or the environment were the most common disincentive among families and least common for elderly and single person households. And as income rises those factors become increasingly significant deterrents to buy. A general picture emerges of three main influences at work. Accommodation type, family circumstances and income will often pull and push in different directions. In other words there is often a mismatch between households' ability to purchase and their desire to purchase the dwelling they occupy.

These results are closely paralleled by the BMRB study (BMRB, 1986) of housing and savings. Those showing a low interest in purchase identified dwelling factors (19%), age (21%) and income (18%) as the main reasons. The only other recent large scale evidence available on this issue comes from a Scottish Office study (Foulis, 1985). Scotland is of particular interest given its large public sector stock and the relatively low level of interest in buying

129

among tenants. The Scottish study comments that non-buyers were aware of the advantages of buying. Prices were recognised as good value, rising rents and deteriorating services were resented, and the financial benefits of ownership were appreciated. The reason these factors had not drawn them to buy was 'partly because the force of these attractions was dissipated by dissatisfaction concentrated on the house type or condition' (p. 52). Insecurity, however, was identified as the key factor. This could relate either to the lack of a job and hence the ability to undertake purchase in the first place (only about half of the non-buyers had jobs) or to concern about future employment. A strong renting tradition, age and political opposition were also identified as factors deterring purchase.

The Scottish study also identifies tenants who applied to buy but subsequently dropped out. Over one third of these had dropped out before an offer was made. The survey evidence shows that these 'failed buyers' were

> . . . barely distinguishable from buyers in attributes and in outlook. This was the case with the valuations and % discounts they were offered, their satisfaction with their home and neighbourhood, the length of time they had been living there, their household composition, employment and income, the head of household's occupation and his age (p. 57).

Some difference was identified in social contact with owners and council house buyers in particular but more reliance can be placed on the reasons given by the tenants themselves. The most common reasons for withdrawal were that they were 'worried about job security' (27%), 'the place needed too much doing to it' (16%), 'could not afford the repayments' (15%), 'change in personal circumstances' (12%), 'valuation too high' (12%), 'did not like the house enough to buy it' (8%), 'the place was not worth the price' (8%) and age (7%).

While Scottish evidence is generally consistent with that from the GHS it does highlight insecurity and employment factors which do not emerge from the latter. This may reflect the nature of the GHS questions or may indicate that there are national/regional differences operating. If this is the case it would be reasonable to suggest that the low rates of sales in the northern regions of England are also affected by insecurity and employment factors.

LIFE CYCLE CONSIDERATIONS

The evidence presented above is not only important in understanding the pattern of sales to date. It also offers the basis for
estimation of future impact. In any such estimate it is important to
acknowledge that household circumstances change. Households
currently unable to buy may move into such a situation. It would
be expected therefore that the family life cycle effect will continue
to 'recruit' new purchasers. In such a calculation, however, dwelling stock factors may come to play an increasingly important role.
Progressively fewer tenant households will find themselves in a
position to purchase a desirable council dwelling.

We examined more closely the relationships between dwelling
type, family life cycle and the allocation system in a case study of
council house buyers in Birmingham. Tenants in the earlier stage
of the family life cycle were more likely to occupy high rise flats
which they would not choose to buy. Similarly, those with the least
bargaining power — the homeless, single parent families and other
disadvantaged groups — were more likely to end up in the less
attractive parts of the stock. The operation of the transfer and
allocation system meant that for the typical tenant purchaser his/her
housing history in the public sector had involved a progressive
upgrading in terms of housing quality. For example, of tenant
purchasers in Birmingham in 1979–80 just under three quarters had
transferred at least once and just under a third had transferred twice
or more. Typically they had moved from a multi-storey flat or
terraced house to a three-bedroomed semi-detached with a garden.
In Plymouth a similar percentage had benefited from a transfer at
some stage. In general, purchasers had moved from a flat or
terraced house to a three-bedroomed semi. When first allocated a
tenancy, 36% of purchaser households had been allocated a flat,
maisonette or bungalow. By the time of purchase only 7% were still
in such property types. This movement through the public housing
system was paralleled by changes in the position in the family life
cycle. As households mature in terms of children leaving home
and/or starting work their optimum income position was likely to
correspond to their optimum housing position. There was thus
inevitably a high degree of correspondence between those tenants
for whom purchase was both most appropriate and feasible and
those occupying the best dwellings.

Without giving due consideration to changes in circumstances
the notion that council house sales have involved a 'creaming-off'

131

of the more affluent and better behaved tenants leads to a crude pathology of different tenant groups. Most simply, static comparisons of who is moving into the public sector with who is moving out through sales might suggest that certain groups of tenants, namely the unemployed, single parent families and others in problematic social and financial circumstances, may never be in a position to buy. This model could consolidate the view that there are 'problem' and 'non-problem' groups within the working class — 'deserving' and 'undeserving' categories. For this reason we traced the housing histories of purchasers. What emerged from this exercise was that many purchasers would have been categorised at earlier stages as 'problem' tenants with little prospect of purchasing. For example, a high proportion of purchasers had been through periods of quite serious rent arrears. The point was that households who were apparently making a smooth and unproblematic move into house ownership had previously experienced long periods of coping with single parenthood, or unemployment, or low earnings. Many had entered the public rental sector in the 1950s or early 1960s threatened with eviction by private landlords or occupying properties in the slum clearance programme. There was clearly not one group of tenants who were able and wishing to purchase and another group who were necessarily *permanently* excluded. But this process will be distorted by the nature of the dwelling stock and this will be subject to local variations. Once again the most obvious contrast is between the less urban authorities with few flats and a generally popular stock of houses scattered in a large number of small towns and villages and the metropolitan centres such as the London boroughs, Birmingham and Liverpool. In the former there is no logical reason why almost all the public rental stock will not be sold off. In the latter, however, as the selective nature of sales raises the proportion of flats and less popular houses and estates remaining in the stock, the propensity to buy among those tenants who remain will undoubtedly be reduced.

LOSS OF RELETS

The housing histories of current tenant purchasers will not be mirrored in the housing histories of those now entering or wishing to enter the public rental sector. As family circumstances change the inevitable decline in transfer opportunities will mean that for an

Figure 6.3: Loss of relets

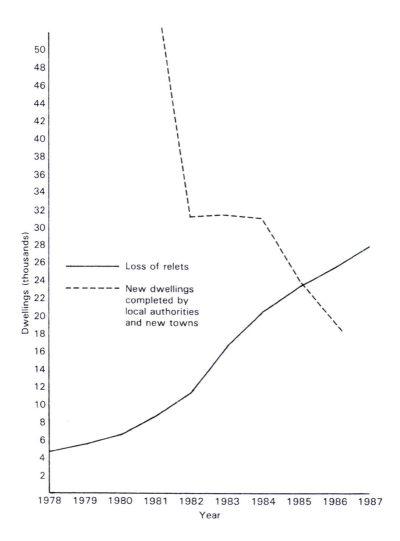

increasing number of tenants their first allocation may be long term or permanent. In the past, subsequent mobility has been significant in enabling initial allocations to be changed to fit preferences and needs. It is in this context that the impact of council house sales in the future pattern of relets is important.

The once-stated view of this was that 'some 30–40 years would typically elapse before there is an effect on the number of houses vacant and available for letting to new tenants' (DoE, 1980). This was replaced in 1980 by a view that the sale of council houses was largely to people who would not have moved and that consequently the loss of relets would initially be low and would build up slowly. Using age-specific data on death and some other reasons for termination the DoE's more considered view was that some 115 to 150 relets would be lost for every 1000 sales over the first ten years. A further 45 to 70 relets would have occurred as a result of death or household dissolution. This figure of 160–220 relets lost per 1000 sales was not accepted by the Environment Committee which concluded that the best estimate for the annual loss of relets calculated in the manner proposed by the Department is 2.6 per cent (House of Commons Environment Committee, 1981). While there is uncertainty and dispute about these figures they are low compared with the average annual rate of relets which stands at some 3.7%. Some of the differences arise from shorter term assessments. Over a longer period and, depending on the age and other characteristics of purchasers, the loss of relets would come to average 3.7%.

Perhaps it is these disputes which have deterred any subsequent calculation of loss of relets. The issue remains relevant, however, and given that the level of sales is substantially higher than many forecast it is appropriate to offer some brief consideration. Rather than present a whole range of alternative calculations we have adopted the Environment Committee's cautious view of the 'best estimate' for the loss of relets (2.6%). This lies between the DoE figure and the average annual rate. Year by year figures are unlikely to be accurate but the calculations based on these provide a reasonable indication of the scale of the loss of relets.

The calculation of the loss of relets relates to council house sales completed in England and Wales since 1960. If the figures for losses are staggered by one year to avoid overstatement, they suggest that by 1987 the loss of relets was almost 28,000. The real decline in opportunities to rent is indicated by this loss of relets which by 1987 is greater than the rate of new council building

(Figure 6.3). In these terms the combined effect of the sale of council houses and cuts in the rate of new building has had the same effect as would the termination of new council building in the absence of any council house sales. Sales of properties do not remove such properties from the housing market but different households are able to buy than would have been allocated a new tenancy.

This picture understates the situation in one obvious way. Relet properties should themselves be taken into account in future loss of relets. Properties which would have been relet (the lost relets) would themselves generate relets. Logically an additional figure for second and subsequent round relets should be added. If a second round relet only is included (and others beyond this are very small) the calculation would be further increased.

This loss of relets will become even more important in the future. Assuming a steady continuing rate of sales of 80,000 a year, the loss of relets in 1991 will be some 36,000. Again, allowing for second-round relets increases these figures. The predicament of households unable to buy and needing to rent and of those authorities with duties to provide housing is illustrated by these figures. Capital investment in council housing has not compensated for this erosion of capacity to provide housing.

CONCLUSIONS

Selling council houses has involved strikingly different rates of claims and sales at regional and local levels. The pattern of North-South and Inner-Outer city variation has been firmly established and is only likely to change with major shifts in policy. The consequence of the policy is a major revision of the geography of housing tenure. But it is a revision resulting in increased tenure polarisation between localities. Sales have been highest where owner occupation is already at high levels. There is also a strong relationship between the pattern of sales under previous discretionary policies and the pattern under the RTB.

The most striking general impression from the analyses presented is of increasing tenure polarisation both between and within localities. This confirms and extends previous findings indicating that sales have been highest in areas where owner occupation is already at high levels. There is a strong relationship between the pattern of sales under previous discretionary policies

135

and the pattern under the RTB. This calls into question the belief that the release of pent-up demand among previous non-sellers would be a significant element of RTB sales. Rather, it seems that higher discounts, rising rents and other external factors related to the uneven impact of the recession and the movement of interest rates may have generated a new wave of sales in areas where many tenants had already bought. Whilst statutory compulsion to sell has accounted for a proportion of the very high levels of sales achieved over the last five years, it may be that the factors referred to above have been of greater significance. Moreover, the high proportion of variation explained by regression analyses suggests that this pattern will continue and will contribute a greater unevenness in the distribution of tenures.

Increasing spatial variation between tenures is occurring at the same time as the tenures themselves are changing. Part of this change is a direct consequence of what has been sold and what has not. The importance of flats and specialist accommodation in council housing has increased. And there is evidence of increasing social polarisation within council housing with broader divisions in British society reflected in the contrasting position of tenant households with multiple earners and households with little or no earned income. It is that former group which constitutes the principal customers for the RTB — providing they are occupying desirable dwellings. Patterns of new building and council house sales have also contributed to an increasingly polarised age structure within council housing with the young and old expanding disproportionately as families and family accommodation is transferred to owner occupation. A privatisation policy for council housing which was reliant on sales to individual tenants would produce diminishing numbers. It is not surprising therefore that government is turning towards less voluntaristic forms of transfer such as the sale of whole estates, the creation of housing trusts and transfers to new landlords.

7

The Polarised City

Longer term social and economic trends have contributed to an increasing polarisation between the main housing tenures in Britain. The impact of contemporary housing policy and of the recent economic recession has strengthened this trend and as outlined in Chapter 4 parts of the housing market have increasingly become associated with marginalised groups. How these processes affect different cities and localities will however differ considerably. The impact of the recession itself is uneven. The structure and development of local housing markets are also different. Who lives where, both in terms of tenure and of dwellings within tenures, is affected by a number of factors. These include historical patterns of growth, demand, rationing and access; mobility between and within tenures; and the relative costs, reputations, quality and other attributes of housing in different parts of the market. Social divisions in the housing market reflect differential bargaining power. This in turn relates to economic status and class and issues of race and gender. Marginalisation operates against different backgrounds and takes different forms. In relation to council housing, in some cases it is associated with inner city areas redeveloped through mass slum clearance while in others it is associated with new building on peripheral green field sites. In these cases the design and age of dwellings are likely to be very similar. In others the least popular estates may be of very different age and form.

It is against this background that the sale of council houses has occurred. In this chapter evidence about social segregation and social mix is discussed in relation to major urban areas. Has the sale of council houses operated to reduce social polarisation between areas and what evidence is there of different rates of sale between areas within cities? The central question being addressed, however, is a spatial one. If the sale of council dwellings in cities breaks up single tenure estates and creates mixed tenure estates then socio-tenurial polarisation will not necessarily have a spatial association. While the marginalised poor will remain in council dwellings they will not be living in single tenure ghetto estates and there will be greater social mix within areas than would be the case if all residential decisions on that estate were managed by local bureaucrats on grounds of social and housing need. Council house sales could then be a key way of preventing local authority estates from becoming what Bevan referred to as 'colonies of low income people' or 'twilight villages', and this view was strongly argued by proponents of council house sales. Three alternative propositions have also been argued. First, that increasing tenure mix does not imply increasing social mix. If sold council houses come to form the lowest demand segment of the owner occupied stock then it is the lowest income and marginal owner who will buy them. Second, without denying a trend towards a residual tenure for marginal groups, council housing in Britain remains far from a one-class tenure. In comparison with public housing in the USA, for example, council housing caters for a wide section of the community. Historical patterns and family and income changes mean that the characteristics of council tenants in general are much more diverse than the characteristics of new tenants. Council house sales could reduce this diversity both by affecting decisions about mobility and by reducing the supply of new lettings. One consequence could be that new tenants were a much more uniform social group. Thirdly, if sales vary by area the propositions outlined earlier could both prove true. Some estates would become mixed in tenure and social terms; others would not and indeed their progress towards one class ghettos would be increased by the very fact that opportunities for council housing became more restricted. It is this third proposition which is most easily addressed. Are council house sales distributed evenly between estates and across the stock and if there are variations what do they relate to? Are all areas becoming more mixed in tenure terms or is there a divergent pattern? Evidence on these questions is easier to obtain and can be seen as a necessary step in narrowing the range of likely outcomes. Propositions about longer term patterns of social and spatial change can be put forward with greater confidence if the initial pattern of sales is clear.

The earliest systematic evidence on spatial patterns of council house sales related to the period of discretionary sales in Birmingham. One conclusion drawn from this research was that sales were exacerbating patterns of socio-tenurial polarisation:

> Rather than reduce the dominance of public ownership in 'council ghettos' the policy does not affect these areas directly. However, it does affect people in these areas by reducing the opportunities available for them to transfer to other areas and house types. (Forrest and Murie, 1976, p. 12)

The volume of sales under the Right to Buy has been very much greater than under the previous discretionary policies. Some of the locally determined elements of policy (e.g. exclusions of flats, estate quotas) which contributed to differential rates of sale have also been removed with the right to buy. The pattern operating prior to 1980, however, appears to hold true for the subsequent period. In the remainder of this chapter evidence on this is presented in respect of three cities — London, Liverpool and Birmingham. It is argued that in each case the unequal pattern of sales is leading to a spatial and social polarisation within the city. Different types of evidence are drawn upon to address these issues.

LONDON

Since 1961 the geography of housing tenure in Greater London has been transformed. The decline of private renting and growth of both council housing and owner occupation have not taken place at an even pace throughout the area. Hamnett (1983) has detailed the emergence of an outer ring predominantly owner occupied and an inner ring predominantly rented. In 1961 private renting was the dominant tenure in Greater London, accommodating almost half of all households. By 1981 more than half of London's private tenants had disappeared. This decline had occurred in both inner and outer London but from a different base — a decline from 64% to 30% in inner London and from 30% to 15% in outer London. But the growth of other tenures to replace private renting has been uneven. Between 1961 and 1981 owner occupation expanded from 17% to 27% in inner London and in outer London from 53% to 62%. It is the public housing sector which has expanded much more rapidly in inner London and in 1981 catered for 43% of households — compared with 23% of outer London households. Rather than the decline of private renting resulting in a levelling of home ownership rates between inner and outer London the differential growth of

139

council housing has left tenure differences as marked as 20 years before but with council housing as the largest tenure in inner London. The distinctions are even sharper at borough level (Table 7.1). In outer London only four boroughs had over 25% of their households living in council housing. In inner London only one borough had fewer than 25% (Kensington and Chelsea where other forms of renting accounted for 54% of households). One factor affecting the differential rate of tenure change before 1979, although only to a minor extent, was the sale of council houses.

House prices in Greater London and South East England are the highest in the UK and this spatial polarisation of housing tenure is associated with a broader pattern of social segregation. The inner London boroughs include the major concentration of economic, social and housing stress. In a recent analysis based on 1981 census data and creating standardised scores to provide a single index of deprivation (a Z-score), only two of the 19 outer London boroughs had basic Z-scores in excess of any of the 13 inner boroughs (excluding the City of London). The same pattern applied in relation to Z-scores for *housing* deprivation. Nationally, it is London boroughs which score highest on this measure. All of the top ten are London boroughs (nine inner London plus Brent) and 16 of the top 20. (*Hansard*, 1986, vol. 99, cols 505–6). In 1981 only three of the outer London boroughs but all of the inner London boroughs (excluding the City of London) had over 10% unemployment.

The most recent survey of poverty in London (Townsend *et al.*, 1987) highlights a continuing and widening fissure between rich and poor. This involves the growth of dependency outside the labour market, the casualisation of large parts of the workforce and increasingly conspicuous wealth and rising prosperity at the top end of the labour market. All of these elements have a strong spatial dimension. Conditions in the poorest and richest boroughs have diverged further. For example, in relation to unemployment, Townsend, *et al.*, state: 'Unemployment has grown in all boroughs, but absolutely, and proportionately by more in the deprived inner London boroughs than in the outer boroughs. The "gap" between boroughs has widened from a ratio of 2.4 to 1 to 3.8 to 1' (p. 17). The picture emerging at this stage is of an increasingly polarised city with concentrations of deprivation and divergence in the way the tenure structure was changing — a divergence particularly between inner and outer London.

Against this background the progress of council house sales, especially under the Right to Buy, has taken a clear pattern. In the

140

period 1974–8 relatively few council house sales were completed. The decision to sell or not was at the discretion of the local authority and discounts to encourage tenants to buy were less generous than under the 1980 legislation. The most active selling authority was the Greater London Council and its sales were particularly concentrated on the cottage estates of outer London. Three inner London boroughs sold over 100 dwellings in this period and five outer London boroughs sold none. Sales clearly were not reducing tenure differences in this period. However, it is the much higher rate of sales after 1979 which represents the most striking restructuring of housing tenure. In the period from April 1979 to mid 1986 over 82,000 council dwellings were sold by London boroughs. These were principally sales under the Right to Buy but included discretionary sales, especially of vacant dwellings. In Greater London as a whole council housing was in absolute decline and privatisation through sales to tenants were more significant in the growth of home ownership than the activities of speculative housebuilders. Table 7.1 details the sale of council dwellings by London boroughs. It does not include sales by the GLC — a factor which means the total sales figure is understated and the spatial impact of these sales is ignored. In this period more than two thirds of all sales were in the outer boroughs.

The London region, as has already been noted, had the lowest rate of council house sales of any region of England. The variation in rates of sale between constituent authorities in the London region is also higher than in any other region of Britain. Sales have been highest in the outer London boroughs and lowest in inner London (Table 7.1). There are clear exceptions to this pattern. The City of London is a minor housing authority with a small stock of dwellings and can be disregarded. The more serious exceptions are Wandsworth which has achieved high sales principally because of the sale of vacant dwellings under discretionary policies; and Brent and Greenwich which are the lowest selling outer boroughs and in this and other respects form part of the real inner London. Figures 7.1 and 7.2 demonstrate the extent to which sales have reinforced the pattern noted by Hamnett (1983). Sales have been highest in boroughs with higher levels of owner occupation and have added to the momentum of demographic, economic and housing market change to widen the difference between inner and outer London. Table 7.1 and Figure 7.3 further demonstrate that sales have been lowest in areas with the highest levels of unemployment and of general deprivation (high positive Z-scores).

The geography of council housing is being redrawn in London and

141

Table 7.1: Households, unemployment and housing in London

	(1) House-holds	(2) % men 16–64 out of employment	(3) Basic Z-score	(4) Housing Z-score	(5) % council dwellings	(6) % owner occupied	(7) sale of public sector dwellings	(8) sale of public sector dwellings	(9) post 1979 public sector sales as % stock[2]
	1981	1981	1981	1981	1981	1981	1974–8	April 1979–June 1986	
Inner London									
City of London	2001	8.2	– 6.33	– 7.60	69.2	4.9	5	659	27.1
Camden	70061	12.2	4.05	5.64	38.9	23.8	5	565	1.6
Hackney	68499	16.1	6.69	8.62	57.4	16.5	–	561[1]	1.2[1]
Hammersmith & Fulham	61057	12.1	4.98	7.04	27.9	30.0	1	1773	8.7
Haringey	77090	11.1	4.86	6.58	28.5	43.6	–	1898[1]	7.4[1]
Islington	64317	14.1	4.80	6.23	55.6	16.9	–	826[1]	2.0[1]
Kensington & Chelsea	56092	10.4	3.34	5.07	14.0	31.7	157	608[1]	6.5[1]
Lambeth	95662	13.7	5.52	7.19	43.2	26.6	–	1045[1]	2.1[1]
Lewisham	88341	11.4	3.46	4.34	43.6	37.1	–	1986[1]	4.6[1]
Newham	14214	13.3	5.84	8.11	39.0	41.6	212	2794[1]	8.0[1]
Southwark	83127	14.4	4.40	5.38	64.8	15.8	47	1482[1]	2.3[1]
Tower Hamlets	53116	17.4	5.53	6.90	81.7	4.6	–	492[1]	1.0[1]
Wandsworth	98208	10.8	4.50	6.15	35.3	35.5	37	8837[1]	18.8[1]
Westminster, City of	73149	10.8	2.97	4.39	29.2	20.7	732	1471[1]	6.0[1]

Outer London

Barking & Dagenham	55773	11.0	1.08	1.27	65.3	31.4	–	6043[1]	15.8[1]
Barnet	106271	6.4	0.63	0.86	19.0	62.1	360	3897	18.2
Bexley	77500	6.3	-1.82	-2.31	19.1	72.9	654	2162[1]	16.3[1]
Brent	89268	10.1	4.62	6.28	22.1	53.9	–	1313[1]	5.8[1]
Bromley	109298	5.7	-1.76	-2.26	17.2	69.7	276	4462	21.5
Croydon	114592	6.6	0.35	0.57	18.8	64.7	277	4209[1]	17.7[1]
Ealing	100294	8.7	2.94	4.28	20.9	57.2	23	4141[1]	17.2[1]
Enfield	95075	7.4	0.56	0.71	22.5	66.2	115	3786	15.4
Greenwich	78070	10.9	2.08	2.54	47.0	38.5	–	2443	6.3
Harrow	70408	5.5	-0.33	-0.47	13.0	74.7	95	1639	16.4
Havering	84715	6.8	-1.89	-2.34	20.9	72.2	305	4829[1]	22.5[1]
Hillingdon	81755	6.0	-0.98	-1.28	26.7	61.3	56	3599[1]	16.9[1]
Hounslow	73112	7.4	1.68	2.46	30.0	53.1	–	2362	10.4
Kingston upon Thames	51435	5.3	-0.82	-0.88	14.3	68.8	81	1403	17.7
Merton	63985	6.5	0.56	0.81	21.8	61.7	60	3053[1]	19.5[1]
Redbridge	82762	6.9	0.23	0.35	15.2	72.9	431	2583[1]	18.8[1]
Richmond upon Thames	64133	5.5	-0.35	-0.24	14.6	62.2	86	1482[1]	13.1[1]
Sutton	63613	5.1	-1.78	-2.18	20.1	68.0	186	1994	14.4
Waltham Forest	81663	9.7	3.09	4.39	25.0	54.9	–	2226[1]	9.6[1]

Notes: (1) Indicates incomplete figure.

(2) Stock has been calculated as stock plus sales.

Sources: cols 1, 2, 5, 6, OPCS, 1981 *Census*; cols 3 & 4 Department of the Environment, *Urban Deprivation Note no. 2*; cols 7, 8 & 9 Department of the Environment statistics on sales progress.

Figure 7.1: Owner occupation in London, 1981

Index
1. City of London
2. Hammersmith
3. Islington
4. Kensington and Chelsea
5. Westminster
6. Lambeth
7. Southwark
8. Lewisham
9. Tower Hamlets
10. Hackney
11. Waltham Forest
12. Richmond upon Thames
13. Kingston upon Thames

50% or more

Kilometres (approx.)
0   5   10

Miles (approx.)
0   5   10

those dependent on council housing are increasingly located in inner London. And it is in these areas that council housing is most likely to consist of flats rather than traditional houses with gardens. Council flats and maisonettes have been heavily under-represented amongst sales in both inner and outer London boroughs and a greater coincidence between tenure and dwelling type is emerging throughout London. It is most pronounced in inner boroughs. One perspective on these trends is the changing pattern of demand for council housing. Rising levels of homelessness in the mid 1980s have resulted in the homeless dominating access and allocation to council housing. The reduced supply of council housing resulting from declining new building and relets is required to house the homeless and is often insufficient to achieve that. Those gaining access to council housing are more likely to have experienced homelessness and to lack bargaining power and ability to wait or

Figure 7.2: London — council house sales, 1979–86

Index
1. City of London
2. Hammersmith
3. Islington
4. Kensington and Chelsea
5. Westminster
6. Lambeth
7. Southwark
8. Lewisham
9. Tower Hamlets
10. Hackney
11. Waltham Forest
12. Richmond upon Thames
13. Kingston upon Thames

over 16%

8 to 16%

less than 8%

choose in housing. To this extent new tenants form a less diverse group than in the past when more routes into council housing were open. A less diverse group funnelled into a less diverse and geographically spread stock is part of the process of polarisation of the city. It is likely to affect future patterns of sale and the general development of council housing in London.

Two final points should be mentioned in connection with data on London. Firstly, high and low rates of sale do not coincide with party political control. While Conservative controlled Wandsworth has used its discretion to boost sales of vacant dwellings, the general pattern of sales does not relate to this. The permanent Conservative strongholds of Westminster and Kensington and Chelsea have not been the highest selling inner boroughs and their performance has been second best to a number of Labour controlled boroughs. The polarised tenure structure is not simply a consequence of different

145

Figure 7.3: London — council house sales and Z-scores

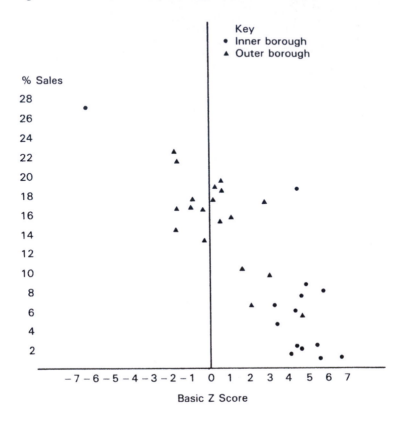

Source: Table 7.1.

political control. Nor does the evidence of administrative delay
suggest a single party-based division. Indeed, complaints referred to
and investigated by the Ombudsman include those levelled at
Conservative authorities (including Wandsworth) as well as Labour
controlled councils (Cochrane, 1986). Secondly, council dwellings
are sold at prices related to a market valuation. Even with discounts
of up to 60% available to tenants this places sale prices in excess of
what many sitting tenants could afford. Evidence from inner London
(Hackney) and outer London (Hounslow and Sutton) suggests that
income and occupation factors are important in determining who
buys and comparisons with less high priced regions suggest that

146

these factors are more important in determining the social and spatial pattern of sales in London than they are elsewhere (Forrest and Murie, 1984a; 1984b). Again this reinforces the inner-outer polarisation but it also implies a tenure polarisation within individual boroughs throughout London. The impact of the higher discounts available under the Housing and Planning Act 1986 to tenants of flats and the higher maximum discount available in 1987 could be important in London. However, the increase in house prices affects valuations of council houses and it seems likely that the interaction of high costs and high levels of deprivation will maintain rather than alter the established pattern of individual sales.

New forms of privatisation are, however, creating new pressures for inner London council tenants. The high valuations and high prices which act against individual purchase create the ideal conditions for the transformation of former council estates into exclusive, executive housing for London's expanding, high earning professional classes. For example, Moravian Tower, a 1969 red-brick, high rise block in Kensington and Chelsea was purchased and refurbished by Ideal Homes. They created one, two and three bedroomed flats selling for between £100,000 and £400,000. Hanging gardens were planted on every third floor set behind a glazed atrium. Usher (1987) gives details of other similar developments in London. He refers to an estate sold by Wandsworth to Regalian Properties. The St John's estate, now renamed Battersea Village, consists of 284 flatted dwellings built in the 1930s. These were bought by Regalian from the London borough of Wandsworth for £3,710,000, representing a cost of around £13,640 per flat. The flats were subsequently refurbished at a cost of around £20,000 per unit, and sold yielding a total profit of around £14 million. Refurbishment work involved general environmental improvements by which internal courtyards were landscaped and internally the walls of the flats were adjusted to enlarge the bathrooms and kitchens. A lift service was installed and security arrangements provided in the form of video entryphone installation in each flat. This form of relatively cosmetic refurbishment work is typical of work on projects around the country. Refurbishment frequently involves the installation of fully equipped kitchens, video entryphone systems and landscaped grounds, and some schemes provide whirlpool spas with communal sports facilities (Usher, 1987, p. 23).

Wandsworth has designated a number of estates as 'special sales areas' and has earmarked over £70,000 for its marketing campaign. The object of the sales area policy is to achieve vacant possession

147

of prime estates and to offer them for sale rather than reletting (see Grosskurth, 1983). The optimum conditions for privatisation through this method exist almost exclusively in inner London. It is only there that council housing is in prime locations and can be converted into luxury homes in a price range which will yield substantial profits. Various political, commercial and financial pressures are combining to favour this form of municipally managed gentrification. The style of management involved is not so different from that associated with private landlords 'winkling' tenants out to achieve profitable disposals into home ownership. The legislative powers provide the capacity for eviction as well as incentives to move. The consequence for London's expanding underclass will be a shrinking supply of council housing in a smaller number of locations.

The gentrification of inner London's council housing could begin to alter the socio-spatial patterns discussed earlier. However, the socio-tenurial patterns are liable to become more pronounced as the remaining council estates become more distinct and ghettoised.

LIVERPOOL

Merseyside, and especially Liverpool itself, has been particularly badly affected by the shift in economic balance. In the period since 1961 there has been a net loss of manufacturing employment in Liverpool. And between 1971 and 1981 the city lost a fifth of its overall employment. There has been a decline in port-related and associated industries located around the docks and city centre and a movement of new manufacturing industry and some established firms to peripheral areas where good environmental conditions combine with modern housing, new industrial estates and access to the national motorway network.

The decline in employment in city centre areas has only partly been balanced by the growth of city centre services. Indeed, Liverpool as a whole has suffered a net loss of employment in the service sector (Champion *et al.*,1987) In any case, many service sector jobs are often unsuitable for those laid off from declining manufacturing sectors. The impact of changes in the structure of employment in the central area on workers living in these areas has been particularly great because of difficulties in travelling to work from these areas. The 1981 census indicates that dependency on public transport remains high in the inner areas. In some districts 90% of households

148

are reliant on the public network of services.

As everywhere, the continuing rise in unemployment has hit some groups more than others. Working-class youth, the unskilled and ethnic minorities are particularly affected. Groups who generally fare badly in the labour market fare particularly badly in Liverpool. In a declining labour market those who have jobs hold on to them and there is less turnover in jobs that tend to have a high turnover under other circumstances. Employers, with a greater degree of choice in recruiting, discriminate against blacks and those with varied and inconsistent work records. The households experiencing this labour market trap, in which those with least skills and most labour market 'impediments' are pushed to the bottom, are particularly those living in inner city areas although it is also evident in other areas including some of the postwar peripheral council estates (Nabarro, 1980). Outmigration, clearance, disinvestment and the concentration of the poorest sections of the working class have created a striking coincidence of physical decay and social disadvantage in Liverpool's inner areas where black households are particularly concentrated. This concentration has changed little since the black community was established there, but council policies concerning clearance and improvement have created a situation of inbuilt racial disadvantage in which black people are concentrated in flats (Commission for Racial Equality, 1984).

Drawing on data from the city's planning department, it is possible to link a number of variables with areas of low status housing in general and public housing in particular. When variables commonly associated with disadvantage (large families, single parenthood, car ownership, overcrowding, unemployment, black households, unskilled employment, junior clerical or manual employment) are mapped at ward level, predominantly rented areas tend to score higher on a larger number of these variables. This association is not limited to areas mainly consisting of council housing. Indeed, inner areas of mixed public and private renting are in the highest percentage group for more variables than any other wards. What is marked, however, is that areas with higher levels of owner occupation are *less* likely to fall into the highest percentage groups on the 'disadvantage' variables. The two variables where this pattern is most consistently broken are single parent families and ethnicity and these variables (especially ethnicity) are those most seriously affected by sampling error. This can be elaborated using cluster analysis. Liverpool City Council has created 128 Basic Data Zones (BDZs) which are, as far as possible, internally homogeneous. The 128 BDZs are grouped into 24 clusters, 23 of which contain a significant level of local authority accommodation. From these, six 'neighbourhood types' have been identified which provide a general perspective on differentiation in council housing. These range from medium status areas to very low status areas. Areas of rented housing and of council housing are differentiated not only in terms of age, type and location of dwellings but in their social characteristics. Those parts of the city which are predominantly council housing areas or areas of mixed council and private renting are sharply distinguished. The areas of lowest status housing coincide with the areas of highest unemployment.

While these differences would be expected to affect the pattern of privatisation of public housing the association between council house sales and social and economic malaise is also crucial in terms of who benefits from sales and in terms of the impact of sales on those trapped in different parts of the housing and labour market. The 'lowest status' areas include more recently built estates with high proportions of flats.

Schemes for the disposal of public dwellings have operated in Liverpool at various times since 1962. Although the details of policy have changed the spatial pattern of sales is remarkably similar. Between 1971 and 1981 over 10% of dwellings were sold in 16 BDZs and of these only four were within the inner city area. Of the 35 BDZs, where over 5% of the council stock was sold, only six were within this inner city area. This pattern of sales reinforced a division between areas of rented housing (public and private) in the inner city and some peripheral estates and areas of relatively high home ownership were becoming more exclusively owner occupied. This was a more striking feature than the trickle of owner occupation into largely rented areas. For those continuing to rent, the spatial distribution of accommodation available to rent was becoming more restricted. The pattern of disposal of publicly owned dwellings between 1971 and 1981 can be compared with the council housing neighbourhoods referred to earlier. What emerges (Table 7.2) is a general trend for sales to be highest in highest status areas and minimal in lower status areas.

The three areas with over 1,000 council dwellings where no disposals occurred between 1971–81 were in the central area where levels of home ownership are very low. The predominantly council areas with high rates of disposal are, with one exception, those areas which exhibit least evidence of social stress. The conclusion drawn from this 1971–81 pattern is that sales have exacerbated polarisation

Table 7.2: Council house sales and council house neighbourhoods in Liverpool

Council housing neighbourhoods	Disposals as a proportion of stock of dwellings 1971–81 %
Medium status (1)	9.2
Low status (2)	5.4
Low status recently built inner area (3)	0.9
Low status recently built outer area (4)	1.3
Very low status predominantly council (5)	—
Very low status mixed rent (6)	0.5

within the city of Liverpool and especially between the high social stress inner city areas and the ring of more affluent, higher home ownership areas immediately outside this core.

Analysis of the pattern of sales since 1981 shows remarkable continuity. Changes in ward and data zone boundaries prevent a simple updating. However, a similar analysis of deprivation based on 1981 data produced five broad types of area. One of these labelled 'poorest council' included areas to the north and south of the city centre and the outskirts of the city. The housing stock in these areas:

. . . is some of the least desirable and most overcrowded in the city. Many of the dwellings are in a poor state of repair and this is reflected in the numbers of repair notices served on the local authority by tenants. It is no surprise that many of the dwellings are difficult to let and vacancy levels are high.

The poor housing conditions in which many of the tenants live are further highlighted by the 'disinfestation' levels which are the highest in the city.

Almost half the workforce is either unskilled or semi-skilled and the unemployment rates for both adults and youths are the highest in the city.

These poor economic circumstances are directly reflected in the high levels of children receiving free school meals and to some extent in the numbers of children taken into care and the above average rates of infant mortality.

The age structure in these areas is also one of its distinguising features with well above average numbers of pre-school and school-age children along with relatively few pensioners. These

151

Figure 7.4: Council house sales by ward — Liverpool, 1981–5

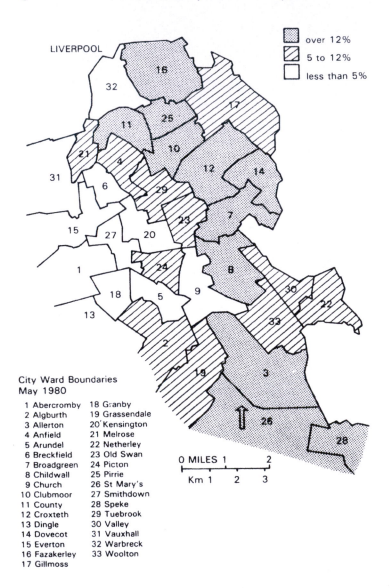

City Ward Boundaries
May 1980

1 Abercromby	18 Granby
2 Algburth	19 Grassendale
3 Allerton	20 Kensington
4 Anfield	21 Melrose
5 Arundel	22 Netherley
6 Breckfield	23 Old Swan
7 Broadgreen	24 Picton
8 Childwall	25 Pirrie
9 Church	26 St Mary's
10 Clubmoor	27 Smithdown
11 County	28 Speke
12 Croxteth	29 Tuebrook
13 Dingle	30 Valley
14 Dovecot	31 Vauxhall
15 Everton	32 Warbreck
16 Fazakerley	33 Woolton
17 Gillmoss	

high numbers of children are reflected in the levels of over-crowding which stand at almost twice city average. (City of Liverpool, 1984)

The evidence on the distribution of council house sales by ward shows that the poorest council areas and especially those in the redeveloped inner core of the city continue to have the lowest rates of sale. Figure 7.4 indicates the variation in sales completed between 1981 and 1985. In 1980 the housing stock in the North City and South City housing management districts consisted predominantly of flats (86% and 84% respectively). It is the wards in these areas (Vauxhall, Everton, Abercromby, Granby, Dingle) which have lowest sales and which remain predominantly council. Of the 7,382 sales completed between 1981 and 1986 only 106 (1.4% of all sales) were flats or maisonettes.

The pattern of sales by ward can be looked at in relation to levels of unemployment and other indicators of social deprivation. Again there is a coincidence between such indicators and low levels of sales. The general pattern is one of very high rates of unemployment in the areas adjoining the city centre and the outer council estates and relatively low rates in the owner occupied belt of the south outer city. The take-up of free school meals is described as 'a reflection of low income and as such presents a similar picture to the distribution of unemployment although with a much wider range. Rates were particularly high in inner city wards and in the outer council estates' (City of Liverpool, 1984).

Table 7.3 presents data on council house sales and social characteristics by ward. Wards are ranked according to the rate of sales (sales 1981–5 as % of council dwellings in 1981) and the following are indicated by a cross:

(i) the ten wards with highest percentage unemployment;

(ii) the ten wards with the highest proportion of the unemployed out of work for over one year;

(iii) the ten wards with the highest proportion of children (5–16) receiving free school meals;

(iv) the ten wards with the lowest proportion of 17–24 year olds receiving higher education awards.

Wards falling into the 'most deprived' category according to these indicators do generally have the lowest rates of sales. This is particularly true for the unemployment indicators and least true for

Table 7.3: Social malaise and council house sales — Liverpool

	% sales	% unemployed	% unemployed out of work for over one year	Children receiving free school meals	Higher education awards
Allerton	19.3				
Pirrie	19.1			X	
Clubmoor	16.9			X	
Croxteth	16.7				
Fazakerley	15.7				
Speke	14.8	X	X	X	X
St Mary's	14.2				
Broadgreen	13.8				
Childwall	12.9				
County	12.6				
Dovecot	12.6	X		X	
Anfield	11.2				
Tuebrook	11.0				
Valley	9.2		X		
Netherley	9.1				X
Gillmoss	7.4		X	X	X
Old Swan	6.9				
Aigburth	6.8				
Woolton	6.7				
Melrose	6.2		X	X	X
Grassendale	5.7				
Picton	5.7				
Breckfield	4.7	X	X		X
Warbreck	3.7				
Smithdown	3.3	X	X	X	X
Kensington	2.8	X			
Dingle	2.7				
Vauxhall	1.7	X	X	X	X
Granby	1.1	X	X	X	X
Arundel	1.0	X			
Everton	0.7	X	X	X	X
Abercromby	0.2	X	X		X

Source: City of Liverpool Planning Department, 1984.

the free school meals indicator. It is also apparent that there is no neat fit between levels of sales and the indicators used. The pattern is consistent with a view of sales exacerbating intra tenure polarisation but it is also compatible with arguments advanced elsewhere that in somewhere like Liverpool the marginal poor are not restricted to pockets of the council sector. Nevertheless, the net effect of the processes indicated here is that the disadvantaged are becoming more spatially concentrated. The other element in this process is one in which among new tenants the most disadvantaged get the worst dwellings (Commission for Racial Equality, 1984).

The geography of council housing in Liverpool is being substantially changed. Its concentration in inner city areas and flats is becoming more pronounced. Those sections of the population with least ability to purchase in the market and with least bargaining power in negotiating access to council housing will have fewer alternatives to housing in these inner city areas. The links between economic circumstances, tenure, dwelling type and location will become more pronounced. Those in a labour market trap are in an increasingly tight housing trap as the supply of properties available to transfer out of the inner city declines. Those able to buy are experiencing an increase in opportunities to move — to starter homes or resold council houses. The implications of this pattern are of an increasingly polarised and segregated city. The areas of the city are sharply differentiated in both housing and employment terms. Increasingly, the housing and employment patterns are coinciding. Areas where economic stress is greatest are least affected by the growth of owner occupation. If present trends continue the more affluent council housing areas will increasingly become owner occupied. Inner city residents are affected by inconvenient location in relation to job opportunities, by reduced opportunities for renting outside the inner area, and arguably, by a hardening of images and social reputation associated with area of residence as disadvantage is increasingly concentrated by area. The impact of high rents, increasing dependence on state rebates and the poverty trap provide the final element tying employment and housing situation into a circular mesh of mutually reinforcing disadvantages which exclude those living in certain areas from a variety of opportunities and privileges available to others.

BIRMINGHAM

Birmingham is widely acknowledged to have been the pioneer in developing a substantial council house sales drive. Policies have varied with changes in political control, but in the period since 1966 the economic circumstances of Birmingham and the West Midlands have change dramatically. It was not, however, until the late 1970s that the underlying economic decline combined with demographic change to produce rising unemployment. And service sector employment increased at less than the national average rate and did not counteract the loss of manufacturing employment (Spencer *et al.*, 1986). Between 1978 and 1982 the manufacturing workforce

155

declined by 20%. At the 1981 census male unemployment in some of Birmingham's inner city areas stood at 30%. By 1985 Birmingham's unemployment rate was 15% and among Birmingham's unemployed a particularly high proportion fell into the long-term unemployed category (Champion, *et al.*, 1987, p. 87). The spatial pattern of employment has also changed. Spencer *et al.* (1986) refer to a 'redistribution of both population and employment from the conurbation to the surrounding areas' (p. 71). The impact of these changes will have been particularly severe for households living in inner city neighbourhoods. It is in this context that the restructuring of Birmingham's housing market should be considered. This is discussed in two sections — sales and allocations. This enables us to examine changes in the distribution of the stock and to look at aspects of the changing social profile of tenants.

COUNCIL HOUSE SALES IN BIRMINGHAM

Evidence on council house sales is more widely available from Birmingham than for other local authorities. A survey carried out in 1973 established that neither dwellings sold nor households buying were representative. Among purchasers neither the youngest nor the oldest tenants were fully represented (Murie, 1975). Subsequent studies have drawn attention to the spatial variation in sales and related this to policy factors, dwelling type characteristics and popularity of estates and properties (Forrest and Murie, 1976; 1984a). The implications of this for transfer and allocation policies and mobility and choice within the public sector were emphasised along with the long-term implication that council housing would become more restricted in terms of location and dwelling type. Evidence on who bought former council houses when they were resold showed that these purchasers were younger than sitting tenant purchasers, had no children or had young families and were more comparable to first time buyers in general than to new council tenants (Forrest, 1980). In this sense the areas where sales had occurred were changing their social composition relative to areas with very low levels of sale.

The city's own evidence to the House of Commons Environment Committee (vol. II, Minutes of Evidence) in 1981 was consistent with this overall picture. This evidence suggested that the Right to Buy would have less impact in Birmingham than in areas which had not previously been selling houses. It was expected that houses would be sold to those tenants who were more financially secure leaving a greater percentage of tenants suffering social disadvantage (e.g. single parent and other low income families). It was not expected that the sale of flats would be significant and fewer sales of houses were expected in less popular areas. Transfer opportunities would be affected, especially for families living in flats. The properties that had been sold were predominantly family houses in the suburbs and not in the inner city areas. Areas of council housing with large proportions of flats had relatively low rates of sale and this was expected to continue in the future. If flats were excluded, the variation in the rate of sale of houses was still considerable. Sales were greater in areas around the city boundary (except in the west). On 8% of estates 30% or more houses had been sold (the highest rate was 56%). On 31% of estates fewer than 10% of houses had been sold.

Birmingham City Council maintains a computer list of sold properties and the pattern of sales can be analysed from this at ward level and according to age, dwelling type and size characteristics of the stock. In May 1986 this source referred to 35,705 sales. Some 22% of the stock had been sold. The highest rates of sale were in Hall Green (41%) and Sutton New Hall and Stockland Green (34%). These are all wards with low proportions of council housing. In contrast the lowest rates of sale were in Ladywood (4%), Aston (6%) and Edgbaston (8%). The first two of these wards have high proportions of council housing and are redeveloped inner city areas while the council stock in Edgbaston is all postwar. These three wards have among the highest proportion of council housing as flats. Figure 7.5 maps this pattern of council house sales. Lowest sales are in wards concentrated around the city centre with two outliers in Sutton Vesey and King's Norton.

Of the 35,705 sales in Birmingham, 35,061 (98%) have been of houses rather than flats, maisonettes, bungalows or other dwelling types. Sales of houses account for 35% of the stock of houses. The continuing low rate of sale of flats is a considerable influence on the pattern of sales. If sales are expressed as a proportion of houses sold, however, the variation between wards is not eradicated. The lowest rates of sale are in Aston (13%), Sparkhill (14%), Ladywood (18%) and Handsworth (18%). The highest rates of sale are in Bournville (53%), Northfield (53%) and Sutton New Hall (49%). Figure 7.6 demonstrates that sales expressed in this way show an even more pronounced split between inner and outer city with only Longbridge and King's Norton in the south breaking the pattern. Thus, the

Figure 7.5: Sale of council dwellings by ward — rates of sale, Birmingham

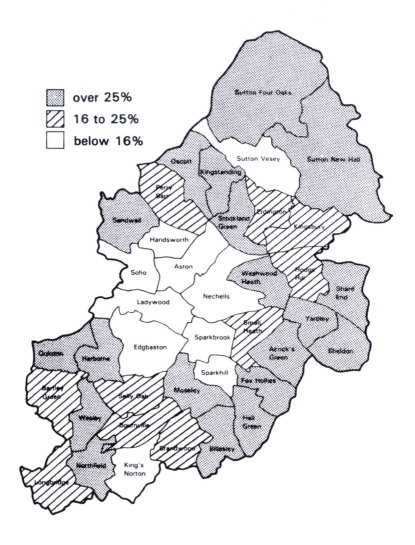

Figure 7.6: Council house sales by ward — rates of sale expressed in relation to stock of houses only, Birmingham

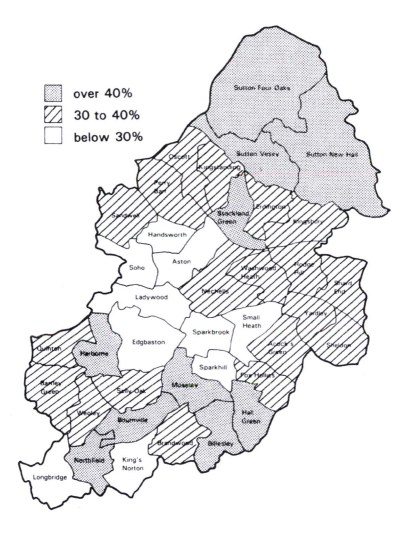

over 40%

30 to 40%

below 30%

Sutton Four Oaks

Oscott

Kingstanding

Sutton Vesey

Sutton New Hall

Perry Barr

Erdington

Sandwell

Stockland Green

Kingsbury

Handsworth

Soho

Aston

Washwood Heath

Hodge Hill

Shard End

Nechells

Ladywood

Small Heath

Yardley

Sparkbrook

Quinton

Edgbaston

Acock's Green

Sheldon

Harborne

Sparkhill

Fox Hollies

Bartley Green

Moseley

Weoley

Selly Oak

Hall Green

Bournville

Brandwood

Billesley

Northfield

King's Norton

Longbridge

variation in sales and the divergent progress of different wards is not explained solely by the distribution of flats. Even when these are removed from the calculus there is a clear spatial pattern. Figures 7.7, 7.8 and 7.9 express some of these relationships in a different way. Figure 7.7 shows that the rate of sales declines systematically with the proportion of flats in the stock. Figure 7.8 demonstrates a similar relationship between rates of sales and rates of unemployment. Finally, Figure 7.9 shows the rate of *house* sales also varies systematically in relation to unemployment.

The various evidence summarised here demonstrates a consistent pattern of change within Birmingham's council housing. In certain areas, and particularly in the outer wards with attractive houses with gardens, council estates have changed significantly and have become mixed tenure estates. There are visible changes associated with porches and frontages. There are also consequences in terms of who lives in these estates, with a greater proportion of younger childless couples than would otherwise have been the case. But in other areas, and particularly in inner city estates with high numbers of flats and maisonettes, the picture is very different. They remain largely one tenure estates and have become more obviously one class estates. Those on the social and economic margins such as the homeless and unemployed have been increasingly funnelled into these estates.

The polarised city involves a concentration of the unemployed and the poor in the residual one tenure estates with a decreasing social mix. And the characteristics and distribution of council tenants are affected by other pressures in addition to the pattern of sales. They involve the allocation of new tenancies and changes in the age and household composition of existing tenants and the pattern of tenancy terminations for reasons other than the sale of council houses. The combined effect of these processes may, for example, increase the extent to which council housing caters for special needs groups and single parent and other low income households.

COUNCIL HOUSE ALLOCATIONS IN BIRMINGHAM

Research on the pattern of new allocation in Birmingham in 1978–9 and 1980–1 showed that new allocations were less likely to involve allocation to prewar dwellings, to houses and to larger dwellings than would have been the case if the characteristics of the stock as a whole were reflected. This is affected by patterns of new building

Figure 7.7: Council house sales and flats, Birmingham wards

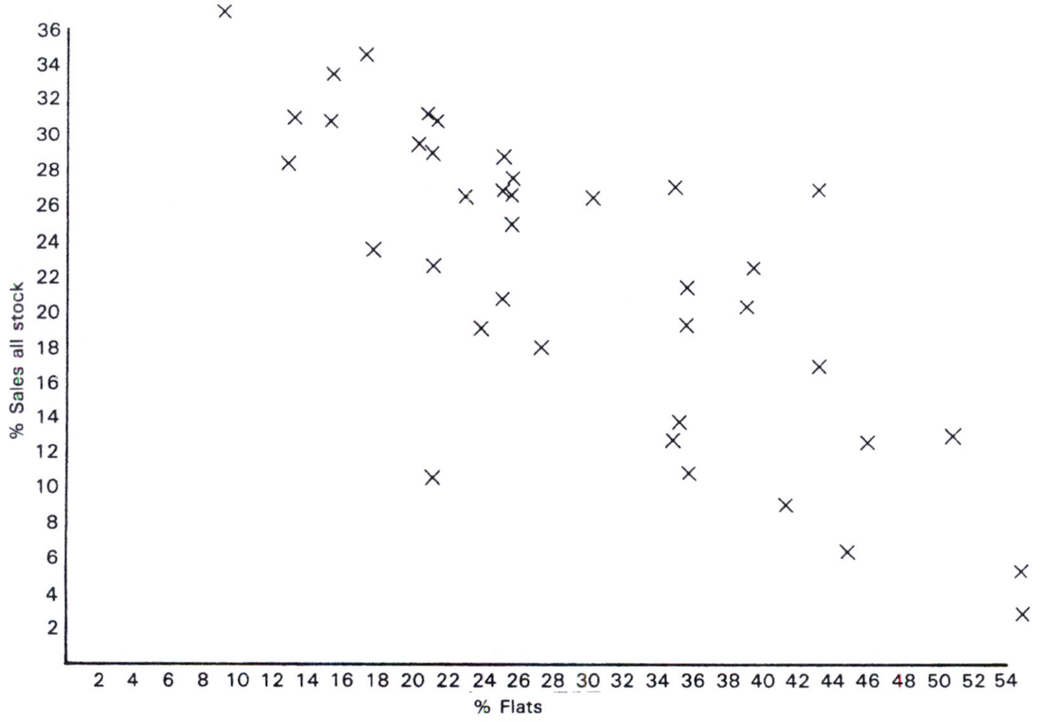

Figure 7.8: Sale of council dwellings and unemployment, Birmingham wards

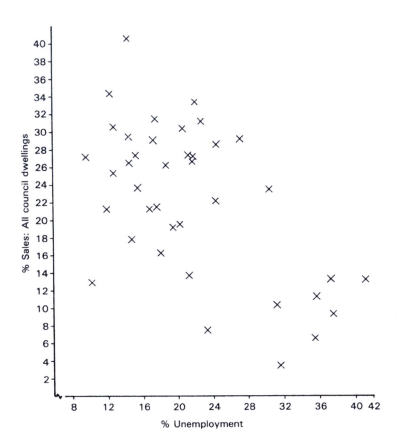

and by capital programmes but also by aspects of mobility and need.

Even in 1978–9 only slightly over one in three of all allocations (including transfers) were to households from the waiting list. This had fallen to almost one in four in 1980–1 when single persons were considerably more important in allocations. It has fallen further since. Allocations to homeless households also were significant and in 1980–1 were of equal importance to waiting list allocations.

Figure 7.9: Council house sales and unemployment, Birmingham wards

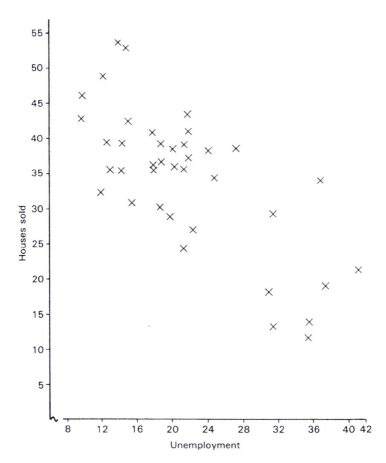

Households moving into the council sector differed significantly from the general profile of tenants (or from those moving out by buying as sitting tenants). In comparison with existing tenants new allocations involved a high proportion of single parent households and small families. Large adult households were significantly under-represented.

When new tenants as opposed to new allocations (which include transfers) are looked at separately in these two periods, differences

163

from the profile of existing tenants become more marked. Small, adult households and small, single parent families accounted for 74% and 72% of new tenants but for less than 59% of existing tenants. Among new tenants and transfers some three quarters of small, adult and small, single parent households were new tenants (and one quarter transfers). In contrast only some 50% of larger households were new tenants. This impression of changing characteristics of council tenants is also affected by other factors including sales, tenancy terminations and family and demographic changes. It implies a general tendency for council housing to play an increasing role in housing relatively deprived sections of the population. There is, however, a wider and more complicated issue connected with new allocations. As the location and characteristics of the council stock change (at present principally as a result of sales) questions of who is in what housing become significant. Those allocated to more saleable properties may subsequently buy. Those in less saleable dwellings are less likely to. However, following the route taken by current purchasers these households might expect to move within the council sector and to buy in the future.

Certain household types are considerably more likely to be allocated to flats and maisonettes. Although larger households and families with children are more likely to be allocated houses the pattern is not a simple function of household type. Substantial numbers of families with children (especially single parent families) go to flats or maisonettes and a small number of small, adult households and the great majority of large, adult households go to houses. This was particularly marked in 1980–1. The small, adult household groups included almost all the households (elderly persons) allocated to bungalows. The greatest contrasts involved clearance and transfer cases and the homeless. While in the former two groups only between 2 out of 10 and 3 out of 10 households were allocated to flats, in the two homeless categories the range was from 6 out of 10 to over 9 out of 10 allocated to flats. Allocation category clearly influenced the type of dwelling obtained.

Additional data on transfers indicate considerable movement between dwelling types and as many as 14% of transfers involved moves from houses to flats (in some cases probably of elderly persons). The general direction of movement is from flats and maisonettes and towards houses and bungalows. Prior to transfer, in 1980–1, 36% of households were in houses or bungalow. After transfer 60% were so housed. Movement away from maisonettes was particularly marked: 21% of all households were in maisonettes before transfer and only 5% after transfer. In 1978–9 there were fewer 'contrary' moves but the resulting pattern was identical and the flow away from flats more marked. The outcome, although inevitably affected by short run fluctuations in supply, is consistent with the past experience of tenants and demonstrates the effects of transfers in facilitating moves within the local authority stock. In 1978–9 and 1980–1 over two-thirds of all transfers involved three bedroomed dwellings. These were being released by households in later stages of the family cycle moving to smaller dwellings (21% of all transfers in 1978–9 and 20% in 1980–1) and being used by 'growing households' and those changing in the same bedroom category (40% in 1978–9 and 46% in 1980–1) with the remainder moving to larger dwellings. The number of properties released by transfers to smaller dwellings will decline as a consequence of purchase. Consequently, the scope for movement by growing families and to facilitate changes in dwelling type and location will decline. As opportunities to transfer are reduced so the first allocation will become a permanent or longer term allocation. Those whose first allocation is to a less satisfactory dwelling will be less likely to remedy this and move to houses which they might subsequently choose to buy. The opportunities afforded by council dwellings to this generation of tenants are as a consequence very different from those of the previous generation.

Both this data and research elsewhere indicate that the operation of the allocation system involves a range of influences. What is clear, however, is that households of different types coming into council housing through different routes will predictably be allocated to particular parts of the stock. Consequently the reduction in opportunities to transfer (especially from flats to houses) has a disproportionate impact on those household types allocated to flats and maisonettes and on households coming into council housing through those allocation routes which are most likely to lead to flats and maisonettes (homeless and waiting lists). The opportunity to relax allocation constraints, to enable a more varied pattern of allocation to particular household types and allocation categories, will decline as sales and reduced new building affect the supply of dwellings to let. At the same time the opportunity to modify these allocations through subsequent transfers will be affected. While all tenants and applicants will be affected by these changes the most severe effects will be felt by those in the least desirable properties, those with least bargaining power and those where family structure or change imply a need for transfer.

165

The impact of sales to sitting tenants prior to 1979 was dampened and delayed, particularly because council house building was sustained at a high level. In addition the loss of relets arising from sales was relatively low in the early years because of the age profile of buyers. These dampening factors are no longer significant. It is now over 20 years since sales were increased significantly in Birmingham and the loss of relets associated with such sales is becoming more marked.

Changes in the council sector are taking place alongside a long established decline in private renting. The net effect of tenure change in Birmingham is a decline in rented accommodation. Those who hitherto would have found accommodation in the rented sectors are competing for a declining supply of less desirable dwellings or in some cases will look to the lower end of the owner occupied market. The changing social role of council housing affects its capacity to offer housing opportunities to the present generation of new tenants and applicants comparable to the opportunities of those who have succeeded in buying their council house. The experience of over 35,000 council tenants in Birmingham is of a public service which initially provided them with good housing and latterly with ownership. New tenancies are more likely to be of second best housing. The new tenants are less likely to be able or want to buy these dwellings. New tenants will find few initial or transfer choices as the council sector declines and is more spatially concentrated. Those unable to buy are becoming more concentrated in parts of the council built stock. The polarisation within council housing becomes part of the polarisation of the city.

CONCLUSIONS

The evidence presented in this chapter of marked spatial variation in sales is consistent with studies of English cities as diverse as Leeds, Bristol, Oxford and Norwich (Bassett, 1980; Forrest and Murie, 1986a; Brough, 1977; Friend, 1980). A similar spatial pattern is apparent in Scottish cities. Sales in Scotland up to 30 June 1985 showed Glasgow as having sold a lower proportion of its stock than other Scottish cities. Properties sold tended to be in the most desirable parts of the city and the rate of sale varied from some 0.4% in Castlemilk and 0.5% in Easterhouse to over 5% in Anniesland and Baillieston. Flatted dwellings comprised nearly 85% of Glasgow's council stock yet only 34% of sales were of flats. The increased discounts for flats under 1986 legislation would result in qualification for very high discounts and the comment in their Annual Housing Review 1985 is that it is likely that the greatest number of sales will be in four-in-a-block property in better areas, which means that the council's stock of good quality housing will be further eroded. Work in Aberdeen (Sewel, Twine and Williams, 1984) showed a variation in levels of applications from 21.3% in Kingswells to nil in four areas. Correlational analysis showed statistically significant links between the level of sales, the proportion of flatted properties, the popularity of the estate and the social profile of each estate. The strongest relationship was with the social profile. No sales had been recorded (at that stage) in those areas of Aberdeen which the council regarded as difficult to let and the implication was that the quality of dwellings available for letting will decline. A subsequent paper on the period October 1980 to June 1984 (Williams, Sewel and Twine, 1986) was still affected by the small number of sales completed in Aberdeen. The evidence presented however was seen as consistent with that of Foulis (1985) and with evidence from England. Sales were stated to have been predominantly of the better dwellings in the more popular areas.

Because of low rates of sale even in the higher quality parts of the stock the rate of polarisation is much slower than in the cities referred to earlier in this chapter. In all of these cities the trends indicate an increasing polarisation between tenures and a divide within the council built sector. This involves a split between the mixed tenure areas of more popular housing and the one class estates of less popular dwellings. The split is more general and more striking than ever emerged previously through allocation policies. With the decline in private renting there are fewer housing options for poorer people. With the recession there is a larger impoverished community dependent on the rented sector. With a policy which leads to differential rates of sale of dwellings and which is not generating new lettings through new build or acquisition those dependent on renting are increasingly funnelled towards a more limited number of estates. And there are fewer chances of transferring from these estates. Those whose economic circumstances improve (and living on stigmatised estates is likely to make this more difficult) may be able to move on — there is little likelihood of escape for the rest. These estates are not all the same. However, they are more likely to be high rise and system built, to consist of flats and maisonettes, to be associated with slum clearance rehousing or particular periods of development, to have been explicit dump

167

estates, or to have been consistently let to households with low bargaining power. In this sense there is an accretion of *households* with problems on *estates* with problems. These parts of the council sector are exhibiting less social mix and a greater concentration of social malaise. They are nearer to the ghettoised estate than they have ever been.

The problems represented by the process of polarisation of the city are not ones of tenure polarisation. There is a partial coincidence between tenure status and spatial location. But this is a product of the historical pattern of building and transfer of ownership. The important element in the polarised city is the increasing *spatial* concentration of different groups irrespective of tenure. The sale of council dwellings increases tenure mix — more so in some estates than others. But the key issue is its impact on social segregation. It is clear that, in some parts of the council stock, ghettoisation is made more pronounced by a variety of trends including sales. In those estates where sales are high tenure mix could have various impacts on social mix. If former council dwellings become the bottom end of the owner occupied market then lower income and marginal owners are more likely to buy those dwellings on resale. Differences in class and income between those purchasers and those who would have been allocated these dwellings as council tenants will be limited. It is still likely that they will differ in family cycle terms. A more likely prospect however is that well built houses with gardens on the edges of estates and next to areas of home ownership will not form the bottom end of owner occupation and tenure mix will not reduce social mix. The consequence of this process is to exacerbate the inequalities between the 'urban priority areas' and affluent middle Britain. The polarised city is not a product of council house sales but they have been a major contributing factor to the emerging socio-spatial divisions in British cities. While a new set of inner city policies may ameliorate these divisions its overall impact will be limited if the main thrust of housing policy continues to reproduce and deepen urban inequalities and their spatial concentration.

8

Contextualising the Sale of Council Housing

So far we have dealt with the social and spatial impacts of council house sales at different levels. Patterns of social and spatial polarisation can be identified within cities and between regions. There is an accumulation of evidence that council housing is becoming more clearly associated with various groups in the population which might be appropriately labelled marginal. British council housing is becoming the form of housing provision for those excluded from the mainstream of social consumption; a mainstream characterised by individualised, commodity consumption fuelled by credit finance. And the owner occupied house occupies a pivotal position in that process. Progressively, being a council tenant signifies relative poverty. From its historical role as a tenure of relative privilege for the skilled working classes, low investment, privatisation and the stigmatised building of particular periods are combining with the growth of the unemployed and the working-class elderly to produce a quite different set of social relations. Underprivilege is not, however, confined to council housing. On the contrary, there are pockets of deprivation in both the privately rented sector and in owner occupation and homelessness, overcrowding and involuntary sharing are prominent features of Britain in the 1980s. But the worst aspects of deprivation tend to be less visible and less concentrated than the mass high rise housing and dump estates which dominate large sections of cities.

Despite the accuracy of these observations it would be erroneous to assume an evenness of change. Council housing has developed at a different pace for different reasons and in different forms. At various stages we have emphasised the local variations in its form and function and we need to situate the provision of council housing within other social and economic dimensions of local communities.

Localities have distinctive features in terms of occupational structure, demography, and history. We cannot ascribe common meanings and features to the impact of privatisation in different areas. The obtrusiveness of high rise developments in the urban concentrations of London and places like Birmingham and Liverpool dominates our view of contemporary council housing. But that view conceals the variety of building types within the tenure. In the past and within limits, local administrations have been able to exercise discretion in the pattern and rate of building for public rental. They have also been able to exercise discretion in its disposal through sales. Whilst it would be misleading to claim that locally based decisions have always been the most sensible in terms of local housing needs, they have nevertheless produced distinct patterns of provision reflecting local social structures. The Right to Buy, as a non-discretionary policy imposed from above, lacks sensitivity to local conditions and local needs. It assumes a common set of values and aspirations and similarities in the structure and role of council housing.

The sale of council houses has quite different impacts and consequences in terms of households and localities because council housing varies significantly between localities. The visibility of the high rise developments of the 1960s and 1970s and their dominance in some inner urban areas, has fuelled prejudice and misconception regarding the social structure of council housing. Recent policy and academic commentary and analysis (see, for example, Coleman, 1985; Praks and Priemus, 1985) risk consolidating a view that there is a necessary and inevitable connection between council housing, uniformity and low quality. Different phases of public provision have produced marked variations in design and quality. It would be mistaken to excuse and underestimate the bureaucratic and paternalistic excesses of public landlordism. But oppressive paternalism, high rise living or entrapment on mass, dump estates has not been the experience of the majority of council tenants. It often seems that judgements and images of council housing derive from mental models which contrast high rise Hackney with suburban Guildford. It would not be less appropriate to compare run down, owner occupied tunnel backs in Saltley, Birmingham, with the council owned, cottage estates of Bromley.

The uneven pattern of council house sales within and between localities which has been discussed in earlier chapters reflects differentiation within the council housing sector. This differentiation is not just about the physical structure of the stock (e.g. flats versus houses) but about the differences in local social and economic structures.

THE TYPICAL PURCHASER? THE TYPICAL PURCHASE?

Before discussing further some of the local dimensions referred to above, it is appropriate to emphasise some of the apparent similarities and consistencies. Since the mid-1970s there has been a steady accumulation of evidence demonstrating the selective impact of council house sales in terms of who buys and what they buy. The earliest academic studies of the effects of council house sales were undertaken in the West Midlands in the early to mid-1970s (Murie, 1975; Niner, 1975; Forrest and Murie, 1976). These studies were essentially policy evaluations focusing on three main questions: what kinds of properties were being sold? how did the profile of purchasers compare with the tenant population as a whole? how would sales of council dwellings affect future vacancy rates?

The debate over loss of relets remains complicated because of the difficulty of isolating sales (as opposed to say lack of new building) as the dominant factor in vacancy losses or growing waiting lists. But as Niner (1975) remarked — 'no continuing policy can remain "short term" and "moderate" indefinitely — both time and numbers are cumulative' (p. 87). It may be that it is only now that we are in a position to make a reasonable calculation of the impact in these terms (see the discussion in Chapter 6). The problem remains, however, that the demands on and the context around council housing have changed so dramatically that to privilege sales as the key factor in reduced housing opportunities would risk underestimating the broader pattern of disinvestment in public housing and the corrosive effects of economic recession on the social and economic fabric. Moreover, the precise impacts of sales and minimal new building will vary according to *local* housing market conditions.

The local impact of sales on relets relates to the issue of the resale of former council houses on the private market. Prior to the Right to Buy, discretionary sales in many localities were recent and limited in number. One counterclaim to the view that sales would inevitably reduce relets was the argument that since former council houses would eventually emerge for sale on the private market there would be no numerical loss. Rossi (1977) suggested, moreover, that some former council houses might be purchased by those on council

171

waiting lists. Birmingham, with its long history of council house sales, has as yet provided the only research evidence on this issue (Forrest, 1980). This work suggested that former council houses did not emerge as the cheapest properties on the market and that when compared with the original sitting tenant purchasers buyers tended to be younger, at an earlier stage in the family cycle and a considerably higher proportion were in white-collar employment. Further in-depth social survey work carried out on an estate in Birmingham produced a similar profile of new purchasers. Those buying former council houses were more comparable to first time buyers generally than new council tenants. This is hardly surprising. As council dwellings become subject to allocation through market processes they become part of a general pool of houses available for purchase. They no longer have any specific function in the local housing market. What is crucial is the price structure of the local owner occupied market. In a high price locality, resold former council houses are unlikely to be affordable by those who would have sought to rent. It is in London where this is most evident. A council dwelling available for rent at £35 per week can a few years later be offered for sale at £100,000 or more.

Where sales of *vacant* dwellings occur the effect on relets is direct and unambiguous. Some of the more enthusiastic selling authorities pursue policies of disposing of dwellings as they become vacant. Prior to the Right to Buy, the Conservative administration in Nottingham only returned vacant dwellings to the rental pool if they remained unsold after three weeks. Wandsworth, the most celebrated seller of vacant dwellings, disposed of 3465 vacant dwellings between 1980 and 1985 — more than all their sales to sitting tenants in that period. There are other effects of sales on housing supply which are impossible to quantify. Most obviously, the steady flow of former council houses on to the private housing market may dampen demand for new housing, especially at the lower end of the market. Certainly the building industry has never been unequivocal in its support for council house sales recognising that it may not be compatible with the need to sell new houses. Moreover, the products of the speculative housebuilding industry do not always compare favourably with former council houses in terms of quality and space standards (Forrest, 1980).

Research evidence on the selective nature of purchasers and dwellings sold is less speculative. Indeed, it has shown a remarkable consistency over the years. In 1975 the profile of Birmingham purchasers was of a long established tenant, in middle age, with a fairly large family growing up, earning above average wages, in a skilled manual occupation and often with more than one wage earner in the household. Niner's research, carried out at around the same time, found a similar pattern in five other West Midlands authorities (Niner, 1975). Further research carried out before and since the Right to Buy was introduced has continued to confirm the significance of the family life cycle in recruiting new purchasers. Council house purchasers have had consistently similar age and family characteristics. In Birmingham, for example, the characteristics of tenants buying in 1979–80 did not differ substantially from those buying between 1968 and 1973. And research in other localities including Solihull, Plymouth, New Forest, Hounslow, Carrick, Hyndburn and Derwentside has produced similar profiles of typical purchasing households with male principal earners in skilled manual work in mid to late 40s and with a grown up family (Forrest and Murie, 1984a, 1984b). Whilst higher discounts under the 1980 and 1984 Housing Acts have drawn in more elderly purchasers (often assisted by children), younger and older tenants remain relatively underrepresented. Factors such as type of dwelling occupied, earnings levels and discount calculations combine with family life cycle effects to produce this pattern. Tenants in their late 40s are more likely to have moved through the transfer system and be occupying an attractive dwelling, their children will be earning or have left home and they will be eligible for a high or maximum discount on valuation. Conversely, younger, newer entrants are likely to be in high rise flats or less desirable houses. And those tenants with the least bargaining power — the homeless, single parent families — are more likely to end up in the less attractive parts of the stock. While elderly tenants may now be eligible for 60 or 70% discounts the inclination to buy will be reduced by age and declining and low incomes. Also, some elderly tenants will be in properties of special design which are exempt from the Right to Buy. Generally there is a coincidence between those households for whom purchase is most appropriate and financially possible and those occupying the more desirable dwellings.

These factors also help to explain the selective nature of sales in terms of dwelling type. This selectivity is most apparent in the small number of flats which have been sold. Under old discretionary policies flats were in fact excluded. Their inclusion under the Right to Buy has, however, done little to alter the skewed pattern of disposal. Flats represent just under a third of the stock but account for only 5% of sales. Some localities have very few council flats.

It is in the major cities and particularly in inner London where this distorted pattern is most evident. Hackney has 83% of its council stock as flats yet virtually none have been sold. A similar pattern can be found in other inner London boroughs. For example, Southwark has some 47,000 flats yet by March 1986 had only sold 377. On the outer periphery, in Hounslow, sales have been almost exclusively of three bedroomed houses — a category which represents only a third of its council stock (see Forrest and Murie, 1984a, 1984b, 1986b). Legal complications and high service charges have undoubtedly hindered the sale of flats. There are predictable difficulties for a prospective purchaser in a block which might remain predominantly tenanted. There is also a strong association in Britain between *houses* and home ownership. Council tenants in flats may wish to become home owners but they wish to own a house with a garden, not a flat on the sixteenth floor of a block in the middle of Birmingham or Liverpool. However, as was noted earlier, the higher discounts now available for flat purchasers may affect overall patterns and individual judgements.

It would be equally mistaken to assume that all council *houses* are desirable acquisitions. Not only is there evidence that sales are higher on more popular housing estates but end terraces and properties on the edge of estates are more likely to sell (Forrest and Murie, 1976; Brough, 1977; Bilcliffe, 1979; Friend, 1980). The pattern is less consistent and less marked than the clear distinction between house and flat sales but nevertheless accentuates the asset stripping effects of the sales policy.

COUNCIL HOUSING AND THE LOCALITY

We have established an image of the typical council house purchaser and the typical purchase. Whilst the relatively privileged section of the working class has benefited from the provision of high quality council housing, those now benefiting from its disposal are drawn from the same group. Conversely, the excluded residuum once crowded into privately rented terraces in the inner city is increasingly accommodated in less saleable, less desirable and less popular council owned flats and houses. But such an image, whilst usefully provocative and evocative, can only indicate the general drift in housing policy and provision. It can overstate the contrasts between those who purchase and those who remain as tenants and over-emphasise the residual nature of council housing. Whilst it is true that a substantial number of tenants regard themselves as too old and too impoverished to consider buying, and would not wish to purchase the dwelling they are occupying (see OPCS, 1985), it is also the case that among non-buyers are those on reasonable income and in attractive dwellings.

National surveys and comparisons across a number of local studies have established the characteristics of the typical purchaser household. Averages, however, conceal significant variations. Once we move beyond broad social categories and dwelling types, differences do emerge. What is being bought, why people are buying and the implications for local housing markets and policies are highly varied. Stated simply, what is on offer is not a standardised commodity and there are different kinds of customers.

The variations in quality and design and the very different social and physical environments are strikingly apparent. The small village estate nestling in the New Forest or the large, solidly built council houses overlooking the harbour in a Cornish fishing village are far removed from the inner city squalor of high rise in Hackney or the isolation of Chelmsley Wood on the edge of Birmingham. This becomes more explicit on resale. For example, an ex-council home auctioned in North Yorkshire was described as having a rural location, gardens of one fifth of an acre and a stable. The mass housing so evident in Liverpool, Birmingham or London should not obscure the variation in what is on offer and what is being sold. Moreover, the transformation brought about by sales on the prime estates shows the possibilities for a social housing which combines high quality construction and user control. Relatively inexpensive and superficial changes such as different paintwork or doors transform the easily labelled uniformity and drabness of a council estate into individualised, highly desirable properties indistinguishable from private housing generally. Such variety of individual expression is not (nor ever was) incompatible with the principles of social housing. It was, however, incompatible with a view that public tenants could not be afforded the luxury of individual expression. Council housing was about satisfying quantitative need through a paternalistic, standardised service. It is only in recent years that more imaginative management styles have developed and tenants have been recognised as active consumers rather than passive recipients of a service. Unfortunately council house sales, broader patterns of disinvestment and the impact of recession have accelerated the general trend for council housing to become a second class service. Changes which could have considerably enhanced British public housing in the past can now appear as rather trivial and cosmetic.

In earlier chapters we have pointed to the uneven impact of council house sales in both qualitative and quantitative terms. Analyses of what council housing is or has become and prescriptions for what if could be must acknowledge the differences in the historical development and social role of council housing in different localities. The changes which have occurred over the last few years have not occurred against a common base. These variations go beyond the observable differences in dwelling types (e.g. flats or houses) or tenure structures (numerical size of owner occupation relative to council housing). They relate to the ways in which local council housing has been shaped to the contours of the broader local social and economic structure. Council housing varies in its strategic role. The age structure of the tenant population varies. The quality and availability of private sector dwellings varies. And there are more subtle distinctions in the image and reputation of council housing.

Rather than continue in this general vein it is more appropriate to draw out some of these differences with reference to *four* particular localities. These are Hyndburn, Derwentside, New Forest and Hackney. They are chosen because they provide contrasts in the nature of political control, the issues raised by council house sales and in their tenure structure. Derwentside and Hackney have above average levels of council housing and are Labour controlled. Conversely, Hyndburn and New Forest have above average levels of owner occupation and are Conservative controlled. The statistical breakdown from the 1981 Census is set out in Table 8.1.

Table 8.1: Households and tenure in four localities, 1981

	Owner occupation %	Council housing %
Derwentside	49.3	42.5
Hackney	16.5	57.4
Hyndburn	78.0	15.7
New Forest	71.0	15.4

Source: Census of Population, 1981.

It would, of course, be quite legitimate to distinguish between these authorities in other ways. For example, whilst in Derwentside and Hyndburn private renting is negligible, in Hackney it is more common than home ownership. And in New Forest in 1981 almost 14% of households remained in the privately rented sector. We might further differentiate the forms and role of private renting in Hackney, as opposed to New Forest. In the former it conforms to the stereotype of transient inner urban bedsit land whereas in the latter much of the private renting which remains is the residue of tied accommodation for agricultural and estate labourers. We could also distinguish between the north and south of England (Hackney, New Forest in the south and Derwentside, Hyndburn in the north) and thus between high and low house price areas. And crucial differences are evident in the council housing stocks of Derwentside (76% houses) and Hackney (83% flats).

Some might argue that these localities are exotics in the sense that they display various extreme variations from the norm but every locality has unique features which could lead to that claim. The purpose of these case studies is to illustrate the very different implications of council house sales in different local contexts.

NEW FOREST: A TRIUMPH OF IDEOLOGY OVER LOCAL NEEDS

Contrary to popular belief not all Conservative controlled authorities chose to sell council houses under discretionary powers. As far back as 1971 Julian Amery, the then Minister of Housing and Construction, announced at the Conservative Party Conference, 'I have a little list of Tory authorities which refuse to sell council houses' (Conservative Party, 1971). New Forest had not sold any council dwellings by 1979 and with only one Labour councillor out a total of 58 it could scarcely be more solidly Conservative. Given the nature of the area the dominance of the Conservative Party is hardly surprising. The district covers 290 square miles of south-west Hampshire of which almost half is the forest itself. This is an area of woods and heathland created originally by Henry VIII as a source of timber for ship-building and as a royal hunting ground, now managed and extensively protected by the Forestry Commission. It is a major tourist attraction (enhanced by the wild and ubiquitous New Forest ponies), a popular area for retirement and a commuter district for Southampton, the nearest urban concentration. There are no major towns in the district itself, the most urbanised and industrialised areas being around Totton, Hythe and Fawley on the western periphery adjacent to Southampton. Major petrochemical industries are concentrated on this western periphery and whilst there is a diversity of industry in Lymington and Ringwood, the bulk of the area is predominantly rural in character with extensive farming and market gardening.

Typically such an area has a highly polarised social structure — a local working class on relatively low incomes competing with outsiders seeking retirement, commuter or second homes. This creates a high priced owner occupied sector. For Hampshire as a whole the average purchase price was £37,500 in 1984 (Nationwide Building Society, 1986). Given the limited availability of privately rented accommodation, much of it tied to employment or reserved for holiday lettings, public renting plays a crucial role in provision for the local working population. There is a high demand for council housing but even in a political climate favourable to public provision, land costs, land shortages and planning restrictions in such an area limit the scope for an extensive building programme.

In 1976 the Housing Committee of New Forest DC considered a report on the sale of council houses (then a discretionary power under a Labour government). Both the pros and cons were discussed and debated. The advantages were listed from (a) to (g), the disadvantages from (a) to (m). Among the advantages cited were that sales to sitting tenants:

> . . . would be likely to improve maintenance standards; that the sale of a council house 'does no more than recognise a fact that a good tenant will be in permanent occupation': and the rather cryptic claim that a 'mix of owner-occupied and tenanted houses has sociological advantages'.

The long list of disadvantages was, however, rather weightier. Among the more important were that:

> . . . replacement costs are likely to exceed any sale price at market value; at some stage the Council can expect in the long term each dwelling to become vacant and available for reletting; low historic capital costs ought to be retained for the benefit of the housing revenue account and not transferred to the private sector;

and, perhaps, the most over-riding consideration that:

> . . . there are problems for small villages in a district like this where there are real planning problems to be overcome before

replacement new council houses could be built, as in those villages the local people living and working in the area tend to be tenants of council houses; also council housing often provides the only means for young local people to have a house in their own village or area.

After some discussion the vice-chairman moved the motion 'That the Council do not sell council houses'. It was carried narrowly by ten votes to nine. A year or so later a similar debate ensued with similar results, although an amendment was carried which stated 'That further consideration of the sale of council houses be deferred until the meeting of the Committee to be held on 31 May, 1978' (five months later).

Paternalistic and local housing considerations continued to override any broader political opposition to council housing. By July 1979, however, the election of a Conservative government had forced the Council to anticipate statutory sales. That month the Housing Committee recommended: '. . .that the Council continue the current policy of not selling council houses but that the officers be asked to make the necessary preparations for possible legislation for the sale in the future'. The Council was not, however, going to acquiesce to national Conservative policy without expressing its misgivings. In November 1979 the Chief Executive wrote to the Permanent Secretary at the Department of the Environment setting out the Council response to the consultation paper on the Housing Bill. The letter outlined a number of specific considerations which applied to the New Forest — principally relating to its attractive rural character and the danger to local housing needs should market forces be given free reign. So concerned was the Council that it requested the Secretary of State to receive a 'deputation' of councillors:

Many members have real misgivings about the long term effects of a more general policy for the sale of council houses which, in their opinion, would be disastrous for local communities where the small stock of council houses is regarded as virtually the only stock of housing for many people (particularly local young people) who cannot normally afford to buy houses in this high cost area. Given present and likely planning policies, it will be increasingly difficult to build new council houses to meet local needs.

Within the terms of the Housing Act 1980 certain special arrangements were available to designated rural areas, such as national parks. These were in two forms. First, a special covenant requiring the consent of the previous landlord (the local authority) should the owner wish to dispose of the property to someone who neither worked nor resided locally. Secondly, a pre-emption period of ten years requiring the purchaser to offer to resell the property to the previous landlord (a local authority or development board) should he/she wish to dispose of it within that period (see Section 19 of the Housing Act 1980 for details). The council applied for special designation, not only for the forest itself but for the southern and western parts of the district excluding only the townships. In February they were informed that special designation had been granted but restricted to the forest. Whilst the council had wished restriction to apply to nearly 13,000 dwellings only about 500 were covered by the designation. But such exemptions and restrictions are in any case unlikely to offer any real protection for local residents on lower incomes who are seeking to buy. At most, they will represent an expensive form of stock replacement for the local authority. This is well illustrated by an article in the local *Evening Echo* (3.10.1980) with the headline 'Thatcher Housing Act Can't Help Me — Village Tenant'. The article began by describing the council house located 'in a quiet corner of the picturesque village of Brockenhurst', the garden was 'beautifully laid-out front and back'. It went on 'A couple of New Forest donkeys stand munching grass outside the gate'. The problem was that this idyllic location had a high market value and even with a 40% discount (for which the tenant was eligible) it was beyond his means. And this particular tenant was not a low paid agricultural worker but a skilled operator on relatively good earnings working in an oil refinery. He was quoted: 'I know we are lucky to live in this area but to expect us to pay the going rate for this village is ridiculous'. The going rate is, of course, what the next prospective purchaser would have to pay without the benefit of discount. If a tenant on reasonable earnings could not afford to buy with a discount what relevance has the 'local' restriction in the covenant to the next in line. And the authority would have to pay the market price should it wish to retain the property for local housing needs. As the same tenant comments in the article: 'Even with the discount, at my age the repayments would be so great I could not afford it. Surely that is wrong'.

Having no previous experience of selling council houses, the council took some time in setting up the various administrative procedures for their disposal. During this time the local Conservative MP became increasingly impatient with the council. With tones and accusations reserved normally for recalcitrant Labour-controlled authorities, New Forest was accused of 'dragging its feet' over sales and of 'harassing and bullying tenants' (*Lymington Times*, 11.4.1981; *Evening Echo*, 21.3.1981). At a meeting of the Christchurch and Lymington Conservative Association the MP, Robert Adley, evangelised that he would fight for the rights of tenants to buy their own homes — even if they did not vote Conservative. The newspaper rather cryptically reported Mr Adley as stating 'It is the greatest single social advance since Lloyd George'.

The first dwelling was sold in March 1981, an event celebrated by the MP but not the council. At his own champagne and ribbon-cutting ceremony the absence of representatives of the council was taken up by the MP as the latest example of the authority's ill-will towards its tenants. A further setback for the council's local housing priorities occurred when it received notification that exemptions had been refused for bungalows it had sought to reserve for elderly and disabled people. In total the council sought to exempt 800 one and two bedroomed bungalows under Section 2 of the Act (around 10% of the stock at that time) because of the high demand for council accommodation from elderly people. As many authorities discovered, however, the conditions for exemption were highly restrictive. The Secretary of State had to be satisfied that applications for exemption were for dwellings designed or specially adapted for occupation by persons of pensionable age and that it was the authority's practice to let it *only* for occupation by such persons (para. 5, Schedule 1 of the Housing Act 1980). It was not sufficient to simply wish to reserve a number of suitable dwellings because of the pressing housing needs of the local elderly population. This was the basis of the New Forest claim. There was a higher than average population of elderly people in the area and there was a growing number of elderly people in urgent need on the housing waiting list. As reported in the *Lymington Times* (16.5.1981) the council was 'perplexed and puzzled' by the rejection of their claim for such exemptions. Once again, however, the local MP took a rather different view. Reacting to the decision by Michael Heseltine, the then Secretary of State, he claimed it was 'a good day for democracy and a good day for Parliament'. He continued: 'If we had reached a stage where Parliament passed laws and then local authorities could choose whether or not to obey them, then democracy would be seriously on the slide' (*Lymington Times*, 16.5.1981).

Democracy triumphed, however — at least if measured by New Forest's implementation of the Right to Buy. By the end of 1982 almost 2000 applications had been received and over 1000 dwellings had been sold out of a stock of 8300. In 1981, 553 dwellings had been sold whilst only 55 new council homes were completed. And this gap has widened. By 1985 the Council had sold almost 20% of its stock and was among the top 50 sellers (as measured by the proportion of those sold). Yet the original reasons for not selling council houses have not changed. Indeed, with the disposal of a large section of the existing council housing stock the needs of the local working class are if anything more pressing. The council's housing strategy statement of 1981–2 noted that: '1234 applicants for rented housing . . . are considered in urgent need of housing — more than half are either sharing accommodation or living in residential caravans where toilet and bathing facilities are provided in communal buildings . . .' In its long term strategy it stated that: 'There is a desperate shortage of rented accommodation in the district and this acute need is unlikely to be met other than by the provision of publicly rented accommodation'.

Rural areas provide a very different context for council house sales. This reflects the specific features of such local housing markets (Beesley et al., 1980; House of Commons Environment Committee, 1981; Winter, 1980; National Council of Social Services, 1980; Shucksmith, 1981; Phillips and Williams, 1982). The chronic lack of privately rented accommodation in these areas means that for newly formed households the choice is between direct access to home ownership or sharing with parents until a council house becomes available. The excess demand for owner occupied dwellings through the demand for retirement and second homes creates a sharp division between the costs of public renting and home ownership. There is a high bottom end to the owner occupied price structure in many rural areas. Former council houses may be simply absorbed into this structure well beyond the means of the lower paid sections of the local working class. This exacerbates the tendency for there to be a dual housing market paralleling a dual labour market. The effect of privatising the public stock in rural areas is thus to widen the choice available to inmigrant and indigenous white collar workers and for those seeking to move in for retirement or to purchase a second home. Working-class couples sharing with parents will have to wait longer for council accommodation or take unsatisfactory low season lettings in cottages or caravans. The strategic function of council housing in small villages is also seriously undermined. A small number of council houses can service the life cycle of the local community. In some areas council housing caters for different generations of the same family and enables individuals to move as their circumstances change. In terms of maintaining family and community links a small stock of council dwellings may have a critical role. And they may also be crucial in providing housing for local workers and in sustaining local demand for education, transport and other services. By retaining families with young children, council housing may play a central role in preventing 'village communities' becoming retirement and commuting zones for the affluent, urban middle classes. Even if it were financially possible the replacement of sold council dwellings in more remote rural areas is made difficult by land shortages and inadequately serviced sites. If any replacement occurs it will tend to be in the larger settlements, thus exacerbating depopulation trends. A reduced public sector will also condemn many people to remain in the decaying remnants of 'tied' privately rented accommodation.

HYNDBURN — (OVER) EXTENDED HOME OWNERSHIP?

Hyndburn, on the northern periphery of industrial Lancashire, has a population of about 80,000. Accrington, the principal town, was once a centre of cotton weaving and displays the familiar characteristics of such an area. With the decline of the textile industry the local economy has undergone major restructuring, and closures in the current recession have increased unemployment. The local population is housed predominantly in a residential environment produced in the last century — tightly clustered rows of Victorian terraces. Almost two-thirds of Hyndburn's housing stock was built before 1914 and most of it in the period 1870–90. This compares with 37% for England as a whole.

On some measures Hyndburn could appear rather similar to the New Forest. It has a similarly low level of council housing (15%) and an above average level of home ownership (78%). Indeed with a total of 84% of its stock either owner occupied or privately rented it has one of the most highly privatised housing markets in the country. And, like the New Forest, it has an above average number of elderly people. Moreover, the local council is in Conservative hands albeit by a majority of one. There however the similarity ends.

In the recent past, various politicians and pundits have offered visions of a future where the vast majority of householders are owner occupiers. This vision of a property owning democracy has on occasion been related to a figure of 80% of households as home owners. Implicit in this view is that those households already in the owner occupied sector generally live in houses, with gardens, that their property values are increasing and that the next layer of home owners will continue to enjoy such benefits. And the sale of council houses has been the favoured and most significant method of achieving a higher level of home ownership since the early 1980s. Council tenants were offered the opportunity to share the benefits already enjoyed by home owners. But this image of suburban affluence, of rapidly escalating property values, of a tenure superior in every way to council housing derives from a partial view of the reality of home ownership. It is the home ownership we find in the New Forest but not necessarily in other parts of the country. Recent correctives to this rosy image of home ownership have tended to concentrate on the problems of marginal owners in inner city areas (e.g. Karn, Kemeny and Williams, 1985) and the increase in mortgage arrears cases (e.g. Doling, Karn and Stafford, 1986). It is this evidence which is published to illustrate the differentiated nature of the owner occupied sector. Such perspectives however, continue to convey a message that *within* any locality the vast majority of home owners do enjoy the advantageous circumstances referred to above. The problems are confined to the marginal additions to the owner occupied population.

The stratification of home ownership is not however the product of contemporary policy developments and the current recession. It is uncontroversial, but rarely expressed, that the development of home ownership (and council housing) has been highly uneven. Owner occupation nationally and within any locality is the product of a layering of policies and changing social and economic conditions. Different groups have entered home ownership under quite different conditions and whilst there has been a general upward trend the pace of change has been extremely uneven — nor has there been a single relationship between affluence and home ownership. And the built environment which accommodated those tenure shifts may have been purpose built for owner occupation or the product of a quite different socio-economic context. Differentiation, therefore, goes far beyond the difficulties of enabling those currently on low incomes to become home owners.

What does home ownership look like in Hyndburn? Most evidently, given that the 80% target has almost been achieved, it is difficult to construct arguments that council house sales are a means of satisfying frustrated desires for home ownership among the local population. Moreover, it is already low cost home ownership. In 1985 an unimproved Victorian terraced house could be purchased for around £3,000 and a fully improved property could be valued at anything between £11,000 and £18,000. It is also of extremely low quality by contemporary standards. In 1984 approximately 40% of the private housing stock was unfit, substandard or in need of major repair. Some 3,000 to 4,000 private sector dwellings lack basic amenities and a further 3,000 are in need of renovation. Every year, a further 150–300 dwellings fall into disrepair. Vacancies are concentrated in the private rather than the public sector. Some 10% of dwellings with rateable values below £75 are empty. The Borough's Housing Investment Programme of 1986–7 stated that:

> At current levels of activity the Authority is dealing with about 130 properties per annum by clearance and 300 per annum by renovation . . . it will be 35 years (2020 A.D.) at least before every owner occupier can enjoy amenities that are considered in a national context to be basic necessities in a property free of major defects.

Moreover, a significant number of owner occupied properties lack front or back gardens thus limiting the scope for improvement and extension. In abstract terms, this means that many properties are inappropriate for the social consumption norms of the 1980s. As a report by the Borough Planning Officer in 1982 noted:

> Between 50% and 60% of the Borough's dwellings are 'two up two down' terraces. Despite falling household sizes . . . these properties are increasingly likely to suffer from social obsolescence. Demand for these properties is likely to fall with increases in the ownership of cars and consumer durables, particularly fridges, freezers, washing machines and tumble dryers. The ability to accommodate consumer durables by kitchen extensions is likely to be limited because of the lack of space around these properties.

The dominant image of home ownership in Hyndburn is of physical decay, low house prices and low rates of accumulation. This has come about through a combination of circumstances. With the declining profitability of the textile industry, mill owners sold off housing to their tenant employees as a means of raising capital. This

185

occurred particularly in the 1930s. A further transfer of rented dwellings occurred particularly in the 1950s and 1960s when private landlords disposed of dwellings to sitting tenants. Low property values in the areas meant that access to home ownership was widespread. High female participation rates in the labour market meant that household incomes were high relative to house prices. The high level of owner occupation has occurred, therefore, through tenure conversion rather than new build. Low property values and low incomes (compared to the national average) have limited the scope for profitable, speculative housebuilding activity. And slum clearance has been limited because of the relatively high durability of some of the stone-built terraces in the area combined with a lack of resources among the constituent authorities. Whilst there have been low costs of access to home ownership, therefore, both households and local authorities have faced the escalating costs of decay and social obsolescence. In neither case have the resources been available to deal with the problems on any scale. And capital receipts from council house sales have been particularly limited because of the low value of properties. Therefore, the problems of home ownership in Hyndburn derive from the *low* costs of entry rather than the price barriers confronting those on low incomes.

The particular features of housing in Hyndburn were discussed in parliament in 1984 (Hansard, 1984, vol. 67, cols 507–15). In that discussion the local MP stated that in areas like Hyndburn:

> . . . the problem is not to promote owner-occupation, but to retain it. While the Government have concentrated on providing effective policies to promote new owner-occupation, they have, perhaps, understandingly, not paid sufficient attention to the problems of boroughs such as Hyndburn with its 80 per cent. owner-occupied properties of which 40 per cent. are substandard and in need of major renovation. Policies such as the sale of council houses, low-cost home ownership schemes and the removal of restraints on private builders, important though they are in the national context, are of only minor relevance in Hyndburn where there are few council houses to sell.

He went on to say: 'Government action is needed to prove . . . that there is a long term future for low income owner-occupation'. He emphasised the need for more government expenditure and suggested a concentration of resources in 'housing stress areas' to assist areas with the highest levels of owner occupied properties that were substandard and in need of repair.

The Minister who responded in the debate acknowledged the 'sheer scale of the problems' and the ready availability of older housing at very low prices. He commented: 'Low cost homes, in such an area, has a different meaning from the usual one. For someone like myself as a London Member used to London prices, the sort of figures that I have just been quoting seem remarkable'. In this context the sale of council houses has peculiar consequences and implications. Firstly, in terms of space and amenity standards, council tenants are relatively privileged. It is the council houses which are three bedroomed, semi-detached with gardens. On resale they are liable to be highly sought after commodities. Secondly, much of the demand for council housing is from owner occupiers, principally elderly home owners. The declining condition of the private housing stock is placing increasing demands on the limited public sector housing. In 1985, the waiting list was equivalent to over 50% of the council stock — and this was despite an exceptionally high relet rate (14.8% in 1984–5). About 55% of dwellings lacking amenities are occupied by aged persons and a further 8% by ethnic minorities.

The sale of council houses in Hyndburn, whilst enabling a limited number of tenants to purchase relatively high quality dwellings at less than market value, is liable to accelerate and exacerbate problems of decay and entrapment within the owner occupied and privately rented sectors.

Public housing has been required to play a strategic role in relation to owners and private tenants and council house sales are liable to limit further its capacity to perform these functions. This will occur directly through a reduction in the number of relets. Between April 1979 and June 1986 Hyndburn had sold 595 dwellings, just over 11% of its council stock. Given Hyndburn's high relet rate this represents a loss of some 80 vacancies. Moreover, low property valuations combined with discounts mean that the capital receipts eventually accruing to the authority are of minimal significance given the scale of the housing problem in the area. And the resource constraints faced by the authority will be exacerbated by the reduction in the number of council dwellings, thus limiting further the number of houses over which to spread the impact of any expenditure on new build and repairs. Council house rents in Hyndburn are already well above the national average. Whilst 80% of tenants are in receipt of housing benefits (the majority on maximum rebates), any upward movement of rents can only increase hardship, and persuade those who can to buy their dwellings.

Council house sales in Hyndburn are, therefore, not about the provision of low cost opportunities to purchase. These already exist in abundance but are of an extremely low quality. Many of those on the council waiting list are either unwilling to purchase unimproved terraces, are unable to do so or are already living in them. In this context, the Right to Buy represents an arbitrary and ill-conceived distribution of housing assistance. Whilst many existing owners occupy decaying properties gaining little or no benefit from mortgage interest tax relief and house price inflation, a minority of tenants reap the benefits of generous discounts on high quality properties. The social and economic fabric of such an area will continue to make it unattractive to the private speculative housebuilding industry. One of the few sources of relatively modern, good quality housing for general purchase is likely to be the sale and resale of council houses. Ironically, in such are elderly owner occupiers look to council housing to meet their changing housing needs, and they will be affected by the reduction in rental opportunities.

DERWENTSIDE — PROPERTY OWNERSHIP FOR THE UNEMPLOYED?

The district of Derwentside, in the north east of England, was formed in 1972 through the amalgamation of the urban districts of Consett and Stanley and of the rural district of Lanchester. The principal town is Consett whose growth was the product of the Consett steelworks which dominated the landscape until its closure in 1980. It was as near to a company town as was possible in contemporary Britain. Some of what is now council housing was built originally by the steel industry to house its workers. As one of the earliest and most prominent victims of the economic recession, the town became a symbol of depression and marginality — and the large 760 acre site in the centre of the town presented a powerful image of changed economic fortunes. Predictably the closure of the steelworks had knock-on effects and further redundancies followed. By 1984 some 7,500 persons were registered unemployed, representing 23.8% of the working population (some 28% of economically active males). In the 'booming town index' produced by Champion *et al.* (1987) Consett comes last. Between 1971 and 1981 it lost 54% of its manufacturing employment. It is controlled by a large Labour majority.

In housing terms, Derwentside provides a considerable contrast to Hyndburn. The impact of unemployment and recession has been similarly evident. But this has occurred within quite different housing markets and on different time scales. There are similarities in terms of low house prices, low rates of money accumulation through the housing market and considerable disrepair and decay in the older owner occupied stock. Derwentside, however, has a large council housing stock of a relatively high quality. According to the Census of 1981 almost 43% of households were in the public housing sector compared to 49% in owner occupation. Only 8% of households were in the privately rented sector. Within the public sector stock there are no high rise flats. Indeed, in 1981, 96% of council dwellings were houses or bungalows — the vast majority being two or three bedroomed houses. In the council's 1985–6 Housing Strategy Statement, it claimed that there were no difficult-to-let dwellings in the council sector and figures on unfitness, vacancy and renovation indicate that physical housing problems were concentrated in the private sector.

In this social and economic context what are the issues which arise in relation to council house sales? The pervasive effects of economic recession would suggest that the conditions for the expansion of home ownership through the disposal of publicly owned dwellings are not particularly propitious. On the other hand valuations are low and the assets on offer are relatively desirable, at least in terms of use value. The level of home ownership is considerably below the national average so that, unlike in Hyndburn, the expectation would be of some pent up demand among tenants especially since Consett District Council (as opposed to Stanley and Lanchester) had not previously sold council dwellings. In fact, between October 1980 and March 1986 some 3,600 tenants applied to buy their council dwellings and 16% of the stock has now been sold.

This could be seen as a surprising rate of disposal in the context of such economic gloom. Moreover it would seem to suggest that contrary to some predictions whilst the owner occupied market is not exactly overheated, it has certainly not collapsed. In Derwentside (and in Consett) properties are still bought and sold and prices do rise, albeit at little more than the general rate of inflation. In some cases prices may be falling in real terms but there is no

189

evidence of a spectacular collapse in property values or pervasive unsaleability. Rather than collapse, the characteristics of a depressed market may involve reduced residential mobility, longer selling times and less investment in the maintenance and repair of dwellings as a consequence of reduced or insecure earnings. Paradoxically, the closure and demolition of the steelworks in Consett has created a much cleaner and more attractive residential environment and may encourage some limited compensatory inmigration. Whilst this is unlikely to be on any significant scale, property values are low and Consett is within easy commuting distance of Hexham (a relatively prosperous market town) and Newcastle. In more abstract terms, Consett may represent redundant productive space but there are prospects of some enhanced value for its use in consumption activities.

Some indication of house price trends and property values is available from the valuations of council houses. The average valuation of dwellings sold in Derwentside in 1980–1 was £9,700 (Forrest and Murie, 1984). The same figure for disposals in the period 1983–5 was £11,610. In that period valuations ranged from £6,250 to £19,650. When discounts are applied to these figures the costs of loan repayments become extremely low. For example, of council house sales completed in 1983, more than a third of purchasing households had gross repayments of less than £60 per month. Among the latest group of purchasers (1984–5) only one house in ten had gross repayments exceeding £25 per week.

These relatively low repayment costs have important implications for the interpretation of council house purchase in an area such as Derwentside. In many cases mortgage payments are less than unrebated rents. For those paying full rent (some 27% of council tenants) and assuming modest house price inflation, rent increases and rising discounts (either with policy change or lengthening tenancy period), it will increasingly make simple *economic* sense to buy rather than continue renting. In other words, regardless of the ultimate saleability of properties, council house purchase for many can represent a means of rescheduling housing costs, renewing housing subsidy and escaping escalating costs in the public rental sector. The relatively high level of sales in Derwentside is not simply an expression of tenure preference.

For the substantial proportion of tenants in Derwentside receiving housing benefit the equation is quite different. Whilst some households on state pensions or benefits have purchased their dwellings, the majority of elderly and unemployed tenants are

190

likely to remain in the public rental sector (at least on present policies). This suggests that there is a relatively finite limit to the number of properties which will become owner occupied through the Right to Buy. Indeed, evidence on the characteristics of purchasers indicates a marked polarisation between households with secure and multiple earnings and those dependent on state benefits. Polarisation is not limited to north-south comparisons but is evident in all localities. To be relatively affluent in a declining and depressed locality can be extremely advantageous given the low cost of living (provided you are not planning a move to the south east). Purchasing households in Derwentside tend to be multiple earning and in apparently stable employment. For example, of a sample of purchasers in 1983–5, only a third of principal earners had been in the same job for less than three years (and they were younger purchasers). More than a third had been in the same employment for more than eleven years. And 90% of those households had second earners who were typically females in part time employment. A striking feature of tenant purchase in Derwentside, however, is the proportion of principal applicants who are females. This rose from 11% in 1980–1 to 21% in 1984–5. This is unusually high and is likely to be explained by an increase in households where females are the principal or sole earners. In this context Champion *et al.* (1987) note an above average increase in the participation rate of married women in the labour market in Consett.

The issues surrounding council house sales in a locality like Derwentside are complex and in sharp contrast to areas in the south (typically London boroughs) with chronic unemployment, large public rental sectors and high house prices. In Derwentside, properties of relatively high quality are on offer at low cost. Typically, these are houses with gardens. Critical considerations relate less to chronic housing shortage and the consequences of sales for relets and transfers and more to the benefits conveyed by home ownership and the motivations for purchase. In terms of household income there is an evident polarisation between multiple earning and state dependent households within the public sector. For the former to remain as rent paying tenants makes little financial sense given the relative costs of renting and owning. Indeed, for those households, that could be a more powerful expression of tenure preference than the decision to purchase. In Derwentside, however, households with marked differences in levels of earnings are unlikely to be (or find themselves) in highly polarised situations as regards housing standards, conditions and opportunities. Whether public sector

191

tenants buy or continue to rent they will be occupying similar dwellings in similar locations. And given the general economic climate and only limited house price inflation sharp contrasts in the housing prospects of tenants and tenant purchasers are unlikely. The evidence for residualisation in the public housing sector in Derwentside is to be found in the economic marginality of the tenant population rather than in their housing standards and conditions. A large section of the productive working class has become redundant and state dependent but in the short term at least their housing situation is unlikely to deteriorate. Contrary to many commentaries about council house sales, Derwentside demonstrates that the unemployed and those on low incomes can take advantage of the sale policy. Whether or not they gain something of long-term value remains to be seen. In the absence of a revival of the local economy house values may remain low and householders may find it difficult to repair and maintain their homes. In the long term, buying a council house could mean deteriorating housing conditions, limited asset appreciation and a lack of resources to take full advantage of user control.

HACKNEY — SALES IN THE INNER CITY

On the face of it, Hackney represents precisely the kind of locality which council house sales were designed to transform. Much of the early rhetoric referred to in Chapter 3 was about breaking up council house ghettos and extending opportunities to purchase in areas with low levels of home ownership. Hackney, in inner London, has one of the lowest levels of home ownership in the country. It remains a rental housing market with 57% of households in council housing and 26% in the privately rented sector. Less than one in five households are owner occupied. And in seven years of statutory sales some 561 dwellings have been sold — just over 1% of the total council stock.

The explanation for this is rather simpler than the explanation for the high level of sales in Derwentside (which also has a council stock considerably larger than the national average). In the early years of the Right to Buy when Hackney achieved minimal sales, the government attributed much of this slow rate of progress to intransigent and recalcitrant behaviour by local Labour councillors. There was certainly little enthusiasm for the policy in the authority. However, the small number of completed sales cannot be attributed to local political factors. The fact is that the vast majority of council tenants in Hackney either cannot afford to buy their council dwelling or do not wish to. A number of factors combine to create probably the least propitious conditions for council house sales anywhere in the country. The high level of economic and housing stress in Hackney has already been noted (Chapter 7). As Harrison (1983) has observed Hackney: '. . . is less than four miles from Hampstead and Highgate, but if social distances were measured in miles it would be half-way round the globe' (p.21).

Such dramatic assertion is based on evidence of chronically high levels of umemployment and severe deprivation in the area. On almost any measure, Hackney emerges as one of the most deprived areas in the country. And, unlike Derwentside with similarly high levels of unemployment, in Hackney poverty and deprivation co-exist with soaring property and land values, gentrification and conspicuous wealth. In 1981 two-thirds of Hackney households were dependent on public transport. Of Hackney's 46,000 council dwellings 83% are flats. The relationship between the nature of the stock and the low level of sales is clear. No flat sales have yet been recorded. In this sense a more valid comparison of rates of sale between authorities might be a calculation of the percentage of *houses and bungalows* sold. On this calculation Hackney has sold over 7% of its stock. And there is selectivity among the types of houses sold — larger four bedroomed dwellings and acquired properties are over-represented among sold dwellings when compared to the stock as a whole. As in many London boroughs a number of dwellings are acquired houses located on predominantly owner occupied streets. These can be extremely desirable properties free from the stigmatisation of a location on large council estates. They can also be very expensive.

What is on offer through the Right to Buy in Hackney, and in other inner London boroughs, varies dramatically. The general picture is of a highly polarised social structure, a highly differentiated council stock, increasing marginalisation and a deterioration of housing opportunities and conditions for a majority of tenants. For a minority who can afford to buy the desirable properties there is the potential for substantial money gains. In view of the high cost of purchase it is not surprising that purchasing households in Hackney tend to be larger, multiple earning families — one reason why the larger dwellings tend to be over-represented in sales. And a house, not untypically valued at around £50,000 in 1983, bought for £25,000 with a discount of 50%, could now be worth twice that

193

amount. But for council tenants in the high rise estates the possibilities of a transfer to a house are remote (especially with the further depletion of the stock of houses through sales), purchase on the private market is impossible, and the purchase of their flat likely to be beyond their means and of uncertain benefit.

Beyond the fact that both Derwentside and Hackney have large public housing sectors and high levels of unemployment, the contrasts between the localities are striking. Sales in Hackney occur against a backcloth of high exchange values but often low use values, excess housing demand, rising homelessness and a close relationship between tenure and social divisions. If you are marginalised from the labour market in Hackney you are more likely to be marginalised in the housing market. In Derwentside, however, there are high use values but low exchange values, relatively low housing demand and a less clear and marked relationship between marginality and council housing. In Derwentside the loss of employment may find some compensation in the cheap acquisition of a desirable house with a garden. The prospects of money gains through home ownership may be limited but housing costs may be reduced. In Hackney, the tenant purchaser will almost certainly experience increased housing costs but house price inflation is likely to be rapid.

MARGINALITY AND FORMS OF RESIDUALISATION

In this chapter we have attempted to draw out some of the varying impacts of council house sales by focusing on four contrasting localities. It is evident that there are major differences in terms of local social and economic structures which reflect and act upon the local housing market in general and council housing in particular. Variations in the housing stock, housing quality and the characteristics of council tenants reflect current and past variations in local labour markets, demography, social structure and the uneven impact of economic change and recession. The nature of council housing in any locality represents a layering of histories of local and national housing policies, local political structures, the vicissitudes of capital investment and the relative bargaining power of local working classes. In this context the built-in residualism of Hackney's council housing can be contrasted with the relatively high quality council housing in Derwentside provided for a powerful, highly unionised labour force which was in a key sector of the economy.

However, whilst local case studies provide an important

corrective to top-down generalisations they always run the risk of degenerating into an 'everywhere is different' analysis where key features of social and economic change are obscured by a mass of local descriptions. In the strict sense every locality is unique. There are nevertheless a number of general processes at work which can be abstracted from the detailed case studies. Moreover, as we have illustrated elsewhere (Forrest and Murie, 1986b), local housing market factors such as the relative sizes of the tenures, the level of differentiation within the council stock, and the buying/renting cost gap can interact with broader socio-economic processes to produce quite different outcomes. Equally, apparently similar outcomes can be the product of a different combination of factors.

Much of what has been discussed focuses on the relationship between an expanding, marginalised underclass and the tenure structure. It is this relationship which informs the view that council housing is becoming a residual tenure. In representations at the national level, this relationship is expressed as a polarisation between renters and owners with the marginal poor increasingly segregated in council housing as private renting continues to decline. This relationship will, however, vary between localities according to a number of key factors; the size of the marginalised population; the tenure structure; the relationship between use value and exchange value. The ways in which these and other factors combine involve different patterns of social and spatial polarisation and varying degrees of coincidence between them. There may also be a coincidence with tenure but this reflects and can be more directly and immediately manipulated by policy and legislative change. For example, the transfer of ownership of an estate may change tenure status but do little to change socio-spatial inequalities. Figure 8.1 contrasts the representation at national level with four representations of 'forms of residualisation' of council housing derived from the case studies. *A* describes a locality where a large marginalised population is spread across all tenures but is disproportionately represented in a large public sector. In what might be described as a marginalised locality, house prices are low and the council stock has a high use value but a low exchange value. Access to home ownership is therefore possible for low income groups either through council house sales or (to some extent) 'normal' market processes. Council housing therefore performs a *major* residual role but there is not a marked social distance between the tenures. Moreover, the existence of a large stock of high quality council housing means that there is a *dislocation* between labour market position and housing situation.

195

Figure 8.1: Forms of residualised council housing — diagrammatic representations

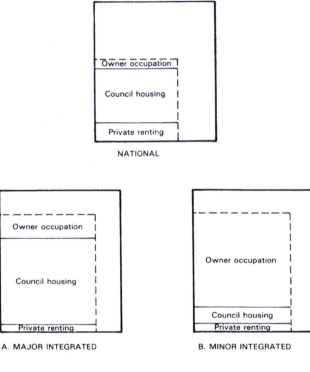

NATIONAL

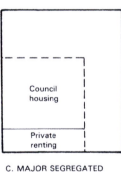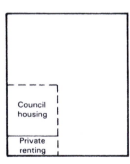

A. MAJOR INTEGRATED   B. MINOR INTEGRATED

C. MAJOR SEGREGATED   D. MINOR SEGREGATED

The whole block represents total population and that within the dotted line the marginalised section of that population. The representations of tenure categories indicate where the marginalised sections live.

Exclusion from the labour market does not necessarily correspond to exclusion from good quality housing.

In the case of *B* owner occupation dominates in an area with a large marginalised population. There is extensive residential decay, low exchange values and council housing performs a minor residual role catering for low income and elderly owner occupiers and the marginalised young. In both *A* and *B* the form of residualisation is termed *integrated* because there is a low degree of socio-tenurial polarisation and socio-spatial segregation.

Both *C* and *D* describe *segregated* forms of residualism. In *C* the large marginalised population is accommodated in both forms of renting. Exchange values are, however, high (as in an inner London borough) and there is a high degree of exclusion from owner occupation. This housing market segregation is liable to reflect and exacerbate labour market exclusion. Use values in the council sector are low and spatial polarisation is marked.

D typifies a locality with a small marginalised group in an affluent, high demand area. Within the council sector, both use values and exchange values are high. Access to home ownership is therefore restricted to those in employment with council housing catering increasingly for those who cannot buy. Whilst the privately rented sector continues to perform a parallel role in accommodating the small marginal population the expectation would be of low use values in that sector. In what is a representation of a rural locality with high demand from inmigrant and commuting middle classes the social distance between owners (and tenants who buy) and the marginalised poor will be marked but spatial polarisation will be limited.

These representations and the varied implications of further substantial privatisation are summarised in Table 8.2. What this illustrates is that privatisation of council housing can have different effects on different groups in different localities. And different levels of privatisation have different implications for the quality of the housing service available to marginalised populations. Residualisation does not necessarily correspond to social exclusion and spatial segregation. Equally, it can imply poor people in poor housing in an increasingly ghettoised situation.

Whilst these representations are not exhaustive it seems likely that most local areas will fall within one of the broad categories. For example, the pattern of economic change has tended to shift the centre of economic gravity away from the older industrial centres where council housing is most concentrated. Affluent areas with

197

Table 8.2: Forms of residualised council housing

	Nature of council sector	Implications of further substantial privatisation
A. *Major integrated*	Large share of market High use value Low exchange value Caters principally for local demand for permanent housing Affected by relatively dispersed sales	Reduced housing investment and expenditure following transfer of ownership. Long term consequences for condition of stock and problems in home ownership.
B. *Minor integrated*	Small share of market High use value Low exchange value Important role in catering for potential and former 'owner occupiers' choosing to rent at different stages in life cycle	Short term improvement of owner occupied stock. Marginal and elderly owners left with no escape route. Homelessness. Increased problems within home ownership including disrepair.
C. *Major segregated*	Large share of market Low use value High exchange value Highly differentiated stock Caters for those who cannot buy Strong spatial variation in housing status	Selective gentrification and redevelopment. Displacement, homelessness and ghettoisation. Emergence of new forms of housing for low income groups — sharing, squatting etc.
D. *Minor segregated*	Small share of market High use value High exchange value Caters for those who cannot buy	Gentrification. Displacement of local workers. Impact on local services and structure of communities. Emergence of new low cost/low quality forms of housing — e.g. mobile homes.

smaller marginalised populations are consequently likely to have small stocks of council housing and to fall into the *minor segregated* category. Not all areas, however, with small stocks of council housing are affluent and especially in northern England the *minor integrated* form is likely to be typical. The declining industrial centres will tend to be areas where houses have a low exchange value and will fall into the *major integrated* category. There are, however, areas where relative affluence coincides with a large stock of council housing, and it is in these localities where the *major segregated* category is typical. These different forms of residualism signify different degrees of exclusion and stigmatisation and a varying pattern of social division where housing market processes may exacerbate the inequalities generated elsewhere.

9

Radical Centralism and Local Resistance

The impact of the Right to Buy extends beyond consideration of socio-tenurial divisions, the changing geography of tenure, and the changing structure of local housing markets. At various stages in this book we have referred to a centralisation of policy and the changing nature of central-local relations. This change has not come about without conflict and resistance. In this chapter we shall examine this dimension in greater detail, both as an input to the formulation and implementation of the policy *and* as a consequence of the policy process. In this respect the privatisation of council housing links to broader analyses of the erosion of local autonomy, constitutional change and the role of different levels of government in the delivery of welfare services.

The compulsion on local authorities to sell council dwellings regardless of local housing circumstances, the lack of discretion available to local administrations and the general framing of the Right to Buy signified a shift in relations between central and local government. The provision, management and allocation of council dwellings has been one of the most significant and visible of local government activities. It has been one of the major areas in which local councils could exert a real influence on local social and economic circumstances. Its erosion through a statutory Right to Buy was seen, therefore, as not only a threat to locally determined housing policies but an undermining of local democracy and autonomy. While this concern was expressed most vociferously by Labour controlled councils it was not limited to them. As we saw in the previous chapter, some Conservative authorities were by no means enthusiastic at the dominance of central dictat over local paternalism. Privatising the council stock and low replacement rates diminished a council's capacity to provide homes for locals. And

200

some Conservative backbenchers recognised that with political change the enhanced power of central government could be used to impose a rather different set of housing priorities on local administrations. Resistance to the Right to Buy was anticipated by Section 23 of the Housing Act 1980 which contained a powerful measure for intervention by the Secretary of State if any local authority were slow or reluctant in implementing the Right to Buy. Referring to this clause, one Conservative backbencher remarked in parliamentary debate: 'It is all very well making the Secretary of State the gauleiter of housing, but on these Benches we should remember that the next gauleiter could be a commissar' (*Hansard*, 1980, vol. 976, cols 1510–11).

According to Bulpitt (1983), however, the Conservative government objected to what it perceived to be an increasingly corporatist style 'carve-up' of local affairs between councils and trade unions. From this perspective, the Housing Act 1980 and other legislative measures such as the Transport Act 1980, the Education Act 1980 and the Local Government Planning and Land Act 1980 represented the opening up of local government to ordinary citizens — a strong central state creating greater political space for individual choice and expression. Within New Right thinking the Housing Act 1980 opened up local housing provision to greater influence from private enterprise, and the Right to Buy asserted individualism over collectivism. Far from representing an erosion of local democracy the Right to Buy was an escape from bureaucratic oppression, a more potent and purer form of decentralisation than was on offer from the left. This positive view of the erosion of local government involvement in housing provision is explicit in a recent publication of the Adam Smith Institute.

There is scope, also, for taking the whole problem of housing out of the local political arena, and contriving a situation in which both ownership and rent are regulated not by political whim but by demand for them and the supply which can be generated to meet it. (Butler *et al.*, 1985)

In practice, however, as Green (1987) has observed, the overall shape of the measures recommended by the Adam Smith Institute remain highly interventionist. Conflict and debate over the introduction of the Right to Buy, the tone and nature of the legislation and the manner of its implementation sit therefore within a much broader theoretical and policy debate. The perceived progressive centralisation of state power and the dilution and constraining of localised power has been a dominant theme in theoretical accounts of structural change in a contemporary capitalism as well as among those more directly concerned with policy-making processes and the role of local government in Britain. For example, Jones and Stewart have suggested that a Bill of Rights is needed to give constitutional protection to local government (Jones and Stewart, 1981).

Conflicts between central and local government are not limited to housing. The history of central-local government relations in Britain has involved a continuous friction between central and local priorities and demands, between the legitimacy of local mandates and the policies of elected national governments, between local discretion and central control. Occasionally these tensions erupt, gain wider prominence and become symbols of deeper conflicts, variously defined as class struggles, opposition to authoritarian centralism, the erosion of local autonomy or the products of structural discrepancies in contemporary capitalism.

The dominant image is of the radical local administration resisting cuts, or wishing to increase expenditure on local services confronting a reactionary, insensitive central government. Such an image may be consistent with current events but presents only a partial account of central-local conflicts and is in danger of erecting party political differences as the key explanatory variable and local actions as the source of conflict. Inevitably the political complexion of the national government in power produces conflicts which appear to be party based, and the progressive 'nationalisation' of local politics with increasing use and compatibility of political labels at national and local levels has highlighted this aspect. And there are, of course, instances where the political labels are reversed as in the case of the maintenance of selective schooling involving a confrontation between the Secretary of State for Education and Science and the Metropolitan Borough of Tameside. Nevertheless, the most prominent conflicts have been between Conservative central governments and Labour controlled local governments. At its simplest level this is because at times of economic crisis it is expenditure on council housing, state education, the health services and other items of social consumption which are often hit hardest. Labour controlled local authorities are more likely to be resistant to those pressures and are more likely to have greater investment in those items. Historically, resistance to such pressures has resulted in legal action by central government to enforce the implementation of particular policies, legislation to control the expenditure patterns of local government more tightly or, indeed, to remove entirely the provision of a service from local political control. And this process has a long history. Whilst such conflicts have a particular prominence at the present time a tendency towards greater control by the centre can be observed since at least the 1930s (Dearlove and Saunders, 1984).

And centralism is by no means exclusively associated with Conservative administrations in Britain. Nor are local autonomy and democracy such unambiguously enlightened and progressive features. Indeed, enlightened local autonomy and dissension in one era can become reactionary obstruction in the next. Faced with a right wing central government local enclaves of socialist resistance have been heralded as the new terrain of class struggle — as prefigurative of a broader based socialist transformation (Boddy and Fudge, 1984). But the rules of the game constantly change and conflicts and struggles find new institutional expression at different levels of the state at different times. In the 1960s and 1970s the radical left mounted a sustained critique of the role of local bureaucrats and elected members in the allocation of resources, and Cockburn's influential book characterised local government as the local state, 'a key part of the state in capitalist society' (Cockburn, 1977), primarily an instrument of class domination and control. Such an analysis has been correctly criticised as being crude and unidimensional, mainly because it involved an inappropriate transposition of theories of the central state to the local level. Nevertheless, some of those critiques have been rather easily forgotten with the general onslaught on local government services in recent years. And it is council housing which has been perhaps the area of greatest political and theoretical confusion.

The rather timid campaign against council house sales by the Labour Party reflected a lack of clarity over what it was that was being defended. It reflected also a recognition of political realities. The mass mobilisation of tenants was unlikely because those in the better council housing would want to buy, and those in the dump estates would not think it was worth defending. Indeed it *was* unclear what was being defended. It was certainly questionable whether an unqualified resistance to sales was a struggle for the working class or the preservation of local paternalistic, bureaucratic empires. In their discussion of the development of council housing in Sheffield, Dickens and Goodwin comment:

Council housing, while it is under attack from a right wing central government, has at the same time, become a peculiarly repressive form of tenure. It has become far removed from the ideals of, for example, John Wheatley in the 1920s and Aneurin Bevan in the 1940s: ideals which were substantially upheld. But rather than continue glorifying past achievements, perhaps we should now ask: is council housing *as we know it* really something worth going to the wall for? (Dickens and Goodwin, 1981)

As we have stressed elsewhere, people 'know' council housing in different ways. What it was, or has become, varies between localities. This is not to underplay its oppressive and repressive elements but to guard against accepting too readily its blanket condemnation. In fact, despite some initial posturing, few local authorities chose to go anywhere near the wall when the Right to Buy became law. It might be argued, however, that Norwich, the authority which ultimately came in to sharpest conflict with central government, had council housing rather more worthy of defence than many others. Indeed its housing stock had once been referred to as the 'jewel in the crown' of council housing in the region by Department of the Environment officials.

THE POWER TO INTERVENE

The new Conservative government had revised the general consent on the sale of council houses to enable local authorities which so chose to offer the more generous 'manifesto' terms of sale. But the major innovation in 1979 was the pursuit of legislative action to enforce the Right to Buy. Any hesitation about local autonomy, or housing need, or the terms of sales, had been overcome and the drafting of the Housing Act 1980 represented a determined attempt to ensure that neither the aspirations of those tenants wishing to buy nor those of Conservatives with respect to council house sales could be frustrated by local opposition or reluctance to act. The new mechanism to achieve privatisation in housing was Part I of Chapter 1 of the Housing Act 1980. This involved major changes in policy and practice towards council house sales. Among other things Section 23 of the Act contained very strong powers for the Secretary of State to intervene over the implementation of the Right to Buy. These and other details of the legislation were generally regarded as providing wide powers of intervention in order to influence local action and to maximise the incentives to purchase. Indeed, the Act represented a thoroughly centralist, compulsory approach to policy implementation.

In summary, Section 23 of the Act stated that where it appeared to the Secretary of State that any tenants of a particular landlord were having difficulty in exercising their Right to Buy effectively and expeditiously, the Secretary of State could give notice in writing of intention to intervene. It is worthwhile noting that the basis for intervention was that tenants were experiencing delays and not a comparison of progress between authorities. The Secretary of State was thus under no obligation to select the most dilatory authority. Also, financial penalties were involved in respect of lost income from processing sales and interest on sums received on their completion.

Despite the scope and severity of the power of intervention, this section of the Act did not arouse enormous controversy during the passage of the legislation. This may have been because it was generally regarded as a power of last resort which was unlikely to be used. During the second reading of the Housing Bill, the Secretary of State, Michael Heseltine, had referred to it as follows:

> Tenants wishing to become owners will expect the House to ensure that they have a right to buy which cannot be circumvented or ignored. If Parliament enacts this legislation it is right to expect all councils and landlords falling within the provisions of the Bill to carry out their duties responsibly and speedily. If it appears, however, that a council is not taking adequate steps to facilitate a sale under the Bill, I shall be able to take over the transaction. Clause 22 gives me the powers and discretion necessary to do so effectively.
>
> Let me say at once to the House that I regard that as a reserve power. I shall use it only when I find that I have to protect tenants from the illegal behaviour or deliberate delaying tactics of the councils under which they live — [Interruption]. As the hon. Member for Salford East (Mr Allaun) says from his sedentary position, it is democracy. We have a mandate to do precisely that. (Hansard, 1980, vol. 976, cols 1447–8)

During this debate, other contributors made little reference to this section, concentrating their attention on the financial and housing policy aspects of the legislation rather than on issues of local autonomy and centralism.

Inevitably, there was more direct discussion of the powers

available to the Secretary of State in the Standing Committee on the Housing Bill. Gerald Kaufman for the Labour Opposition referred to the clause providing the power for the Secretary of State to intervene as: '. . . the most objectionable part of the Bill. Some of the clauses bestow upon the Secretary of State powers which are little short of dictatorial. . .' (House of Commons, 1980). After some discussion the debate moved on to how the financial and other arrangements would operate in the event of an intervention by the Secretary of State. The Minister of Housing's concluding commendation of the clause as a whole referred to the equivocal position of the Labour Party which had failed to make it clear whether the legislation should be implemented or whether the Right to Buy should be denied to many tenants. The debate in Committee on later parts of the Housing Bill was foreshortened following a guillotine motion. The government's reasons for introducing a guillotine included concern that the opportunity to buy houses should not be further delayed for those 'unfortunate' council tenants in predominantly Labour controlled areas where councils were still refusing to sell.

In view of the subsequent use of the powers of intervention contained in the legislation (and the pervasive threat of their use), the relative lack of debate and controversy during the legislative process is perhaps surprising. It is, however, relevant that the use of default powers in housing legislation had rarely been used in the past. Even the famous Clay Cross episode had not involved housing powers. Moreover, some legal experts took the view that action of this kind would be slow and difficult. Arden (1980), for example, suggested that because of the financial consequences of intervention the Secretary of State would have 'to comply with the requirements of natural justice, or at least fair administration, before exercising these powers'. Arden also considered the words 'effectively and expeditiously' to have a degree of obscurity. And he observed that:

> . . . it can hardly have been intended that at a time of staff reductions in the name of public spending cuts all authorities and housing associations should take on extra staff — and, especially, legal staff — to cope with these difficulties. It would seem that something more than bureaucratic delay must be shown to exist before these powers can be used: perhaps as much as actual wilful obstruction, or a declared intention to obstruct. (Arden, 1980, p. 23)

He was not alone in underestimating the scope of the powers contained in the Act and in misinterpreting their nature.

THE IMPLEMENTATION OF THE RIGHT TO BUY

From the outset, central government took an active part in implementing the Right to Buy. The political and financial importance of this legislation meant that the task was not completed with the passage of legislation. The expectation of local obstruction, the desire to appeal over the heads of local administrations, and the desire to publicise the Right to Buy involved the central department with a substantial continuing role. Initially the government appears to have been satisfied to concentrate on publicity. In the financial year 1980–1 £530,000 was spent on advertisements on television and in national newspapers telling public sector tenants of their new rights. A further £125,000 was spent later in the same financial year on newspaper advertisements to remind tenants of the need to serve Right to Buy claim forms by 5 April in order to qualify for an 8 August valuation. In the financial year 1981–2, £239,000 was spent on publicising the Right to Buy. Information given following a parliamentary answer in May 1985 showed that the £2.3 million spent to promote council house sales was the largest publicity campaign since 1979 (*Guardian*, 30.5.1985).

Considerable press coverage was also given to local housing authorities which expressed an intention not to implement the Act. Most prominent among these were Greenwich and Rochdale. Rochdale were reported to have written to the Secretary of State inviting him to send in a commissioner to effect Right to Buy sales at no cost to the council (Skinner, 1980). At this stage Norwich City Council, which subsequently became most prominent in the conflict, rejected a proposal that they should refuse to implement the Act. The Minister of Housing was at the same time making it clear that the government would use its powers. He was reported as saying these powers would be used 'to ensure that tenants in Labour-controlled areas were not denied the right to buy' (Municipal Journal, 1980).

Despite the potential significance of council house sales for local housing provision and housing opportunities, government expressed little interest in the social and financial impact. It was almost solely preoccupied with the number of sales. The Department of the Environment required local authorities to make regular statistical returns on the number of council houses sold and in the process of being sold. Impressions of progress or delay were also obtained from letters of complaint from or on behalf of tenants, from press reports and from informal discussions between the Department and local authorities. If the information obtained suggested delays were occurring (or were likely to) in implementing the Right to Buy, a formal approach was made to the authority. This would request further details on progress and would typically involve a meeting between Department of the Environment officials and local officers and members. Such a meeting would either produce the necessary assurances on future progress or would result in a formal warning that the Secretary of State was contemplating intervention in the local administration.

Contrary to expectations, and certainly in contrast to the implementation of other pieces of housing legislation, this formal scrutiny and pressure were pervasive. Indeed, by the end of 1983 central government was in contact with some 200 local authorities. This represented a much more active and interventionist stance than had generally applied in the housing area.

The first authority to receive a formal approach about progress was Greenwich. This was in November 1980 only some five weeks after commencement of the Right to Buy. As Table 9.1 indicates, a further three authorities were formally approached in January 1981, eleven in February, and twelve in March. By the time Norwich joined the list, 33 local authorities had already received a similar approach.

In December 1981 reference was made to 70 authorities which had been approached formally about their progress with Right to Buy claims. Some 22 of these had made satisfactory undertakings (or in one case provided satisfactory information on progress) and no further action was contemplated by the Secretary of State. In a further 15 (mostly recent) cases correspondence and discussions were continuing. A further 23 authorities which had not initially made satisfactory undertakings had subsequently done so and the formal warning had been withdrawn.

The crucial measure of progress was the issue of Section 10 notices. These notices stating the landlord's view of valuation, discount entitlement, price and provisions in the conveyance, and informing the applicant of the right to a mortgage and the right to have the house valued by the District Valuer, were to be issued 'as soon as practicable' once the Right to Buy had been established. In addition to the rate of issue of Section 10 notices, the Secretary of State considered the absolute number of admitted Right to Buy claims, the authority's housing stock and the relationship between

Table 9.1: Formal approaches from the Secretary of State over the Right to Buy

Local authority	Date of 1st formal approach	Timetable subsequently agreed without formal warning	Formal warning issued Subsequently withdrawn	Still in force at Oct. '81
Greenwich	12.11.80			X
Barking	27.1.81		X	
Sheffield	30.1.81		X	
Sunderland	30.1.81		X	
Doncaster	5.2.81		X	
Stoke on Trent	10.2.81		X	
Wolverhampton	10.2.81		X	
Bolsover	10.2.81	X		
Leeds	11.2.81			X
Camden	16.2.81		X	
Great Yarmouth	23.2.81		X	
Kingston upon Hull	23.2.81		X	
Bristol	24.2.81		X	
Manchester	25.2.81	X		
Newham	26.2.81			X
Lambeth	4.3.81			X
Middlesbrough	6.3.81		X	
Barnsley	27.3.81		X	
Wakefield	27.3.81		X	
Crawley	30.3.81		X	
Leicester	30.3.81		X	
Carlisle	30.3.81	X		
Thamesdown	30.3.81	X		
Hackney	31.3.81			X
Lewisham	31.3.81		X	
Walsall	31.3.81		X	
Waltham Forest	31.3.81		X	
Gateshead	15.4.81			X
Haringey	15.4.81		X	
Blyth Valley	15.4.81	X		
Newcastle upon Tyne	15.4.81	X		
North Tyneside	18.4.81	X		
Birmingham	29.4.81			X
Burnley	30.4.81		X	
Norwich	30.4.81			X
Tower Hamlets	30.4.81			X
Brent	30.4.81	X		
St Helens	30.4.81	X		

Source: Derived from Department of Environment evidence at the Divisional Court, 17.12.81.

these two figures.

The reason for focusing attention on the issue of Section 10 notices was that this was the last formal step wholly within the authority's control and not dependent on the response of the tenant or solicitor. The proposed price and the draft terms and conditions to be included in the conveyance or grant were also vital pieces of information for the tenant in deciding whether to proceed with the purchase.

THE NORWICH SAGA

By mid-1981 Norwich City Council had become very much the front runner for intervention by the Secretary of State. This might appear surprising given that Norwich was hardly in the vanguard of the more exotic and well publicised brands of local socialism. The city was, however, relatively unusual in having experienced 50 years of local Labour dominance. Such continuity and stability had produced a balanced stock of relatively good quality council homes and a pride in the professionalism of its housing management. Contrary to some commentaries, Norwich may not have wanted to sell council houses but the council were not *refusing* to implement the legislation. Rather it was a question of priorities. They would proceed at their own pace, observing scrupulous legal and administrative procedures, paying due regard to what they considered more pressing problems such as the homeless and the council waiting list. Moreover, Norwich pointed out on a number of occasions that they could hardly be expected to take on more staff to deal with council house sales at a time of public expenditure cutbacks and general pressures on local authority resources. At the heart of the conflict was therefore the discretion available to local government to determine its own priorities within an overall legislative policy and fiscal framework determined at central government level.

The position adopted by Norwich may have been provocative and intransigent but on measures of comparative performance in the implementation of the Right to Buy there were a number of other potential candidates. This is not the place to enter into a detailed account of the case which is provided elsewhere (Forrest and Murie, 1986a). It is, however, appropriate to make some comment on why the Norwich case went to the High Court.

Norwich was exceptional in offering the least satisfactory indication of future progress on sales. It took the view that certain

210

procedures were necessary and could not be circumvented if the disposal of public assets was to be carried out in a way which was democratic and accountable. It insisted, for example, on the involvement of councillors in valuation procedures. The council refused to use private valuers to speed up progress because it was partly regarded as an unreasonable use of council finances. Arguments over these and other details of policy implementation continued over a number of meetings. Although they modified their position Norwich felt unable to comply with all the department's demands and the tone of the meetings become more hostile. As intervention became progressively likely so the political and official status of those involved became progressively higher.

Whilst a meeting in July 1981 was between officers of Norwich City Council and the Department of the Environment, John Stanley, the Minister of Housing, attended a September meeting and by November local MPs and Michael Heseltine, the Secretary of State for the Environment, were also involved. Close scrutiny of these events reveals an extraordinary level of intervention by senior government ministers. This is most easily understood if the sale of council houses is seen to be of unusual ideological, fiscal and electoral importance. It is also easily explicable if the political priority relates to a view that there are more votes in the Right to Buy and the expansion of home ownership than in rates of council house building or provision for the homeless. For the Conservative Party the rapid and successful transfer of a substantial number of houses from the public to the private sector was an early test of political strength, political will and political credibility. And it was anticipated that many local authorities would react to a statutory sales policy with a marked lack of enthusiasm. Implementation had therefore to be heavily policed and enforced. The government's general election victory in 1979 gave a strong mandate for council house sales. From this point of view the time and resources devoted to detailed scrutiny and the involvement of senior politicians was both understandable and defensible, if somewhat unusual.

Norwich, however, had a rather different perspective. They had never sold council houses but had promoted home ownership through other means, such as build for sale schemes. The evidence available before and after the Right to Buy was introduced indicated that the desire to purchase was of paramount concern to only a minority of tenants. Indeed, at the time of the court proceedings only 4% of tenants had applied to buy and Norwich remains among the low sellers in spite of its high quality stock. The council could therefore claim with some justification to be giving priority to the needs of the vast majority of their tenants and to those on the waiting list. Moreover, on the same day as the general election of 1979 local council elections produced an increased Labour majority on an explicit anti-sales platform. This conflicting local mandate encouraged and indeed added legitimacy to the council's stubborn resistance to making adjustments to its own system of priorities. Constitutionally and legally there is, of course, no doubt that in a non-federal system parliament can override any local mandate — but the point remains that Norwich could not be accused of frustrating the apparent desire of the vast majority of its tenant population.

The conflict finally came to a head in the last months of 1981. After the meeting with Michael Heseltine, the then Secretary of State for the Environment, the Norwich delegation carefully considered its position. Neither side was prepared to compromise further. At a meeting of the General Purposes Committee of the council on 10 November, the history of the conflict was carefully outlined and the various options closely scrutinised. Legal advice suggested that the council's position on the sales issue was not an unreasonable one and that the case was winnable should it reach the courts. Moreover the Chief Executive of Norwich advised: 'It will not be in the best interests of the Council, or of members in their personal capacities, to allow a Section 23 notice to be issued and run its course unchallenged' (Norwich City Council, 10.11.81). Thus, both senior officers and the majority of elected members concluded that any intervention in their local management and implementation of the Right to Buy would be challenged in the High Court.

The next day, the Leader of the council conveyed this response to Michael Heseltine and restated the council's general position:

It simply will not do, in our judgement, to neglect the problems of the homeless, and other statutory housing obligations — and the work we are doing to create employment — and combat other problems — just to enable a relatively small number of people, who are already comfortably housed, to buy a property a few months earlier than they otherwise could, when they will lose nothing by waiting. . . For myself, I do not see how local government in this country (and I have been a Councillor for 20 years) can continue except on the basis of co-operation between central and local government — within a tradition in which the Secretary of State makes reasonable requests and a local authority makes a reasonable fist at complying with them — to a degree, and on a timescale, which may be different from that of the authority next door whose circumstances are different. But Ministers, in this case, have chosen not to stand on this traditional ground. (Norwich City Council, 11.11.81)

It was this privileging of sales above other statutory obligations which for Norwich lay at the heart of the conflict. At a time when they were being urged to restrict staffing and expenditure in general they felt that to direct further resources to the processing of council house sales did not represent 'good housekeeping'. A few days later a formal reply was sent by the Secretary of State. In it he repeated his view that tenants were being subjected to unacceptable delays. He referred to the complaints which had been received by the Department of the Environment since the previous February. Reference was made to various aspects of the council's behaviour which could be construed as obstructive and delaying. What was presented was a general climate of unreasonableness on the part of Norwich. A further letter, a formal notice of intervention, was on its way.

Norwich resisted this intervention and sought leave to apply for judicial review. They were granted this leave and the application came before the Divisional Court on 17 December. The judgements on this were unanimous: the intervention by central government was both justified and reasonable. Norwich then went to the Court of Appeal in late January. Without entering into a detailed blow by blow account of the court proceedings it is instructive to note some of the comments made by Lord Denning who delivered the leading judgement. Earlier in the proceedings he had referred to Section 23 of the Housing Act 1980 as a most 'unusual' power. He now described it as 'a most coercive power'. This power, he said:

. . . enables central government to interfere with a high hand over local authorities . . . Local self-government is such an important part of our constitution that to my mind the courts should be vigilant to see that this power of the central government is not exceeded or misused. (Transcripts of judgements delivered in Court of Appeal, 9.2.82)

Denning then went on to identify the three parties concerned in the case. These were the tenants who had a statutory right to buy their council house, the local council who were under a duty to carry through the sale to the tenants and the Minister who was empowered to ensure that the council carried out that duty effectively and expeditiously. Norwich had been pleading their case in terms of a contest between democratically elected little government versus centralist, insensitive big government. But this David and Goliath image took on a different form for Lord Denning. The concern of the court was to protect the individual from the abuse of institutional power. Tenants in Norwich wishing to exercise their Right to Buy had met with 'intolerable' delay. The council had been 'misguided' and 'ill advised'. In Denning's view too little concern had been shown for the rights of tenants, and in that sense Norwich had acted unreasonably. The interests of tenants were defined narrowly and equated with those wishing to purchase their council house. Denning dismissed the appeal. Similar conclusions were reached by Lords Justice Kerr and May. Norwich had in fact lost all five judgements, two in the Divisional Court and three in the Court of Appeal and a further appeal to the House of Lords seemed a futile exercise.

Moreover, it was evident from the court proceedings that the scope for legal resistance to intervention under Section 23 was severely restricted. This was brought out clearly in part of the judgement delivered by Lord Justice Kerr: 'Section 23 has clearly been framed by Parliament in such a way as to maximise the power of the Secretary of State and to minimise any power of review by the court'. And he went on:

> The governing words are . . . 'where it appears to the Secretary of State . . .' These words make it clear that the determinative factor is the view of the Secretary of State; not the view of the local authority in question; nor any abstract standard of reasonableness to be determined by the court. (Transcripts of judgements delivered in Court of Appeal, 9.2.82)

As Laughlin (1983) has observed: 'Government lawyers obviously had learnt their lessons from previous cases reviewing the exercise of discretionary power by Ministers' (p. 62). They had taken no chances with a piece of legislation of such central political importance which was almost certain to be challenged in court. Moreover the judiciary were curiously, if predictably, susceptible to the central government view. For example, Lord Denning referred to a three month wait for a house valuation as wholly unacceptable. But in relation to waiting periods for the homeless and those seeking to rent, or for those seeking transfers within the public sector, such a wait is relatively short. Such measures are arbitrarily and conveniently applied and do not extend across the whole range of housing services.

BROADER LESSONS AND IMPLICATIONS

At the time of the legal battle, the Norwich case was seen as a *cause célèbre*. It was seen as a serious threat to the Thatcher government's aspirations, as a potential terminator of Ministerial careers and as one of a small number of testing acts in defence of local government and local control and in defiance of creeping centralism. To see the conflict narrowly in terms of housing policy is to strip it of its real political context. The legal outcome represented a clear statement of a shift in the balance of power between central and local government. What leading actors and commentators had failed to appreciate was the nature and extent of the shift facilitated by the powers of intervention which were framed in an entirely new way. The legislation in origin and draughtsmanship represented a determined break with consensus and with the belief that local authorities were the best judges of local needs and policies. It represented an attack on social ownership and was part of a wider policy to encourage owner occupation. In these terms it represented carrying forward onto the statute book the arguments, victories and defeats which had been experienced by Conservatives over a long period of time. And it represented a view that reasonable action by local authorities should be judged by their commitment to council house sales rather than in relation to their general discharge of powers and duties.

Local authorities are obliged to carry out duties laid on them by statute — but how they carry them out will vary and is subject to judgements over administration, staffing and costs. Such judgement is subject to legal action but tests of 'reasonableness' apply. It is this kind of test which Norwich felt they could survive, especially in a period when central government's overriding emphasis was on efficiency and expenditure restraint. But Section 23 of the Housing Act 1980 did not involve a test of this type. Rather, the issue was whether a group of tenants was experiencing difficulty over exercising the Right to Buy. In this way, new duties were placed on a different plane from those under other legislation. They were 'priority' duties, their implementation was subject to different types of scrutiny and performance was accountable in a different way. The Secretary of State had a duty to scrutinise tenants' complaints. The

Housing and Building Control Act 1984 further increased Ministerial control and the rate-capping measures in the Rates Act 1984 took more substantial steps along the same route — albeit using a different mechanism. The balance of power in determining what is done and how it is done has been shifted significantly towards central government. Central government is placed in a position to decide whether actions to carry out a range of duties are balanced, correctly prioritised, extravagant or insufficient. In relation to housing, over recent years central government has learned and developed new mechanisms for asserting its dominance. The Housing Act 1980 was an 'advance' on the Housing Finance Act 1972. The wider range of mechanisms and grounds for intervention included in the Housing and Building Control Act 1984 represented a further sophistication of measures available to central government.

Much of the literature concerning central-local relations is constructed around local government as the 'problem': there is a problem variously of efficiency, economy, calibre, political responsibility or radicalism; the problem resides in local government, and central government has to cope and respond. But this kind of perspective bears little relation to the Norwich case. Here the new departures, radicalism and push against traditional relationships came from central government. It was central government that posed and was the problem. This was even apparent in the style of meetings. Councillors with long experience as members of the ruling party represented continuity and had 'learned how to behave'. The confrontations were with Ministers enthused by the recent acquisition of office and the zeal of election victory associated with new policies. Central government determination to achieve certain targets in relation to the Right to Buy involved an unprecedented degree of determination, scrutiny and intervention. In other areas of housing policy (such as homelessness) where, it might be argued, needs are rather more pressing such commitment has never been apparent. The housing policy agenda was dominated by the overriding political priority of ensuring that recalcitrant local authorities could not hinder the transfer of substantial numbers of dwellings from the public sector to owner occupation.

The Right to Buy has proved to be merely one episode in a procession of legislative and policy measures designed to affect increased central control over local authorities. These developments have been variously justified in terms of central government's fiscal priorities, the need to curb the overspending tendencies of certain local administrations, the extension of citizenship rights and freedom of choice. Such justifications continue to be employed in relation to new forms of housing privatisation and to developments in public transport, education and the health service. In each case what is involved is a diminution of local control of services. The methods employed to achieve this, the consequences in terms of responsiveness to local circumstances, and the effects on the morale and motivation of representatives of the local community, will further weaken local administrations. This progressive assumption of power by central government raises a number of key questions. For example, as illustrated by the Right to Buy itself, central government cannot have the knowledge, competence and experience to cope with local administration and the variation in local circumstances. Moreover, the increased concentration of power through legislation and other policy action has political implications beyond those of the individual policies themselves. As central government becomes more directly responsible for local service delivery so it becomes the butt of criticism and complaint. It becomes more directly and obviously responsible and is less able to shelter behind other organisations. Thus, in achieving one set of objectives, central government could be diminishing the mechanisms which strengthen and legitimate its role. Finally, it is arguable whether these developments can be represented as a diminished role for the state. Rather than the state being 'rolled back' it may be that in housing, as in other areas, it is withdrawing into a centralist shell which is less accountable and less open to democratic demands.

10

Rights to Buy and Beyond

Council house sales is not a new policy but it is only in the 1980s that it has become sufficiently important to merit the term 'social revolution'. The sale of over one million dwellings in six years has involved a rapid change in ownership and control of housing and significant redistribution of assets from the state to individuals. By 1987 the policy appears to have passed its peak. Sales are in decline and the government is looking towards other ways of demunicipalising housing. The possibility that the Right to Buy will be withdrawn from the statute book has become increasingly remote. Ironically in 1987 it is most under threat from Conservative policies to break up council housing through disposals to other landlords. Such intentions were clear from the terms of the Housing and Planning Act 1986 and more obviously from the Conservative Manifesto in the 1987 General Election. This stated:

> We will give groups of tenants the right to form tenant co-operatives, owning and running their management and budget for themselves. They will also have the right to ask other institutions to take over their housing. Tenants who wish to remain with the local authority will be able to do so.
> We will give each council house tenant individually the right to transfer the ownership of his or her house to a housing association or other independent, approved landlord. (Conservative Party, 1987)

The Manifesto and subsequent White Paper referred to powers to create Housing Action Trusts to take over areas of poor housing, renovate them and pass them to different tenures and ownerships, including housing associations, tenant co-operatives, owner

218

occupiers or approved private landlords.

To retain the Right to Buy for tenants whose landlord changes under these policies will undoubtedly complicate the process of sales and the financial procedures involved. Even though the Right to Buy will continue, the viability of the new measures would seem to depend on the erosion of this right. Where a council has disposed of properties to an approved landlord and a tenant subsequently wishes to exercise the Right to Buy there are administrative and financial complications including issues of compensating the landlord or implementing the right to a mortgage. But more important than this, the Right to Buy would seem unlikely to be perpetuated for *future* tenants of transferred properties. To this extent the Right to Buy may become more tenuous for many tenants. Over five million tenants had not exercised their Right to Buy by 1987. The numbers still having the chance to exercise it could rapidly decline through transfers of ownership and subsequent tenancy turnover.

With no major political party proposing a direct withdrawal of the Right to Buy, sales of council dwellings are likely to continue. The rate of future sales will however depend on various factors. Changing family structure and economic circumstances will continue to recruit new purchasers. Changes in the relative cost of buying and renting will also affect the rate of sale. This feature makes arrangements for rent policy and rent increases as crucial as sale discounts. The impact of the legislation of 1986 appears to account for an upsurge in sales especially in Scotland where higher discounts for those living in tenements (and continuing increases in rents under the different legislation in Scotland) affect more households than in England and Wales.

The relative costs of renting and buying are also affected by changes in valuation. Recent house price inflation especially in the South East has considerably increased the cost of exercising the Right to Buy. The static house prices which were so favourable to the Right to Buy in the early 1980s when rents were being increased under pressure from central government have been succeeded by rapidly rising house prices and slowly rising rents. The relative financial attractions of buying have declined much less in areas where house price inflation has been lower and rent increases have been higher. The general movement of house prices has increased problems of 'affordability' — of council tenants unable to afford to buy even under generous discount arrangements. But it is in areas where house prices have increased most that the right to buy can

219

deliver the promised benefits of accumulation and inheritance. In the North, where affordability problems are less apparent, these benefits of purchase are less evident. Maintenance and repair costs may outstrip increases in value and could make the real gains from purchase much less than the promise. The way that house prices have changed has in this sense eroded the potential of a policy which implicitly assumed that the contours of house prices and valuations would not become more uneven and render the discount mechanism insufficient to bring prices down to affordable levels.

The increase in house prices in London and the South East at the same time as creating an affordability problem for tenants has increased the profitability opportunity for those who could take advantage of other forms of privatisation. It is in London in particular that builders and developers are likely to have opportunities for substantial profits from the sale and refurbishment of council estates. The way house prices have moved has made these other forms of privatisation more possible. Where these develop the pattern of benefit will be very different from that under the Right to Buy. As indicated in previous chapters the consequence of such further privatisation will increase the problems of those unable to buy. Displacement, homelessness, increased sharing and a reduction in standards in the private rented sector will become more evident consequences in a growing affordability problem. Ironically the most effective response to such a problem would be a public building programme for subsidised rental housing. This would be the best way to ensure that standards of building were higher than would obtain through speculative building for the bottom end of the market and to ensure that dwellings (and subsidies) were channelled to those caught in the affordability trap.

EXPECTATIONS AND OUTCOMES

The impact of council house sales has sometimes been consistent with expectations. Table 10.1 indicates some of the assumptions explicitly voiced to and by the House of Commons Select Committee on the Environment in its investigation into the sale of council houses in 1980–1. In terms of who buys, what properties are bought, and where, the outcome is as expected. However, the volume of sales has been higher than anticipated and consequently the impact of the policy on the council housing sector and on the loss of relets has been greater. As was outlined in Chapter 6 the loss of relets has been equivalent to the termination of all new council house building and the combination of low building rates and an accumulating loss of relets will increasingly affect access to council housing. Even this view, however, has to be related to varying local circumstances. In areas with an ageing population of council tenants or a low demand for council housing the loss of relets may be easier to cope with. In other areas with small stocks and growing local employment the position may be much more critical especially if new building is low.

Three financial factors have emerged as much more important than initially acknowledged. Firstly, the variation in valuations from area to area received relatively little attention in early debates. The implicit assumption was that council dwellings were of similar age and design and the Right to Buy involved a relatively uniform offer throughout the country. But the Right to Buy has been carried out on a formula related to valuation and the value of what is on offer varies greatly. The local authority with the lowest average sale price (after discount) for all council houses sold in 1981–2 was Calderdale (£4,200) followed by Derwentside (£5,400). The highest average sale prices were in the City of London (£40,000) followed by Kensington and Chelsea (£28,900). The ratio of the highest to the lowest is therefore 1:95 or 1:5.4 if the extreme cases are excluded. This is a much greater local variation than applies in rents, but, more importantly, has implications for the value of discounts provided for similar periods of tenancy. These anomalies in this respect call into question the discount formula used in selling council houses. A lump sum related directly to years of tenancy or rents paid would be more equitable in certain respects. The variation in values also has implications for the nature of the redistribution of wealth and the opportunities opened up to purchasers in terms of access to credit, capital accumulation and subsequent position in the housing market. Those buying in higher house price areas and especially where house price inflation occurred subsequently could experience a real transformation in their ownership of wealth and their ability to obtain good housing in other areas. Those buying in low price areas and especially where house price inflation was low subsequently could experience little substantial change except in control over their existing dwelling. These differences are further complicated by costs associated with maintenance and repair. The relationship between these costs and the capital gains involved in different localities will vary enormously. In some areas they may outweigh such capital gains while in others they will be easily financed by

221

Table 10.1: The Right to Buy — expectations and outcomes

Issue	Expectation	Outcome
1. The extent of sales	Various. Some local authorities anticipating low sales. DoE HIP calculations based on 120,000 sales in England 1981–2. Environment Committee's central calculations assumed 100,000 sales annually.	Considerable regional and local variation. National figures higher than many expectations, especially if discretionary sales included.
2. Types of property sold	Better properties will sell. Few sales of flats and maisonettes.	Pattern of sales broadly conforms with this and low rates of sales of flats not attributable to service charges and delays affecting flat sales more than others. Also some desirable houses and flats too highly priced to sell.
3. Loss of relets	Age based calculations. Some expectations that more younger buyers than past evidence indicated.	Most buyers are later in family cycle but the range of ages for calculations extended downward, implying greater loss of relets in early years.
4. Special groups	Elderly, ethnic minorities, single parent families not likely to share in sales substantially (where properties not excluded e.g. as elderly persons' dwellings).	Effect of higher discounts has been to encourage more elderly buyers (often with assistance from children) but elderly, single parent families still under-represented among purchasers. Households concentrated in flats and inner city estates are also under-represented.
5. Inner city and urban areas	Increasing segregation and polarisation associated with dwelling type.	Broadly confirmed and exacerbated in areas affected by high unemployment and economic dependency. High prices further limiting sales in some inner city areas.

6. Rural areas	High level of sales especially in villages.	Evidence of high rate of sales consistent with expectations, but villages less attractive where relatively isolated.
7. Changing role of council housing	Exemptions would enable role for elderly to be maintained but sales of houses rather than flats could restrict ability of stock to meet other needs.	Properties used by elderly not generally excluded. Loss of houses with gardens and ground floor leaving dwelling stock less suitable for needs of families and the elderly.
8. Extent of redistribution of wealth	No estimates of likely valuations of dwellings but average of 40% discounts referred to.	Average discounts substantially higher even under 1980 legislation. Valuations vary significantly between localities and the extent of redistribution varies as a result. Subsequent house price inflation involved increase in asset values — with a strong regional pattern.
9. Equalisation of wealth	Poorer households and those in lower social classes probably less likely to buy.	Unskilled workers are under-represented among purchasers and these and other groups (economically dependent of working age) not sharing in redistribution but being left behind in a more unequal situation.
10. Comparison between rents and mortgage repayments	Unusual for mortgage repayments to exceed rents.	Changes in rents and mortgage interest rates have significantly changed this situation especially in low price areas and for those with high discounts. Later house price inflation increasing relative cost of buying in some areas.

Table 10.1: contd.

Issue	Expectation	Outcome
11. Mortgage default	Concern that policy, by pulling in the marginal owner, would lead to increased default.	Purchase price as a multiple of income indicates that purchasers in some high price areas are stretching resources but in most areas and cases council purchasers are less marginal than lower income private sector purchasers. Movements in interest rates have also reduced the likelihood of this except where associated with a change in economic or family circumstances. Where cost of renting is near or greater than that of buying lower income households buying to reduce housing costs — with implications for default and maintenance problems.
12. Volume of capital receipts	No clear assumptions on valuation levels but average discount 40% and initial cash payment below 30% (possibly very much lower). Consequently amount of capital available for immediate reinvestment between 7½ and 10% of selling price.	Average discounts higher than expected and immediate capital receipts initially substantially higher (45%). Consequently amount of capital reinvestment around 12½% of selling price. Subsequently even greater role of private sector in mortgage provision and rising valuations further increased volume of capital receipts.

increased asset value.

The second neglected financial feature relates to the comparison between rents and mortgage repayments. In the prior discussion of the Right to Buy there was some challenge to assumptions that exercising the Right to Buy would cost more than renting. In a speech in April 1979 before he became Secretary of State Michael Heseltine had said:

We would not allow the initial mortgage repayments to be less than the rent a tenant currently pays. In the case of cheaper and older properties there will undoubtedly be tenants of long standing whose mortgage repayments will be no higher than they currently pay in rent, and mortgage terms consequently may be shorter than normal if their rent payments exceed the level of instalments that would cover, say, a twenty year mortgage term. (quoted in House of Commons Environment Committee, 1981)

In spite of a recommendation by the Environment Committee no Secretary of State took action to implement this undertaking. In practice, exercising the Right to Buy has in some cases involved reducing housing costs. In these cases the advantages of buying will have been associated with housing costs as well as (or perhaps rather than) increased user control or dwelling ownership. In some areas the relative movement of rents and the costs of purchase have meant that home purchase involves an *immediate* cut in housing costs. Comparisons given elsewhere for one of the lowest house price areas (Derwentside) have illustrated this (Forrest and Murie, 1984b, pp. 69–71).

Exercising the Right to Buy has bought some tenants out of a financing system over which they have little control and which is determined through central and local government decisions on subsidy, management and maintenance expenditure and on the structure of rents and rent pooling. The new system they enter into involves some initial decisions on type, term and size of mortgage. It is then tied to historic costs (with no pooling) and maintenance expenditure can fluctuate wildly. The least controllable element relates to interest rates.

The experience of households who continued to rent and those who have bought involves some sharp contrasts. Since 1979 central government has achieved substantial cuts in general subsidy to council housing largely through increasing rents. Although the interest earned on the proceeds from council house sales has become an

225

important additional source of income and has enabled some local authorities to limit rent increases, such increases have still been substantial. The council tenant who is not in receipt of means-tested housing benefits has experienced a substantial real rise in rents and has in most cases ceased to benefit from any Exchequer or rate fund subsidy. In 1979–80 44% of the income of Housing Revenue Accounts in England and Wales came from central government subsidies and 12% from local authority rate fund contributions. By 1986–7 the estimated comparable figures were 7% and 8% respectively. Tenants not in receipt of housing benefit had experienced an enormous withdrawal of subsidy. In many localities subsidy was non-existent or negligible and in some cases (whether or not subsidy was paid) Housing Revenue Accounts were in substantial surplus, were making transfers to the general rate fund or covered costs which would more appropriately be charged to ratepayers in general rather than council tenants. For tenants not in receipt of subsidy this package represented a real erosion of the advantages of council housing. Even where for example maintenance services were valued this financial regime put a high price on this.

In contrast, since the introduction of the Right to Buy the housing costs of council house purchasers have followed a different pattern. While subsidies for council tenants have been significantly restructured, tax relief arrangements affecting the housing costs of home owners have not been changed. Council house buyers have, however, qualified for additional and substantial subsidies relating to the value of discounts associated with length of tenancy. The value of these discounts varies substantially between areas (Forrest and Murie, 1984b) but has averaged over £6,000 for each transaction. For tenants not qualifying for benefit buying the house has been a means of maintaining and increasing subsidy when renting would involve losing subsidy.

The increased discounts to buy council houses in 1979 coincided with a period of rising mortgage interest rates. However, for most of those who bought in the early years of the Right to Buy mortgage repayments by 1987 were near or below rent levels. Based on this and on the experience of earlier buyers (Forrest and Murie, 1984b, p. 66) purchasers would be beginning to benefit from lower expenditure as well as considerable increase in the value of the housing asset. The removal of the requirement to repay a portion of discount on early sale (Housing and Planning Act, 1986) made realisation of this increased asset value feasible. In these terms the experience of the often more affluent council house purchaser contrasts sharply with the tenant. It is important to acknowledge that the comparison does not take maintenance and related expenditure into account and it may be argued that a false impression is gained. It may equally be argued that for many households with no maintenance 'plan' and with an inclination to postpone or minimise maintenance expenditure it is the comparison in terms of regular monthly outgoings and of asset appreciation which is most appropriate. *When* tenants bought has direct implications for discount entitlement, valuation and price and for the experience of changes in interest rates. In any one locality accidents of timing will have meant that purchase delivers more benefits for some more quickly than for others.

The costs and meanings of purchase can be very different. For some, ownership is achieved and sustained at very considerable immediate expense. For others council house purchase has meant a reduction in immediate outgoings associated with housing. In this latter situation any other advantages of owner occupation are augmented by cash considerations. And cash considerations could form a major factor in decisions to buy. The financial realities could be expected to generate a demand to buy rather than that demand reflecting an innate preference to own. The shifting relative advantages of owning and renting are not just related to interest rates and rents. The level of inflation, the movement of house prices, the value placed on the opportunity to use income in other ways and the advantages associated with this opportunity at different times are all significant factors.

The third neglected financial factor relates to capital receipts. These have been dealt with in some detail in Chapter 5. In summary a combination of factors meant that council house sales consistently exceeded expectations in terms of the generation of capital receipts. The fiscal advantages of the policy have consistently been greater than anticipated. And even when sales are in decline and the policy is benefiting fewer households by enabling them to become owner occupiers, capital receipts have remained high. In retrospect, one of the major advantages of council house sales from central government's perspective has not directly had anything to do with housing or home ownership but has been in relation to the generation of capital receipts.

OTHER FINANCIAL ASPECTS

The discussion of financial issues in this book has largely

227

concentrated on capital receipts. However in the period prior to 1980 and especially in the period 1976 to 1981 much energy was expended on the financial aspects of sales. Increasingly sophisticated discount calculations of the financial effects of council house sales were carried out. The most thorough appraisal was that provided through the evidence and memoranda submitted to the Environment Committee of the House of Commons and published in 1981. It is not intended to rehearse the many elements in such an appraisal here. However one important point in any of these appraisals is that many of the variables included are subject to policy decision by central or local government. The movement of such key variables as rent depends on policy decisions.

The Environment Committee's appraisal was based on the assumption of a 40% average discount for sold properties. In practice discounts have been considerably higher (starting with an annual average of 42% and rising to 47%). The effects of the two year option do not seem to have been significant (numerically, and therefore in their effect in increasing discount). The increase in rents between 1980 and 1982 was greater than the increase in earnings and since then rents have risen broadly in line with prices. Rents foregone have consequently been considerably higher than assumed in most appraisals. These factors will tend to increase the losses or reduce the gains associated with council house sales. In some localities rents foregone are immediately greater than monthly receipts from associated mortgages. When Webster's 20 year or 50 year appraisals are reconsidered (House of Commons Environment Committee, 1981) in light of these two changes it is apparent that in both cases, and allowing for different economic assumptions, there is a substantial loss associated with sales. Inevitably these arrangements have made sales more questionable in financial terms. Sales involve a substantial loss to local authorities in terms of the difference between sale price and market value. But, in terms of the conventional appraisals of the financial impact of sales, larger discounts and higher rents both increase the likelihood of and the level of losses associated with sales.

Discount arrangements represent decisions to grant part of the capital value of housing assets to the purchaser. This capital grant is not an explicit feature of other privatisation policies and does not occur in private market transactions. While some other sales of assets have been at less than market value this has resulted from problems of estimating what values are rather than an intention to discount value. A transfer from the local authority or the ratepayer to council house purchasers is without parallel in other areas of housing policy. It does not occur to the advantage of any other group of house purchasers and forms a payment in addition to other grants and subsidies available to all home buyers. The size of this grant can be referred to in terms of lost investment opportunities in the housing sector or other opportunity costs.

The initial arrangements to prevent purchasers realising the benefits of their 'grants' within a short period were changed in 1986 with the period being reduced from five to two years. The way the housing market works may mean that most purchasers will reinvest any financial gain in housing so that it will not be realised for a substantial time and possibly not by them. Nevertheless there is a capital loss to the local authority. This loss in England amounted to some £5.6 billion between 1979–80 and 1985–6. In each of the last three financial years in this period it was £900 million. These are very substantial figures compared to the levels of capital investment by central and local government in housing. Clearly if discounts were not granted at the rate they have been, the volume of sales and receipts would have differed. The implications of such figures for public expenditure planning or policy making are by no means simple. Nevertheless it is undeniable that the level of payments to private individuals is vast in comparison with total public expenditure figures.

GAINERS AND LOSERS

The picture of who benefits from council house sales has remained remarkably consistent especially in family cycle terms. The converse of who benefits is who loses. Again there is a familiar picture of groups under-represented among those buying council housing — including younger and older households, women and single parent households. It is important to acknowledge in this discussion that changing family circumstances result in a recruitment of new purchasers from among those previously unable to buy and that some purchases are made for and by other members of a household. The longer term effects of changing demand and supply for council housing should also be acknowledged. Various studies show that households with least bargaining power tend to be allocated to the less popular dwellings in the public sector. The decline in transfer opportunities resulting from the decline of council housing will mean that for an increasing number of households their

229

first allocation will become a permanent or long term allocation. Council house sales policy has only been the final stage in a process through which council housing has benefited a particular generation of tenants. The next/new generation of tenants will not only not have the same opportunities to buy (unless properties comparable to those sold are added to the council stock) but they will not have the same opportunities to move and to graduate to desirable dwellings as tenants. The policy benefits one generation of tenants at the expense of the next.

This perspective has another important dimension. Gains to one group do reduce the opportunities for another. The council house sales policies of the early 1980s have coincided with limited new building. The size and quality of the sector have declined and rents have risen. What is on offer for those seeking to become tenants at the end of the 1980s is very different from 30 or 40 years earlier when new tenants (after a long wait in unsatisfactory housing) were most likely to be housed in newly built high standard, high amenity, large houses with gardens. At the end of the 1980s they are most likely to be housed in relets — especially in low demand flats and maisonettes on less attractive estates. The other part of this equation is that the households involved are very different. Thirty to forty years ago new tenants were white families with children, with a skilled or semi-skilled male wage earner in stable employment. At the end of the 1980s they include more women, single parent families, black persons, single person households and more households without jobs or on the fringes of a depressed labour market. These groups in general have been discriminated against in attempts to gain access to council housing. But at the point when this discrimination has come under increasing challenge and greater access is being gained the service concerned has been altered almost out of recognition. Stated crudely it was white households who benefited from the development of a high quality, subsidised, council housing sector and it is white households who have largely benefited from sales and discounts and the shift in subsidy and expenditure towards owner occupation. At the point when black households were increasingly likely to benefit from council housing the resources going to, and the quality of, the sector declined.

While the immediate gainers and losers from policy can be identified any policy of this type has wider repercussions and 'system effects'. These have been referred to in relation to impacts on the nature and structure of the council sector. But the discussion should not end there. The policy crucially changes the nature of owner occupation. It changes the age and characteristics of the population and the housing stock in the owner occupied sector. This is particularly important for calculations about the future condition and disrepair of that stock. The transferring council stock tends to be of an age where maintenance costs are high and it has not always been well maintained. There are other repercussions on owner occupation and it is reasonable to suggest that council house sales have meant that some who would have bought anyway have bought as council tenants — reducing some demand for new building in other parts of the private sector; and that sales have increased the demand for mortgage borrowing and, as a result, the cost of such borrowing — affecting costs for all those with mortgages.

The discussion of who gains and who loses from policy does not have any necessary policy implications. It does not follow that the policy should be terminated because the majority of tenants do not gain directly, or because important groups lose out. The impact of council house sales is determined by the wider pattern of policies — and these rather than the sales policy itself could be reviewed. Nor is it clear that it is in the interests of either gainers or losers to see the appropriate response in terms of defending council housing. Jacobs writing in 1981 and critical of attempts to launch an anti-sales campaign accepted that sales would inflict further damage on an ailing public sector and would jeopardise the interests of those on the waiting list. However Jacobs argued against campaigns which assumed that the expansion of home ownership would divide or dampen opposition to the political *status quo* and against an opposition which assumed that the interests of the working class or of council tenants equated with council landlordism. This is an important perspective returned to later in this chapter. The identification and recognition of problems with the policy of selling council housing should not be assumed to imply termination of sales or defence of the *status quo* in relation to council housing provision.

LONGER TERM QUESTIONS

Some of the other questions raised by the sale of council houses can only be addressed in the longer term. These longer term impacts of council house sales are of direct policy importance because of the number of council houses sold. Typical council house purchasers are in their mid to late 40s and this affects the pattern of households becoming home owners for the first time. Because of discounts those who sell in order to move will have relatively large capital sums released. Their children are often adults and may already have left home. This is likely to affect decisions to move and what kind of dwelling they will wish to move to. Discount and cost factors may encourage some tenants to buy dwellings they are not committed to staying in for a long time — or even to buy in order to enhance ability to move. Given the high level of sales we could expect a high and effective demand for certain dwelling types in certain areas after a number of years. In these ways the large number of sitting tenant purchasers is not in general either like first time buyers or council tenants. They have different characteristics and opportunities. How they will respond in the future is not easily assessed from other evidence but is of considerable interest.

Questions about the longer term impact of council house sales arise over a number of issues. Especially in view of the age, occupational and other characteristics of sitting tenant purchasers it has been argued that severe problems of disrepair will follow sales — but will not be apparent for some time. Others have suggested (see Chartered Institute of Public Finance and Accountancy, 1984) that a tenant acquiring a dwelling is more likely to carry out improvements to bring individuality to the property and is generally more likely to be actively concerned about maintenance. Some support for this view derives from external changes carried out by purchasers — but it is also argued that these are immediate and cosmetic changes and may not contribute to good maintenance.

Limited evidence exists which suggests that former council houses will, on resale, be bought by young childless couples and others who would not have been allocated council dwellings on grounds of need (Forrest, 1980). This aspect and the rate of turnover of former council dwellings will affect issues of maintenance and repair and the change in general patterns of access to housing. Especially after the period in which discount repayment could be involved, if the purchaser moved, the opportunities for sitting tenant purchasers to raise second mortgages or other loans are greater than for most first time buyers (because of discounts). But we do not know whether sitting tenant purchasers take advantage of this opportunity, or when or for what purpose. This is an important aspect of how change of tenure would affect family life and resources — but it is not likely to emerge over the first few years after house purchase. Nor do we know how far council house purchasers trade-up or otherwise benefit from accumulation of wealth through housing.

In view of the age of purchasers and the evidence of joint and 'family' purchase a question arises over how often sons and daughters will 'succeed' in ownership (perhaps through inheritance). There are interesting complications in this. Some sons and daughters who would have obtained a council tenancy on succession may not be able to become owners in the same way — other members of the family may have a claim or other financial factors may arise. Conversely some sons and daughters who would have no claim to a council property on termination of tenancy do benefit where an owner occupied property is involved. Again these aspects are not likely to become clear for a number of years after purchase.

Questions about coping with financial and family crises arise, especially in relation to mortgage arrears. Problems arising from marital breakdown, family crisis, unemployment, redundancy or loss of income exist irrespective of tenure but the mechanisms for resolving them differ. Former council tenants do not appear to experience higher mortgage arrears than other purchasers (Association of Metropolitan Authorities, 1986) but information is patchy and heavily weighted by recent purchasers. The longer term pattern is unclear. One hypothesis would be that in areas where the local economy is buoyant and house prices are high and appreciating there will be fewer of these problems and of problems of repair and maintenance, and council house purchase will increase mobility and choice generally. However, in areas where the impact of economic recession has been more severe and where house prices are low relative to repair costs and not appreciating as rapidly as elsewhere more problems for property and households will emerge.

AN ANALYSIS OF POLICY

The earliest substantial analysis of council house sales emphasised housing policy and different party attitudes and beliefs about housing (Murie, 1975). It was argued that the policy originated between the wars and had been a consistent point of dispute between political parties. This issue had been 'symbolic' of differences in the attitudes of the major parties to the role of the State at local and national levels, and had been symbolic of more than housing issues. Shifts in policy had been considerable and had reflected party disposition rather than any consensus over changing needs or circumstances. The example of Birmingham indicated that the symbolic elements and the shifts in policy existed at local as well as national levels. The

233

particular historical and political traditions of Birmingham as well as its social and economic development gave it particular attributes which will not necessarily be replicated everywhere.

More than ten years later the discussion is more complex. The development of legislation and of the Right to Buy, as well as the way that legislative powers have been used by central government, justify a greater emphasis on central-local government conflicts. The continuing erosion by Conservative central governments of local autonomy in housing focuses attention on the electoral and ideological aspects of the policy and on broader debates concerning the legitimate role of the state in capitalist societies. The housing policy dimension has become more tenuous and less prominent. The merits of owner occupation and the Right to Buy are increasingly expressed in general terms and in terms of the merits of ownership *per se* rather than as a means of improving housing circumstances or increasing housing investment. It may be argued that this is a necessary feature of a policy which, because of the scale of its impact, itself changes the nature of home ownership. Council house sales were initially justified in terms of an image of home ownership which has become less true because of the impact of these sales and other housing developments occurring alongside. Sales have been promoted through greater direct subsidy (discounts) and growing tax relief expenditure. The owner occupied sector has become a state sponsored, subsidised sector rather than a deregulated private sector. As council housing subsidies have been reduced the contrasts between public and private sectors have changed. The process of increasing discounts and removing disincentives to buy has generated various anomalies and inconsistencies — not least in the very different advantages being offered by an apparently even-handed policy. The momentum of sales has been maintained by subsidy and by increasing centralisation of policy through advertising, monitoring and direct intervention. As outlined in Chapter 3 new legislation (The Housing Defects Act, 1984) was required specifically to maintain the view that purchasers could not be worse off by buying.

A policy initially concerned with translating tenants into owners has increasingly lost sight of this and become concerned with other methods of privatisation. By the late 1980s a new phase of privatisation and corporatism in housing policy with a greater emphasis on the role of building societies, builders and landlords has begun to replace the emphasis on households and individual ownership. One interpretation of these developments is that they reflect the need to

234

protect the investment of those who have bought council houses by injecting more private finance and market mechanisms into council estates. However, it is difficult to avoid a view that there has also been some displacement of policy goals.

Various other comments on the process of policy making and development have been made in this book. In particular aspects of central-local government conflict and local variation have been emphasised. The observation that a uniform policy has not led to similar policy outcomes relates to a further aspect of policy which merits a brief mention. In spite of involving a major policy innovation or experiment, council house sales' policies have never been accompanied by a research or evaluation element. Central government's concern has focused on the collection of quarterly statistics and on the numbers of sales. Latterly the General Household Survey and other specific research were used to identify why people did not buy or to inform policy makers over how to extend or develop policy. An important study by the Scottish Office (Foulis, 1985) was the only piece of government research concerned to detail patterns and problems in relation to the policy published before 1988. There is no tradition of research and evaluation accompanying major policy changes. And in this case the policy change has involved a significant erosion of local autonomy. The view that local authorities are the best judges of local needs and demands and of local priorities has been effectively overturned. Central government's willingness to pursue an anti-municipal stance has been evident in various policy developments in the 1980s. In housing, its continuation was apparent in 1987 in threats to intervene in the administration of the Right to Buy in up to eleven local authorities (*Inside Housing*, 1.5.87) and in post-election proposals to establish Housing Action Trusts. These developments, the neglect and costs of a rising problem of homelessness and the increasing emphasis on the use of private funding for housing association development continued to demonstrate the major change in the nature of the welfare state in housing.

The impact of government policy over the last few years may not have been as dramatic as some would have wished but there has been a major transformation of the tenure structure. To recreate the previous structure of tenure would involve a major reversal. But it is not clear why we would wish to make such a reversion. Whilst there are clear advantages in collective housing provision council housing has been as strongly associated with failures as with these advantages. Public landlordism erected in opposition to private landlordism,

235

operating a pathological model of tenant behaviour with implicit or explicit 'rough' and 'respectable' categorisations and preoccupied with managing shortage, has been an albatross around the neck of social housing. It has been relatively easy for the present form of owner occupation to be presented as the preferable alternative. There have been a number of important commentaries which are relevant to this.

Jacobs (1981) criticising the form of opposition to council house sales argues the case for defending council tenants rather than council housing. It might further be argued that a defence of potential and future tenants is needed. Phrased in any of these terms, the policy response to defend tenants and others is not necessarily opposition to sales but it is almost certainly opposition to a policy package which does not embrace policies to increase and extend housing rights and choices to those unable to benefit through sales. The interests of working-class households or those unable to buy should not automatically be equated with council housing but neither can it be assumed that the needs of such households will be met through some unspecified filtering or market process.

A second important proposition equates council house sales with the extension of dweller control. Ward, for example (1983, 1985), has argued that dweller satisfaction relates to the degree of dweller control and that selling council dwellings will push up standards of environmental maintenance and guarantee that someone is going to benefit from public investment in housing. A clear concern and accurate critique of the failure of council housing in terms of dweller control can be seen as compatible with support for certain changes in council housing as well as with the development of co-operatives. Ward's neglect of this puts him into the 'inherent failings of council housing' school. His writing also falls into the 'uncritical view of owner occupation' school. Both of these themes are continually represented in a range of publications by various authors. They present a sterile debate which involves exchanging half-truths about tenures and does not attempt to address the ways of improving the circumstances of the majority of owners or tenants. Generalised denunciations of council housing or owner occupation are of as limited value as are defences of council housing which neglect the council tenant. A more constructive stance recognises that the majority of households in each tenure is not totally dissatisfied but would and do respond to changes in the opportunities available to it. The council house sales issue itself clearly illustrates this. Purchasers' decisions to buy publicly built housing which they have rented for years and regarded as their home do not best represent the alienation of the dweller from the dwelling. Reintroducing the dweller's perspective into the debate would not mean a perspective that always conformed to Ward's. Attitudes to and choices between dwellings and tenures are contingent on a range of factors. They vary over time, according to place and in relation to the family life cycle. They are influenced by previous housing history, and the meanings and practices involved are learned in a local environment. The generalised attack on council housing has lost contact with local variations and increasingly misrepresents the real nature of council housing and attitudes to it.

Undeniably misrepresentations do begin themselves to change such attitudes. In Chapter 2 of this book the variations in the quality and standards of council housing when it was built were stressed. This theme of variation within and between localities and parts of the stock has remained. Problems of design, construction, repair and maintenance have become more apparent in recent years and require urgent action. Local authorities' estimates of outstanding repair costs were some £20 billion in 1985 and the imagery of a crumbling or obsolete stock of undesirable dwellings is correct — for some of the council sector. The bulk of council dwellings are still houses with gardens and tenants regard them as satisfactory. Tenants' decisions to buy are at least in part demonstrations that public authorities built dwellings that people want, and in which they want to continue living. Organisational and management deficiencies in council housing have received more attention in recent years and there can be no doubt that there is considerable room for improvement. However, it is important (and not apologist) to recognise that the task faced by local authorities has changed, is constantly changing, and has become more difficult.

It is unfortunate that it has become fashionable in recent years to indulge in grand generalisation and denigration of council housing. The consensus of denigration lends support to simple centrally determined solutions including various approaches to privatisation. The view that the nature and problems of council housing vary and should be analysed in a local context and that 'solutions' should be built from such analysis and an awareness of local circumstances and needs is less easy to present as a dramatic panacea but should not be rejected for that reason. While there are important failings in council housing, in 1987 it still provides the bulk of rented housing and the major way of obtaining housing for those who must, or who prefer to, rent. Nor is it a sector which typically provides high rise or other flats. It is not accurate to pursue a logic which equates council housing with high rise and which explains this in terms of the defective vision of local government. In general the housing which has been built through local state bureaucracies is good, traditional, popular housing. And the shift to high rise and systems building has occurred under strong pressure from central government, the architectural professional consensus and the private sector construction industry. The kinds of analysis and the conclusions drawn from, for example, Coleman's work (1985), cannot be regarded as significant contributions to a general debate about the experience of local authority intervention in housing. While the failings of local authorities in respect of management and maintenance are serious, it is not clear that the general standard is worse than that in owner occupation. It is certainly better than that which generally has applied in the private rented sector. The repair costs in council housing are generally linked to age, with the need for work greatest in older dwellings of any type (Department of the Environment, 1985). The largest element of need for works is in respect of the ageing inter-war traditional dwellings. The picture is much the same as for the private sector — of deterioration of properties with age. The strongest criticism of local authorities is that they have not been able to anticipate and avoid a decline in repair which in the owner occupied sector is associated with advancing age and declining health and income. On this and other grounds there is a strong argument that local authorities should review and change their housing management. They should decentralise and devolve control and they should concentrate on facilitating and enabling tenants to take decisions and to manage their own dwellings. One advantage of this would be to release the political and professional energies in local authorities for strategic and production/investment related policy making.

The experience of council housing in Britain shows that local authorities can complement private activity to build what is wanted, where it is wanted, when it is wanted. Local authorities are also more accountable in terms of who is allocated dwellings, and are more open to scrutiny than other landlords and agents. However, beyond this they have not proved superior to other landlords. They have not adjusted better to a changing stock profile or to an increasingly residual role. Existing forms of privatisation have speeded the process of residualisation, and made the task yet more difficult. But decentralisation, local estate management, maintenance and refurbishment of run-down estates, the development of equal opportunities policies and the relaxation of paternalistic, bureaucratic habits show that the sector is not inflexible and moribund. For the

238

sector to adjust more quickly or fundamentally requires resources and detailed systematic implementation and evaluation of coherent policies. In some cases the guidance from central government (say, through the priority estates project) recognises this. Other contributions from the centre reflect the preference for simple cure-alls, and the concern to limit public expenditure and generate capital receipts. Privatisation may deliver in these terms (assuming the financial packages which would be attractive to the private sector do not involve too substantial 'discounts' on valuations or too substantial grants of other types). Privatisation will not, however, automatically resolve the management and maintenance problems that exist in a residual sector. One scenario would be that future privatisation will fragment the sector, and will more clearly stratify it. In order to float off some estates (through sales) other estates will become even more uniformly second best. The poor would be moved around in order to realise the asset value of the property portfolio. Indeed local authorities may orchestrate such a movement by decanting estates for sales and obtaining vacant possession in order to enhance sale price.

The sale of vacant dwellings and indeed the sale of estates is not new. By 1987 over 15,000 dwellings had been sold to developers. More than half of these involved two large scale disposals of tenanted property — the GLC Thamesmead development and Knowsley's Cantril Farm estate. With the exception of one small tenanted estate in Oldham the remainder were disposals of empty property. The implications for those who are decanted and for those living or wanting to live in rented estates are of a more pronounced ghetto effect and of less chance of moving within the sector. It is conceivable that the discussion of residualisation would cease to refer to this as a trend or direction but that a uniform welfare sector would have arrived.

A POSTSCRIPT OF PRIVATISATION

Immediately after the general election of 1987 the Conservative government identified housing and the inner city as key areas for policy development. It was in these areas that work remained to be done to create choice. Electoral calculations were prominent in this approach. In 1987 the inner urban areas had remained Labour strongholds. The new emphasis in policy represented a considerable shift in policy and involved a recognition of the failure of the Right

239

to Buy and other elements in the government's policy package to benefit the whole council sector and larger urban estates. Previous policies had not provided real choices to all tenants and had not prevented an increasing concentration of housing, social and disrepair problems on certain estates. The Government response in the Conservative election manifesto was to offer more comprehensive and far reaching policies for demunicipalisation.

Where local authorities wished to pursue estate privatisation they would continue to be encouraged — and indeed financial pressures could also be expected as an inducement. However two new elements were to be added. The first would provide tenants with rights to determine their own tenure arrangements. As expressed by the new Minister for Housing in 1987:

> One way of moving towards more diverse communities, and to give tenants an effective voice in determining their own future, is for the Government to introduce a right for local authority tenants to choose to transfer, either individually or collectively, to other landlords. Appropriate landlords might for example be tenant co-operatives or housing associations. Those who are content with their landlord, and are happy with the service they get, may of course choose to stay as council tenants.
>
> This new right will extend the principle established by Section II of the Housing and Planning Act 1986, which requires local authorities to give a reasoned response to tenants' proposals for new forms of management or transfers of ownership. This gives a good model on which to build our additional right for tenants to choose between competing landlords (Waldegrave, 1987a).

The second new element was specifically aimed at inner urban areas with major social and environmental problems. The Government proposed a major injection of management skills and capital investment, and co-operation between the public and private sectors. William Waldegrave referred to the 'success achieved by the Urban Development Corporations (UDCs), particularly in London' and claimed:

> . . . they have shown that a body single-mindedly devoted to redeveloping a run-down area can achieve massively positive results of a kind that local authorities have in the past been unable to achieve. Urban Development Corporations have been able to bring a new drive, as well as resources, to the single-minded

achievement of their tasks. I agree that they must work alongside the local authorities and in co-operation with them to achieve the best results.

He went on to state:

The Government has decided that it is in the national interest that a similar approach should be adopted for a few of the most difficult urban areas. We will legislate so that I have powers to establish similar bodies in specified areas to take over responsibility for local authority housing with a view to managing it and improving it and also improving the local environment.

Following this, in September 1987, a White Paper (Department of the Environment/Welsh Office, 1987) laid out the government's view of the way in which the UDC model could be applied in the housing field. The principal vehicle was to be Housing Action Trusts (HATs). These would 'have a limited life span'. Their remit would be to secure the improvement of the stock transferred to them in their area and then hand it over to other owners and managers (p. 16). The White Paper also confirmed the government's intention to limit further the scope of municipal housing and encourage the 'independent' sector, through deregulation of new lettings and the development of new financial regimes. It further confirmed the choice of landlord provisions previously in the election manifesto and proposed detailed changes to stimulate further the Right to Buy.

These new privatisation measures offer the prospect of demunicipalisation, drawing private finance into council housing and generating capital receipts. In many cases it is possible that the capital receipt per dwelling will fall short of the outstanding capital debt per dwelling leaving the local authority financially worse off. New measures to reform the finance of council housing — including preventing rate fund subsidy to housing revenue accounts — offered the prospect of higher and more variable local authority rents. These changes, changes in housing benefits and a relaxation of limits on rents in private (independent) and housing association properties were all likely to affect decisions on whether to rent or buy, and on whether to rent in the council sector. One of the detailed changes to the Right to Buy proposed by the government in 1987 — the abolition of the cost floor — could generate a further round of sales. Those unable to benefit to the full extent of their discount entitlement because this would have reduced sale price below the cost floor (relating to costs incurred since 31 March 1984) could find purchase price dramatically reduced.

The Minister for Housing had stated (Waldegrave, 1987b) that the test for the government would not be in terms of housing starts or completions but in establishing 'a new balance of forces' in the housing market. The most striking passages of his speech emphasised the role of private landlords and housing associations in providing rented housing. Ironically one of the arguments against council housing was expressed as 'Do we really want the state to build new saleable houses which it will then sell at a discount? For what? As a way of providing subsidised houses for first time buyers? That would be a very elaborate way of doing that, and very random in whom it helped . . .' It would be more consistent to argue that this is exactly what selling council houses has involved and to see this as the logical way of providing equivalent benefits to the next generation of households. This strange epitaph from a Conservative minister has similarities with the decision in 1987 by the London Residuary Body (which replaced the GLC) to sell houses and flats on premium sites in the Covent Garden area, partly because a policy of renting (as planned by the GLC) would allow tenants to exercise their right to buy and reduce the gain to local authorities (*Guardian*, 1987).

The shift of emphasis away from encouraging home ownership as the sole element in privatisation and towards dismantling council housing is strongly reflected in the Minister's statement. He could:

> . . . see no arguments for generalised new build by councils, now or in the future. Receipts should not be used for new build and sale as if councils were a sort of property company. They can and should be used for repair of existing stock, some for sale and some to retain. But how much of the latter is there? And of what type?
> My belief is, there should not be much of it at all. It is an oddity confined largely to Britain amongst European countries that the state goes landlording on this scale. The next great push after the Right to Buy should be to get rid of the state as a big landlord and bring housing back to the community. If you want to buy and can buy, so much the better; if for example flats are more likely to continue to be rented, then the landlords should be the sort of social housing organisations we see overseas. They can represent tenants more closely; they are not caught up in the

electoral swings and cycles of party politics; they can be single minded about housing and as skilful about it as only specialists can be; they can in many cases be smaller and more local. The British Housing Association movement can provide these organisations, either directly or as foster parents. Meanwhile the councils can concentrate on their front line housing welfare role, buying the housing services they need, or subsidising those who need help, and undertaking the wide range of regulatory, enforcement, planning and other tasks which are the essence of the public sector.

It is too early to say what effect new legislation on these matters will have on council tenants or applicants or on the role of council housing. Four broad comments are however appropriate. First, the new policy package does not offer the prospect of substantial new public sector investment and continues to be preoccupied with tenure rather than problems of supply and quality or dwelling choice. It is implied that capital receipts will be used for this purpose but it seems unlikely that gross capital expenditure by local authorities will significantly increase. New building or acquisitions are unlikely to be developed to generate supply or offset the local effects of sales. At the same time the other structural influences on the role of council housing — the broad system of housing finance and the process of social, economic and demographic change — seem certain to exert pressures in the same direction as over recent years. The role of council housing as such seems likely to change further towards a residual, welfare role for the marginalised poor. This will vary from place to place and parts of the private sector will also perform such a role.

Second, if Housing Action Trusts, estate privatisation and transfers of landlord operate on any scale council housing as such will decline more rapidly, will become more fragmented and will cease to be as distinct from other tenures as in the past. Purpose-built council dwellings and dwellings on council estates will increasingly *not be* council dwellings. Insofar as tenure is less identifiable from where people live or the design of their dwelling, stereotypes associated with tenure should become less easy to apply and less damaging. But it is at least possible that, as with the right to buy, new forms of privatisation will not have a uniform or random impact. There is little evidence of any pent-up tenant demand to change their landlord and there are problems of organisational capacity and finance which may deter housing

243

associations and other bodies from enthusiastically seeking to offer themselves as alternative landlords. Depending on the impact of rent increases will it be more affluent tenants or those on better estates who will opt for co-ops or new landlords? Will those on the worst estates be more inclined to see their escape as through moving house? Will the impact of tenant initiated changes be relatively small and concentrated on better estates and in certain localities where special (valuation?) factors apply? At this stage the impact is uncertain and will depend on how housing associations respond, how strongly central government structures choice through manipulation of grants, subsidies and expenditure controls, how (and how strongly) local authorities seek to influence decisions and whether they make (and are allowed to make) creative use of the legislation to protect tenants and applicants. This might, for example, involve the ideas being pursued by Rochford D.C. to transfer their housing to a newly formed housing trust with a clear, but arm's length, relationship to the council. Whatever the outcome, a further centralisation of policy and loss of local control is likely. Furthermore monitoring of the quality of service will be of key importance. There is early evidence in relation to the operation of privatised telephone and gas services of differences in quality of service and of inadequate safeguards built into privatisation. The scrutiny of new landlords to ensure quality of service requires explicit standards being established prior to privatisation.

Third, the new form of privatisation may draw attention to the varied interests of those working in the housing service. The Right to Buy has involved a shift in housing management responsibility and in the long term implies declining employment in local authority housing departments and a growth in employment in the private sector. Substantial transfers of control of whole estates offer a more dramatic shift with implications for those working in the service. The phenomenon described by Dunleavy (1986) in which the shift to contracting out forms of privatisation represents 'a continuation of the strategies already well developed by senior policy-level bureaucrats for advancing their class (and frequently gender) interests against those of the rank and file state workers and service consumers', may become more apparent and set up new tensions not obvious in the Right to Buy. Emerging disagreement among housing management professionals is evidence of this.

The fourth and final perspective on new privatisation measures is concerned with access to housing. A break up of municipal ownership must reflect the real preferences of tenants (not heavily distorted by short term loading of options) if it is to be regarded as of benefit to them. However, as with the Right to Buy the new privatisation involves other considerations. Arrangements for accountability, standards of service delivery and arrangements for rents will depend on the form of transfer adopted. Issues of succession, the rights of successors, other rights, and the resources available to facilitate transfers and exchanges could be considerably eroded by exercising the right to choose a landlord. As with the Right to Buy it may be argued that these potential difficulties are not grounds for removing the right to choose but do suggest that the right should be backed up by other measures. These issues are more critical for new applicants for council housing. The fragmentation of ownership could involve a complex of arrangements for nominations from the local authority waiting list. But as with transfers it seems more likely that different landlords, trusts and co-ops will operate different access and allocation policies. These could nicely complement one another and provide a system which would stand up to evaluation in terms of who is able to gain access to rented housing. Again, however, it is more likely that there would be more systematic discrimination against certain groups or that the process of reviewing and changing policies to widen access or prevent discrimination would also be more difficult. In this way one of the principal concerns about a new system must be about its implications for equal opportunities in housing. In more general terms new larger 'independent' landlords could in practice reproduce all the worst features of municipal management. It is how they operate as landlords which is crucial and not whether they are 'independent' or municipal.

These perspectives beg and raise questions about the actions of both central and local government. The political prominence and commitment to the latest scheme for privatisation is as great as in earlier phases. Logically, central government will seek to prevent local authorities from obstructing their intention and will publicise tenants' new rights, monitor and pressurise local authorities. On the basis of past performance it is too much to expect a broader programme of research and evaluation by central government to examine the impact on access to housing or to consider whether the extension of choice to one group is eroding that of others. Local government's position is less clear. It could seek to defend council housing by opposing legislation, by implementing it reluctantly and by mobilising tenants to defend council housing. But, if central government takes up such a challenge, the legal powers and financial mechanisms enable it to intervene (if only through Housing Action

Trusts) and to appeal to tenants over the head of their landlords. Various devices could be developed to overcome the lack of enthusiasm of tenants for new arrangements and to persuade housing associations, building societies and other potential landlords to become involved. The consequence could and probably would be fragmentation and a downward spiral as outlined above.

The alternative for local authorities' response to these new measures is not to seek to defend council housing but to defend council tenants (and prospective tenants). It may be that aspects of the new legislation provide the opportunity to negotiate with tenants a system which delivers what they want (without adverse consequences for applicants). The scope to use the legislation creatively is, however, restricted by the whole approach of central government which is geared to a limited public sector role — irrespective of the interests of tenants. Indeed a key area of creativity is ruled out by restrictions on new council house building or acquisition for tenants and applicants. It would be more likely that the whole policy would meet the range of choice and need in housing if central government adopted a positive attitude to municipal activity in housing — even seeing municipal activity as a necessary preliminary to privatisation would be an advance on a view of council housing as an unnecessary evil.

While the effects of future privatisation will depend on the form it takes a number of issues seem likely to arise. If housing management outside council housing is better staffed and more expensive, increased costs will fall on the tenants. Alternatively, they will fall on the Exchequer through general forms of subsidy (tax reliefs, grants to landlord bodies, grants for improvement and repair) or through housing benefits. Moreover the structure of private agencies will not necessarily ensure an adequate future level of investment. Analyses of the dynamics of the speculative housebuilding industry (Ball, 1982) suggest that direct state intervention will still be needed to build new dwellings, to replace obsolete dwellings and to respond to changing patterns of economic activity. In general, the new policies emerging in 1987 leave considerable doubts about their relevance to current or future housing problems. These doubts are as evident for rural areas where there is a shortage of houses for the local working class as for inner city areas marked by segregation and decay. An inner city policy which assumes that all housing stress is confined to the inner city would be misconceived. It is also likely to have little impact on inner city housing if it neglects the range of factors contributing to polarisation in the city — including the operation of high priority policies such as the sale of council houses.

246

CONCLUSIONS: USER INTEREST AND HOUSING PROVISION

By 1987 the number of dwellings being sold under the Right to Buy had declined significantly and a new phase of policy was being embarked upon. This new phase was less centrally concerned with extending home ownership than with demunicipalisation. The mass of council tenants — in excess of five million — who had not exercised the Right to Buy would continue to be able to exercise that right or to change tenure arrangements in some other way. One striking element in this development is a continuing preoccupation with tenure. In Chapter 6 tenants' reasons for not exercising the Right to Buy were discussed. Important among these reasons were household characteristics (particularly age) and dwelling characteristics. Rising valuations, especially in London and the South East, mean that being unable to afford to buy the dwelling currently occupied will have become a more important factor, along with not wanting to buy the particular dwelling (usually because of its design, neighbourhood, etc). Providing a choice of landlord to these non-buying households hardly seems relevant.

If the concern was to enable these households to become owner occupiers, one precondition would be to give them access to a dwelling which they would want to buy. Unless Peter Walker's no-choice strategy was adopted (giving tenants ownership of the dwelling they occupy, including undesirable, unsaleable, difficult to maintain dwellings) the conversion of tenants to owners involves recognising that in housing decisions households consider the package of services provided by a dwelling — and not just its tenure. A strategy to extend the qualities associated with home ownership would not be one which isolated or privileged tenure. It would be one which was concerned with the quality and location of housing — with adjusting the stock to enable people to occupy (and perhaps buy) the dwellings they want. Historically, the expansion of owner occupation has been sustained and made possible because people have decided to buy dwellings built by public and private landlords. As has been stated earlier, the expansion of home ownership has been contingent on the existence of a stock of dwellings which people wish to live in and speculative building alone has not provided this. Owner occupation has grown through and because of state intervention to influence the quality and nature of the housing stock. In view of this, and directly contrary to the stance being taken by Ministers in 1987, policy for home ownership beyond the Right to Buy would involve state action through new building, conversion and repair to increase the supply of high quality housing. It would involve new public sector building and other investment as well as action to encourage other agencies.

There is a further argument that as home ownership expands, changes its role and moves down market, state intervention to sustain the sector will continue to be needed. This is not only likely to involve a continuation of state subsidy for home ownership but will involve specific interventions to ease mobility, and to overcome shortages, bottlenecks and problems of access by acquiring and selling properties. The Right to Buy and other forms of privatisation will be one-off extensions of owner occupation available to a privileged generation of tenants who are in the right houses at the right time *unless* the state has a continuing role in building and acquisition through which it can deliver similar benefits to later generations. The state also has a continuing complementary role if the problems and inequalities generated through privatisation (say, in relation to loss of relets or social segregation) are to be offset.

In these ways, the choice between policies concerned with the individual interest in quality of housing, as well as ownership, and those concerned with a collective interest in the long term quantity and quality of the housing stock, is not a choice between opposites. The individual and collective interests are not best represented by privileging tenure but do involve privileging user needs — by developing a housing stock which people want to live in. This is not best achieved through deregulated speculative production where small, badly constructed units aimed at the bottom of the market do not perform well on either count and where private landlords' responses to shortage are also likely to involve an erosion of standards and quality of housing. In addition, government has still not considered that it can *require* the private landlord to sell to tenants. In this sense a strategy based on state intervention in the production and improvement of housing is more compatible with the expansion of individual rights to ownership than is a policy which rests on the revival of private landlordism.

The new proposals outlined in 1987 are likely to further exacerbate processes of spatial segregation. The Right to Buy has resulted in 'gentrification' and social and tenure mix in some council built areas but has increased the coincidence between tenure and income, wealth and social position in others. This divergent experience of different areas of council housing is likely to be reinforced and institutionalised under new policies. While Housing Action Trusts may develop in the least popular, most excluded estates the process

248

of reclaiming and selling on these estates may be accompanied by other estates becoming the new last resort areas. At the same time management and financial considerations are likely to encourage housing associations and other landlords which take over areas of council housing to be 'choosy' both in terms of properties and tenants. The variation within council housing between 'rough' and 'respectable' estates is likely to become less marked if the management of respectable estates is assumed by other landlords. Institutionalising social differences into landlord differences will have more serious implications where relocation and transfer policies and opportunities for pooling of finances reduce the policy options available to prevent the pattern being reinforced.

A more responsive social housing sector, including municipal and other forms of housing, is more consistent with claims to meet user demands than is the new phase of privatisation with its reassertion of landlord interest without any emphasis on accountability and standards of service. This kind of approach is also a more constructive response than attempts to eliminate the unfairness in the Right to Buy. That policy, based on accidents of tenancy and valuation is inherently unfair — as would any extension through the alternative of transferable or portable discounts. The latter has the advantage of providing more choice to more tenants than does the Right to Buy. But as the sole extension of policy it does less than a more imaginative development of the municipal role. The development of the production role to provide a real right to rent would involve producing and allocating dwellings and is compatible with choices of landlord *and* dwelling. If offers a prospect of providing an extension of user interest beyond a simple polarity of buying or renting. The aim in developing housing provision would be to transcend emergent and existing problems in the major tenures such as barriers to mobility, excessive bureaucracy, paternalism, lack of choice, problems of resale, transaction times and costs and problems in the supply and price of dwellings.

The most positive way of extending and developing accountability (and choice) to tenants is to develop processes *within* municipal housing rather than to provide a one-off choice of landlord. Similarly new building and acquisition to meet housing needs, the development of co-operatives, repairs services, exchange and estate agency services can all be developed within a framework of municipal activity. There is no argument to support a municipal monopoly in these developments. However, the prospects for housing, for developing a viable rented sector, and for a viable choice

249

between renting and owning are greater if municipal enterprise and initiative is made use of alongside other agencies. It is appropriate to concentrate on how municipal landlordism should evolve and to build in mechanisms of scrutiny of performance — not least by tenants and applicants — to develop municipal landlordism in ways which accord with user interests as well as other objectives. A developing municipal role — building on the financial advantages associated with a substantial stock of dwelling with low historic costs and operating within a framework which provided resources to respond to housing need and which did not privilege home owner-ship financially — offers the best prospect of both developing a viable rented sector and of shifting the debate in British housing away from tenure and towards issues associated with investment, standards, access and poverty.

11

Selling Whose Welfare? — Polarisation and Privatisation

This book has drawn on research which has been undertaken in various locations and at various times over more than ten years. And research methods have varied from broad statistical analyses at national level to more detailed qualitative work in local contexts. It would be appealing to call upon some elegant theoretical framework to justify the methodology and the issues addressed but decisions on method have been more typically pragmatic and the theoretical backcloth somewhat eclectic. In the period that the sale of council houses has moved from being a minor and highly localised policy to a major element in the transformation of welfare provision and life chances there have been dramatic shifts in policy, academic discourse and the British social and economic landscape. The points of contact between research on council housing and council house sales, debates in other policy areas and more fundamental theoretical arguments, have changed substantially. The issues addressed in this book, and the way they are addressed, reflect those developments. Moreover, these points of contact have become more numerous as issues of privatisation, social and spatial polarisation and concern about the evident underlying divisions in Britain and other advanced capitalist societies have moved to the centre of the political agenda and become more prominent in the academic literature. And both the physical and social aspects of housing are significant in debates around social and spatial mobility, the distribution of wealth, the domestic division of labour, consumption sector cleavages and the centrality of class in contemporary British society. In that sense, it is hoped that this book contributes on a number of levels.

Because of what has been said above, this is a difficult book to conclude. Council housing remains in the process of being privatised. At the moment, new legislation is evolving which will throw up new issues and offers the prospect of an even more profound change in the tenure structure. A decade of work in this area has not exhausted the issue but has provided a window on a period of rapid social, economic and policy change. And not untypically in research, issues which began as clear cut and well defined have become progressively more complex and opaque. If the Thatcher administrations have shown a narrow and myopic obsession with the promotion of home ownership, they have also been consistently innovative in producing new measures to accelerate the erosion of council housing. And the left has consistently underestimated the scale of the attack. From a position in the early 1970s where sales were limited to the policy predilections of a few local authorities, we have moved through higher discounts, statutory obligation and larger scale disposals to the current situation where the complete removal of housing provision from local authority control is a distinct possibility.

In the previous chapter we offered an internal analysis of the council house sales policy. This considered some of the problems and contradictions which have emerged in its implementation, the extent to which expectations and claims of the policy matched outcomes, and the likely pattern of future developments in housing policy. It is appropriate, however, to step outside the interstices of council house sales policy and to reiterate some of the more general points from earlier chapters. From the point of view of policy analysis it should be evident that to offer a definitive conclusion regarding the sense or otherwise of selling council housing would be misplaced. A judgement of that kind requires an appreciation of *when* sales occurred and the specific social, economic and policy context in which they occurred. Throughout this book we have stressed that many of the positive claims made of sales (and some of the negative counterclaims) have assumed an erroneous uniformity of housing market conditions, council housing and council tenants. A central problem has been the blanket application of a policy prescription which, given the substantial variation in local circumstances, has produced a set of inequitable and anomolous outcomes. And there has been a more fundamental problem. The sale of council houses could have formed part of an imaginative and socially just restructuring of housing opportunities. Unfortunately, it has been pursued as a political priority to the relative neglect of any significant compensatory or complementary policies. Many former council tenants have (and will) derive substantial financial and social benefit. Central government has certainly gained

252

immensely, politically and financially. The exchange professionals, estate agents, solicitors and others whose economic interests are closely tied to the further extension of home ownership, have benefited from increased business. But for the homeless, the poorly housed in all tenures, and for a substantial marginalised minority the policy has been irrelevant if not highly damaging. Even the most ardent advocates of council house sales have rarely claimed that the benefits go beyond those tenants able to take direct advantage.

So what has been on offer to the others? Reduced new building, reduced subsidy, higher house prices, rising rents, high real interest rates have combined with rising unemployment and a widening gap between the employed majority and an expanding underclass to produce a significant deterioration in the living conditions and life chances of many households in Britain. Developments in housing policy have reflected and acted upon this widening structural fissure between the included and the excluded. Whilst tax cuts, tax benefits and welfare subsidies are re-oriented towards the comfort and security of the affluent and relatively affluent, the marginalised and state dependent are more heavily policed, surveilled and stigmatised. It is *their* welfare state which is being disposed of. In his assessment of 'Social Trends Since World War II', Halsey (1987) comments on 'a new form of polarisation in British society' and the emergence of:

> . . . a more unequal society as between a majority in secure attachment to a still prosperous country and a minority in marginal economic and social conditions, the former moving into the suburban locations of the newer economy of a 'green and pleasant land', the latter tending to be trapped into the old provincial industrial cities and their displaced fragments of peripheral council housing estates. (p. 19)

In a similar vein Gamble (1987) has asserted that the pressures '. . . to maintain public order in civil society and continuing prosperity has produced policies that have increased the freedom and mobility of private capital while strengthening the powers of the state against those groups excluded and marginalised' (p. 16). And Pahl (1986) has suggested that the social structure '. . . is turning from a pyramid into an onion-shaped structure in terms of household income' (p. 9). Whilst those at the top end of the household income structure have fared exceptionally well in recent years those at the bottom have done exceptionally badly. The bulging middle strata of

253

(predominantly) home owners with one or more members in employment have, however, enjoyed a relative increase in their living standards. One of the conclusions Pahl draws from this development is that those on the social and economic margins 'unless they are exceptionally concentrated geographically are in danger of being electorally dispensable' (p. 10).

This pervasive polarisation between social groups and sectors of the economy, within and between cities and parts of cities, is the product of long term and deep seated developments in the international economy. These problems are not confined to Britain, neither are they the product of Thatcherism. But the restructuring of housing tenure and housing opportunities in Britain in recent years conforms to the kinds of images presented above where housing privileges are maintained and enhanced for the majority whilst those in weak bargaining positions suffer the effects of relative disinvestment and neglect. It is within this context that the sales policy must be judged and evaluated. In that sense this study is not about the residualisation of council housing but the ways in which the shape of recent housing policy has impacted upon the housing conditions and opportunities of these marginal groups. For all the recent rhetoric of concern for inner city deprivation and run-down estates, political and fiscal priorities remain unambiguously elsewhere. And in housing terms this is not a simple polarisation of tenures. In the previous chapter, and elsewhere in this book, we have stressed that the perceived problems or advantages of particular forms of housing provision are contingent rather than necessary features. Oppressive management structures and stigma are not inherent features of social housing. And asset appreciation and affluence are not guaranteed or inevitable features of home ownership. Too often, generalisations on the relationship between tenure forms and position in the income and social structure derive from a specific set of historical relationships. What holds true over time is that those on the social and economic margins get the worst housing — and the greater the dominance of market forces the more consistent is that relationship. For all its faults, council housing was probably that part of the welfare state which was most successfully targeted on the working classes. Whilst it is only recently that it has effectively reached the lowest income groups, unlike other forms of welfare provision it has been less open to the accusation that resources were being wasted on the relatively comfortable middle classes. And, as we have stressed earlier, its status as working-class provision forms part of the explanation for its demise.

The particular problems of much contemporary council housing, the impact of economic recession and restructuring, and the evident social divisions which, in many localities, do split along tenure lines have contributed to a crude and wholesale critique of public sector provision which is ahistorical, aspatial and misrepresents the relationship between local government intervention and the private housing market. The new orthodoxy of partnerships, co-operatives and user control develops as if the history of British council housing was one of unmitigated failure. To recognise that times have changed and we must move beyond previous conceptions of the role and form of social housing should not conceal the advances achieved through more than half a century of direct state provision in terms of working-class housing conditions and opportunities. Far from council housing representing a barrier to real improvements in the shape and form of housing provision its very existence has been an essential precondition of the various new initiatives under discussion. Without council housing there would of course be no council house sales and any substantial expansion of working-class home ownership would be likely to require much more inflationary and less well targeted forms of subsidy. The drive to increase effective demand for the new products of the speculative housebuilding industry would require lower production costs and thus lower housing quality. The consequences of such developments are all too evident with the proliferation of starter homes in the early 1980s and the general shift from semi-detached to terraced properties. In 1982, one observer commented that 'new dwellings are now smaller than at any time since the First World War' (Levitt, 1982). And a manager of Wimpey Homes stated:

> In the 1960s the typical first time buyer's house was a three-bedroomed semi-detached of some 1000 ft super . . . Today a home suitable for a first time buyer will have a floor area of 450–500 ft super. It will normally have one or two bedrooms and will usually be terraced. (Stonehouse, 1981)

Adverse publicity, low profit margins and difficulties of selling have now pushed the volume builders and smaller, regionally based companies into lower risk parts of the market. New building is now more typically aimed at higher income families and the more affluent young and elderly. But the disposal of vacant flats and houses by local authorities has opened up new opportunities for the building industry. In this sense the new enthusiasm for partnerships and refurbishment schemes reflects, in part, the problems faced by the housebuilding industry. The existence of council housing has, over the years, helped stabilise the market for new dwellings; in 1974 local authorities eased the impact of the slump in the building industry through the purchase of thousands of dwellings which were proving difficult to sell; and in the late 1980s council housing is again providing a new source of profitable activity for the building industry through various refurbishment schemes. Commenting on such developments a director of Wimpey Homes has claimed that: 'There is no other way you can buy a modern house for as little as £10,000. For several years to come this is going to be a major growth area' (quoted in Mann, 1986). In the same article Mann quotes David Couttie, of the Halifax Building Society, as saying: 'Built to Parker Morris standards, they [ex-council houses] are 25% bigger than new private sector housing and they are 20% cheaper'.

In some areas of the country, therefore, low income households remain dependent on the products of a public housing sector for access to cheap owner occupied housing of relatively good quality. In the South East, however, and particularly in inner London, poorer households remain directly dependent on council housing or are increasingly displaced through rampant house price inflation and the opportunities for the building industry to derive super profits from the recycling of council housing for up-market purchasers. What this underlines is the historical significance of state intervention in the production of dwellings and the continuing and fundamental difficulty of combining *quality* and *affordability*. The overriding emphasis on public-private sector partnerships in current housing policy debates conveys the impression that local government and council housing have somehow constrained the private sector. On the contrary, it could be argued that at times the private sector has been dependent on the public sector and at the very least the relationship has been symbiotic rather than oppositional.

Just as the notion of partnerships conveys the false impression of a new corporatist departure in housing provision (rather than a longstanding relationship) so we must beware of the ideological loading of the term privatisation. The financing and production of council housing has always been privatised and it is certainly becoming more appropriate to describe home ownership as a 'socialised' form of housing provision — heavily dependent on a variety of direct and indirect state subsidies. One view of current developments is that we are seeing a shift from collective welfare state provision concerned with the reproduction of labour power towards a more individualised, substantial and complex structure of occupational and state subsidies to support and maintain the life styles of the relatively comfortable majority. The marginalised, the peripheral, the excluded are offered a reduced quality, heavily stigmatised collective provision. This differentiation has always existed but it is now more pronounced and reflects an ideology of state provision which is concerned with rewards for individuals rather than for social groups. It represents a new selectivity which is less about whether groups or families should receive state support than about what form that support takes.

But a focus on the erosion of the collective welfare state should not lead to a one dimensional view of the way in which the welfare state is changing (George, 1985). The alternative to state collectivism which is emerging is not market liberalism, but rather a strong state corporatism built on regulation, subsidy and close relationships between the central state and key private sector institutions. Nor are these two alternatives to state collectivism (i.e. market liberalism and corporatism) the only alternatives. Indeed the key alternatives would emphasise dweller or user control and a shift of real power. Much of the language of the current pattern of privatisation seeks to claim that such a shift is involved. Home ownership is equated with a real shift in power to the user. The confusion arises because the claimed attributes of home ownership derive from its status as a positional good for a relatively privileged minority — not as a mass tenure accommodating a much wider range of households in terms of income and social status. As we suggested in the previous chapter a rather different vehicle may be required to deliver freedom, choice and housing quality on a mass scale.

It is salutary to reflect upon the continuing and dramatic changes which have occurred in the ownership and control of housing during this century. Since the last half of the 19th century a fundamental change has occurred in the way in which housing has been consumed. In the 19th century the most appropriate mechanism for financing housing production and consumption was private landlordism. One perspective on changes since then is that by the last decades of the 20th century individual private ownership (owner occupation) has emerged as the most appropriate mechanism but that in the period of transition state provision of council housing has been an important safety net or buffer. It has prevented the strains and shortages associated with reorganising private provision from becoming too severe and threatening political or social stability.

Thus the development of council housing has at the same time redistributed housing resources in the interests of the working class and has served the interests of capital and 'social order' by minimising the effects of the restructuring of the private market. By the 1980s it is arguable that the period of transition is over. The transitional role of council housing is therefore being abandoned. The permanent role of council housing is more limited. If this view of the changing role of council housing is broadly accepted then the view that a new era of council housing has emerged is strengthened. What is occurring is not simply another phase in development but a new and changing situation. The coalition of interests which sustained the growth of council housing no longer exists and any attempt to influence or change the future role of social housing will have to face a very different political configuration.

The end of a period of transition for council housing and the maturation of owner occupation to a position where it, rather than private renting, is the dominant tenure also draws attention to another dimension of change. As home ownership approaches a 70 % share of the market, the problems of disrepair, repossession, eviction, and homelessness in that tenure are more apparent. The growth phase of home ownership, in the period in which the form of private housing provision has changed from rentier landlordism to individual owner occupier, is likely to have had different characteristics from a later phase. In the growth phase home ownership has been associated with the younger employed, in a growing full employment economy with an expanding welfare service net. In a later phase, recession, unemployment and declining welfare provision mean that home ownership and home owners have a much more mixed experience. The sector is increasingly dependent on grants and state subsidy. The most vulnerable owners are less likely to be able to sustain ownership status. Housing quality and housing market accumulation will increasingly reflect income, wealth and status in work. Both housing and economic trends suggest that inequalities deriving from consumption in housing will become more closely associated with occupational class. The excitement over the extent to which housing tenure differences cross-cut occupational class should be tempered by a recognition that we are in a system in transition. At the end of the transition there is likely to be a better fit between occupational class and housing situation. Distinctions between major tenures may remain and become sharper but more important social divisions will emerge within housing tenures in relation to gender, race, class and the spatial unevenness of house price inflation and housing market gains.

The emerging package of government housing policies is likely to exacerbate social polarisation. Gone, it seems, are the claims and aspirations to create that ambiguous objective of 'better' social mix. New flags of convenience are unfurled to justify a new round of policies to erode the public housing sector and diminish the role of local authorities. Where people live and what they live in will be increasingly determined by ability to pay thus creating and solidifying residential and social segregation. Deregulation in the private rented sector will produce higher rents and problems of affordability. Few expect an increase in supply unless it is through subdivision of properties, lower standards and growth of multiple occupation. Households on lower incomes seeking to rent will gain little financial assistance. Housing association rents will also rise and cuts and changes in housing benefits are likely to undermine further the position of poorer households. The growing excluded population will depend on the rental tenures and low-quality home ownership. The privatisation of estates and the Right to Buy offers the prospect of further decline and increasing social and spatial segregation within the rental market. New government proposals suggest that tenants will have no power to resist Housing Action Trusts and, unless a transfer of landlord is opposed by a majority, it will go ahead. Individual tenants will be able to have their dwellings leased back by the council but the property will automatically revert to the new landlord when the tenant moves. This cumbersome policy may open up new possibilities for profitable exploitation of the public housing sector but it promises less choice for those who already have little enough to exercise. It also raises wider issues about changing patterns of access and the reduced ability for local authorities to fulfil their statutory housing obligations.

We have emphasised throughout this book that it is a mistake to examine the impact of the right to buy in isolation. It is the combination of the right to buy, other housing policies and deeper social and economic developments which will determine the way the housing market and individual tenures develop. In this context it is irrelevant to change council house sales policy in order to achieve a certain objective (say, to widen access to council housing) if other contemporaneous policy changes (say, in relation to new building or acquisition) work in the opposite direction. The residualisation of council housing is a longer term process involving much more than housing policy and is unlikely to be terminated by changing policy on council house sales alone.

The sale of council housing has mattered in other ways beyond the impact on individual household opportunities, the structure of the housing market or political consciousness. The policy has made a significant fiscal contribution to public expenditure planning. The erosion of council housing has formed part of a broader attack on local autonomy and local political control. And its enthusiastic pursuit in the absence of compensatory measures has been indicative of a hardening of attitudes by those in power towards the marginalised casualties of the recession. The deteriorating position of many black households, single parent families and other peripheralised groups in both the housing and labour markets is open to interpretations of racism and sexism and is symptomatic of a world view, where groups are divided into 'deserving' and 'undeserving' categories.

To what extent can processes of privatisation in the state housing sector inform analyses and expectations of likely developments in other areas of state welfare provision? As we suggested at the beginning of this book the sale of council houses was very much the vanguard policy in a developing strategy and philosophy of more pervasive privatisation. However, the pursuit of a home owning democracy has been paralleled by policies designed to achieve a share owning democracy through the privatisation of public utilities and nationalised industries. The broader edifice of the welfare state has so far escaped a full blooded root and branch transformation, and privatisation has largely been limited to contracting out some aspects of services (Ascher, 1987). But developments in health and education, and the history of privatisation in the housing sphere indicate that the polarisation of the social and income structure will increasingly reflect and act upon polarised forms of provision and, indeed, polarised forms of privatisation. The affluent and relatively affluent majority are likely to be recruited into privatised forms of individual consumption involving the payment of fees for higher status services. This progressive 'creaming off' of the middle classes sets in train a cycle of stigmatisation whereby middle-class support for state provided services is weakened, resources are further withdrawn and sections of the health and education services become labelled as second-class residual services catering for a marginalised underclass. But those residual services are themselves subject to other forms of privatisation. As in housing, state owned land and building assets can be disposed of and revalorised. In economically buoyant and highly pressurised local economies, school and hospital buildings could be redeveloped as newly gentrified middle-class enclaves. And the scope for maintaining or enhancing the standard of service can be further reduced through the privatised management of services for peripheral and marginalised groups.

On this basis the scope for privatisation of the welfare state is much wider than some models assumed. It is evident that profits cannot only be made from privatising services used by the affluent but can be derived from services for the marginal poor. In pursuit of efficiency and value for money objectives and the reduction of a public sector role, prison, social security, education and health services can all become profitable activities underwritten by state subsidies — but typically at the expense of standards of service. The profits derived by the private sector from the provision of bed and breakfast for homeless households is a prime example of ideology overriding hard economic considerations. The highly visible and politically embarrassing response to the reduced standard of service currently on offer from a privatised British Telecom contrasts with the comparative neglect of those who have suffered from reduced standards in housing provision. When it is the business community and the middle classes which are on the receiving end, as opposed to the socially and economically disenfranchised, the response is very different.

Britain has been the laboratory for privatisation experiments with considerable international interest in measures to promote popular capitalism and wider property ownership. It should not be forgotten, however, that in Britain the offer of shares in profitable companies or the offer of ownership of desirable dwellings has been greatly dependent on a history of state intervention. And it is a history of successful intervention which belies some of the critiques of the inherent failings of public provision. The form and pattern of this public provision have reflected the distribution of power in British society, and what has happened in housing and other spheres in recent years reflects and acts upon changes in that power structure and shifting economic imperatives. To see council house sales or other aspects of welfare privatisation as simply responses to consumer demand and the inherent failings of public provision is to be mesmerised by current political rhetoric and ideology. In moving beyond the current forms of housing provision it would be unfortunate if preoccupations with some of the worst aspects of council housing and council housing management were allowed to obscure the real achievements of public provision in the raising of working class living standards.

At proof stage we are able to add a final postscript to this book. The stock market crash of autumn 1987 threatened the privatisation of BP and has occasioned a reassessment of the planned programme of further privatisation through share issues. Coincidentally, a lower level of council house sales has financially over-achieved. Not only have council house sales been the largest element within the privatisation programme, with the greatest capacity to deliver cash receipts over a long period; they have proved to be the most reliable and unproblematic for the Thatcher administrations. However, pressures to accelerate the privatisation of public housing may entail greater reliance on institutional rather than individual investment and expose housing privatisation to the same volatility and uncertainty which has affected other asset sales. Ironically, much of the viability of the council house sales policy has derived from its relative insulation from market forces. At market prices substantially fewer sitting tenants would have chosen to buy and many would have been unable to do so. The sale of council dwellings to sitting tenants has unique qualities involving as it does the sale of individual assets to the direct, sole users of the service. Such a model is not easily transferable to other asset sales and would require a rather different conception of popular capitalism. In the short term, at least, the government is likely to concentrate greater effort on lower risk forms of privatisation — typically the contracting out of services where profitable returns can be guaranteed by continuing state finance or subsidy. Whatever policies are pursued, their overall consistency and coherence in welfare provision is likely to be in a further centralisation of power and the neglect of those regarded as electorally and economically marginal.

Appendix

Notes on Method: Use of Administrative Records

Much of the research reported in this book has been carried out using conventional research techniques, e.g. desk research on published data; social survey; semi-structured interviews with key actors. A considerable amount of the data at local level were, however, generated through the use of administrative files.

The procedure involved initial identification of a number of key records. Their location and form varied from authority to authority. Typically, however, they involved information collected by the Treasurers' and Housing departments in the form of two principal files: a 'sold dwelling' file and a mortgage file. Whilst the dwelling file would include house and household histories and some basic financial data such as price, valuation, etc., the mortgage file provided details of occupation, loan and household income.

Sampling procedure involved identification of a suitable sampling frame (e.g. summary list of all sold dwellings, maintenance records with sold dwellings indicated), calculation of a suitable sampling fraction (depending on overall numbers sold, need for sufficient representation in different time periods, etc.) and identification of key administrative codes linking the sample to the main files.

A coding framework was then devised from a sample of files. The precise form and content varied according to the quality, extent and order of data held. A common core of information for each local authority usually included the following variables:

  (i) area code
  (ii) record number
 (iii) date of first tenancy
 (iv) percentage discount
  (v) current market value

(vi) net sale price
(vii) dwelling type
(viii) dwelling size
(ix) source of loan
(x) size of loan
(xi) term of loan
(xii) occupation of principal earner
(xiii) occupation of secondary earner
(xiv) age of principal earner
(xv) income of principal earner
(xvi) household income

In some cases, data were available on:

(i) household size
(ii) household structure
(iii) number of tenancies
(iv) tenants' improvements
(v) year of construction of sold dwelling
(vi) occupational histories
(vii) tenancy histories

With the exception of occupation details (which required reference to the Registrar General's Classification or other classificatory schema), all variables were precoded and data recorded on computer coding sheets. Statistical Package for the Social Sciences (SPSS) was used to analyse the various data sets.

The principal advantage of this method is that it enables the generation of a large sample in a relatively short time and provides limited information on dwelling and household characteristics at considerably less expense than conventional survey techniques. Moreover, in some cases the quality of information is superior. This is particularly true of verified income data required for mortgage purposes.

The general disadvantage is in the rigidity of the data sets constructed as they are for administrative rather than research purposes. A specific problem occurs where the mortgage has been granted by a private sector institution. In these cases, income and occupational data are more limited. This varied between authorities according to the pattern of lending but became more evident over the life of the research as banks and building societies increased their lending activity on council house sales.

In most cases the dwelling or tenancy files contained ephemera of various types (e.g. letters, old application forms, details of previous allocation procedures) and provided additional and unanticipated qualitative data. Whilst providing interesting background to the sales policy and the development of council housing in particular localities, the qualitative information in the files offered some valuable insights and, on occasion, indicated important new lines of inquiry. This was true of our developing interest in housing and dwelling histories. Unfortunately, increased computerisation of records is likely to reduce the richness of administrative files for subsequent researchers.

References

Allen, P. (1982) *Shared ownership*, HMSO.

Arden, A. (1980) *The Housing Act, 1980*, Sweet and Maxwell.

Arden, A. and Cross, C. (1984) *The Housing and Building Control Act, 1984*, Sweet and Maxwell.

Ascher, K. (1987) *The politics of privatisation*, Macmillan.

Association of Metropolitan Authorities (1986) *Mortgage arrears, owner occupiers at risk*, AMA.

Audit Commission (1985) *Capital expenditure controls in local government in England*, HMSO.

Ball, M. (1982) 'Housing provision and the economic crisis', *Capital and Class*, vol. 7, pp. 66–77.

Bassett. K. (1980) 'Council house sales in Bristol, 1960–1979', *Policy and Politics*, vol. 8, 3, pp. 324–33.

Beesley, M. *et al.* (1980) *The sale of council houses in a rural area: a case study of South Oxfordshire*, Working Paper, no. 44, Oxford Polytechnic.

Beesley, M. and Littlechild, S. (1983) 'Privatization: principles, problems and priorities', *Lloyds Bank Review*, July, pp. 1–20.

Bilcliffe, S. (1979) 'Leading evidence', *Roof*, November.

Boddy, M. and Fudge, C. (1984) *Local Socialism*, Macmillan, London.

Boleat, M. (1982) 'Home ownership in inner city areas' in *Policy analysis for housing and planning*, Proceedings of PATRAC summer annual meeting.

Bowley, M. (1984) *Housing and the state 1918–1944*, Allen and Unwin.

British Market Research Bureau (1986) *Housing and savings*, Building Societies Association.

Brough, A. (1977) *The sale of council houses in Oxford city*, Unpublished thesis, Oxford Polytechnic.

Brown, C. (1984) *Black and white Britain, the third PSI survey*, Gower.

Building Societies Association (1983) *Housing tenure*, BSA.

——— (1986) *Bulletin*.

Bulpitt, J. (1983) *Territory and power in the United Kingdom*, Manchester University Press.

Burton, P., Forrest, R. and Stewart, M. (1986) *Living conditions in urban areas*, The European Foundation for the Improvement of Living and Working Conditions.

Butler, D.E. and King, E. (1965) *The British General Election 1964*, Macmillan.

——— (1966) *The British General Election 1966*, Macmillan.

Butler, E., Pirie, M. and Young P. (1985) *The omega file*, Adam Smith Institute.

Byrne, D. and Parson, D. (1983) 'The state and the reserve army: the management of class relations in space' in Anderson, J., Duncan, S., Hudson, R. (eds) *Redundant spaces in cities and regions?*, Academic Press.

Central Housing Advisory Committee: The Dudley Committee (1944) *Design of dwellings*, HMSO.

CES Limited (1984) *Outer estates in Britain, Interim report*, CES, London.

Champion, A.G., Green, A.E., Owen, D.W., Ellin, D.J. and Coombes, M.G. (1987) *Changing places*, Edward Arnold.

Chartered Institute of Public Finance and Accountancy (1984) *Review of the Right to Buy provisions of the Housing Act 1980 and subsequent developments*.

Church of England (1985) *Faith in the city*, Church House Publishing.

City of Birmingham (1939) *City of Birmingham handbook 1939*.

City of Liverpool (1984) *1981 social area study: the results in brief*.

Clapham, D. and Maclennan, D. (1983) 'Residualisation of public housing: a non-issue', *Housing Review*, vol. 32, pp. 9–10.

Cochrane, A. (1986) 'Complaining about council house sales: a study of local ombudsman's report', Unpublished paper, Department of Social Administration, University of Bristol.

Cockburn, C. (1977) *The local state*, Pluto Press, London.

Coleman, A. (1985) *Utopia on trial*, Hilary Shipman.

Commission for Racial Equality (1984) *Race and housing in Liverpool: a research report*, CRE.

Conservative Party (1967) *Annual conference report*.

———— (1968) *Conference '68*.

———— (1970a) *A better tomorrow*.

———— (1970b) *88th Conservative conference*.

———— (1971) *Annual conference report*.

———— (1972) *Conservative party conference*.

———— (1974) *Conservative party election manifesto*.

———— (1979) *Conservative manifesto*.

———— (1987) *The next moves forward*, Conservative Central Office.

Cooney, E.W. (1974) 'High flats in local authority housing in England and Wales since 1945' in Sutcliffe, A. (ed.) *Multi-storey housing: the British working class experience*, Croom Helm.

Cullingworth, J.B. (1963) *Housing in transition*, Routledge and Kegan Paul.

———— (1965) *English housing trends*, Bell.

Daunton, M. (1983) *House and home in the Victorian city*, Edward Arnold.

Dearlove, J. and Saunders, P. (1984) *An introduction to British politics*, Polity Press.

Department of Health and Social Security (annual) *Social security statistics*, HMSO.

Department of the Environment (1971) *Fair deal for housing*, Cmnd 4728, HMSO.

———— (1977) *Housing policy*, Cmnd 6851, HMSO.

———— (1980) *Appraisal of the financial effects of council house sales*, DoE.

———— (1985) *An enquiry into the condition of the local authority housing stock in England, 1985*, DoE.

Dickens, P. and Goodwin, M. (1981) *Consciousness, corporatism and the local state*, Working paper no. 26, Urban and Regional Studies, University of Sussex.

267

Doling, J., Karn, V. and Stafford, B. (1986) 'The impact of unemployment on home ownership', *Housing Studies*, vol. 1, no. 1, pp. 49–59.

Donnison, D. (1967) *The government of housing*, Penguin.

Dunleavy, P. (1981) *The politics of mass housing in Britain 1945–75*, Clarendon Press.

———— (1986) 'Explaining the privatisation boom: public choice versus radical approaches', *Public Administration*, spring, vol. 64, pp. 13–34.

Dunleavy, P. and Husbands, C.T. (1985) *British democracy at the crossroads; voting and party competition in the 1980s*, Allen and Unwin.

Dunn, R., Forrest, R. and Murie, A. (1987) 'The geography of council house sales in England — 1979–85', *Urban Studies*, vol. 24, pp. 47–59.

English, J. (1979) 'Access and deprivation in local authority housing' in Jones, C. (ed.) *Urban deprivation and the inner city*, London, Croom Helm.

———— (1982a) (ed.) *The future of council housing*, London, Croom Helm.

———— (1982b) 'Must council housing become welfare housing?', *Housing Review*, vol. 31, pp. 154–6, 212–13.

Ermisch, J. (1984) *Housing finance: who gains?*, Policy Studies Institute.

Field, F. (1981) *Inequality in Britain: freedom welfare and the state*, Fontana.

Forrest, R. (1980) 'The resale of former council houses in Birmingham', *Policy and Politics*, vol. 8, 3.

Forrest, R., Lansley, P. and Murie, A. (1984) *A foot on the ladder?*, Working paper no. 41, SAUS, University of Bristol.

Forrest, R. and Murie, A. (1976) *Social segregation, housing need and the sale of council houses*, Research Memorandum 53, CURS, University of Birmingham.

———— (1982) 'The Great divide', *Roof*, November/December, pp. 19–21.

———— (1984a) *Right to Buy? Issues of need, equity and polarisation in the sale of council houses*, Working paper no. 39, SAUS, University of Bristol.

———— (1984b) *Monitoring the Right to Buy*, Working paper no. 40, SAUS, University of Bristol.

———— (1986a) *An unreasonable act?*, SAUS Study no. 1, University of Bristol.

———— (1986b) 'Marginalisation and subsidised individualism', *International Journal of Urban and Regional Research*, vol. 10, no. 1, pp. 46–65.

———— (1987) 'The affluent home owner: labour market position and the shaping of housing histories', *Sociological Review*, vol. 35, no. 2, pp. 370–403.

Forrest, R. and Williams, P. (1981) 'The commodification of housing: emerging issues and contradictions', Working paper no. 73, CURS, University of Birmingham.

———— (1984) 'Commodification and housing', *Environment and Planning A*, vol. 16, pp. 1163–80.

Foulis, M.B. (1985) *Council house sales in Scotland*, Central Research Unit paper, Scottish Office.

Friend, A. (1980) *A giant step backwards*, Occasional paper no. 5, CHAS.

Friend, A. and Metcalf, J. (1981) *Slump city: the politics of mass unemployment*, Pluto Press.

Gamble, A. (1987) 'The great divide', *Marxism Today*, March, pp. 12–17.

Gauldie, E. (1974) *Cruel habitations*, Allen and Unwin.

George, P. (1985) 'Towards a two-dimensional analysis of welfare ideologies, *Social Policy and Administration*, spring, vol. 19, no. 1, pp. 33–45.

Green, D.G. (1987) *The new right*, Wheatsheaf.

Grosskurth, A. (1983) 'Special sales area in Wandsworth', *London Housing*, December, no. 35.

Guardian (1987) 'New GLC-built homes go on the market for £2 m', 24 August.

Halsey, A.H. (1987) 'Social trends since world war two', *Social Trends*, no. 17, pp. 11–19.

Hamnett, C. (1983) 'The new geography of housing', *New Society*, December, pp. 396–8.

—— (1984) 'Housing the two nations; socio-tenurial polarisation in England and Wales 1961–1981', *Urban Studies*, vol. 43, pp. 389–405.

Hamnett, C. and Williams, P. (forthcoming) 'House price inflation and personal equity', Greyhound Press.

Harloe, M. (1978) 'The Green Paper on housing policy' in Brown, M. and Baldwin, S. (eds) *The yearbook of social policy in Britain 1977*, Routledge and Kegan Paul.

—— (1981) 'The recommodification of housing' in Harloe, M. and Lebas, E. (eds) *City, class and capital*, Edward Arnold.

Harris, N. (1973) *Competition and the corporate society*, Methuen.

Harrison, M. (1986) 'Consumption and urban theory: an alternative approach based on the social division of welfare', *International Journal of Urban and Regional Research*, vol. 10, 2, pp. 232–42.

Harrison, P. (1983) *Inside the inner city*, Penguin.

Heald, D. (1985) 'Will privatisation of public enterprises solve the problem of control?', *Public Administration*, spring, vol. 63, pp. 7–22.

Heald, D. and Morris, G. (1984) 'Why public sector unions are on the defensive', *Personnel Management*, May, pp. 30–4.

Heald, D. and Steel, D. (1981) 'The privatisation of UK public enterprises', *Annals of Public and Co-operative Economy*, September, pp. 351–67.

—— (1982) 'Privatising public enterprises: an analysis of the government's case', *Political Quarterly*, 53, 333, 349.

Heath, A., Jowell, R. and Curtice, J. (1985) *How Britain votes*, Pergamon.

H.M. Treasury (1987) The Government's Expenditure Plans 1987–88 to 1989–90, Cm. 56, HMSO.

Henderson, J. and Karn, V. (1987) *Race, class and state housing*, Gower.

Hillyard, P. and Percy-Smith, J. (1987) *The coercive state*, Fontana.

House of Commons (1980) *Parliamentary debates*, Official Report, Standing Committee F, Housing Bill, Eleventh Sitting, 21 February.

House of Commons Environment Committee (1980) *First report from the Environment Committee*, Session 1979–80, HC 714, HMSO.

—— (1981) Second report of the Environment Committee, Session 1980–81, *Council House Sales*, HC 366-1.

Howe, G. (1965) 'The waiting list society' in *The Conservative Opportunity*, Batsford.

269

Inside Housing (1986) 'Pattie speech provokes major storm', June, p. 5.

Jacobs, S. (1981) 'The sale of council houses: does it matter?, *Critical Social Policy*, vol. 1, no. 2.

Johnston, R.J. (1987) 'A note on housing tenure and voting in Britain 1983', *Housing Studies*, vol. 2, 2, pp. 112–21.

Jones, C. (1982) 'The demand for home ownership' in English (1982a).

Jones, G. and Stewart, J. (1981) *The case for local government*, Allen and Unwin.

Jowell, R., Witherspoon, S. and Brook, L. (1986) *British social attitudes: the 1986 report*, Gower.

Karn, V., Kemeny, J. and Williams, P. (1985) *Home ownership in the inner city*, Gower.

Kemeny, J. (1981) *The myth of home ownership*, Routledge and Kegan Paul.

Kemeny, J. and Thomas, A. (1984) 'Capital leakage from owner occupied housing', *Policy and Politics*, 12, pp. 13–30.

Labour Force Survey, OPCS (1986), HMSO.

Labour Party (1967) *Report of the Annual Conference*.

―――― (1968) *Report of the Annual Conference*.

Lansley, S. and Fiegehen, G. (1974) *One nation? Housing and the Conservative Party*, Fabian Tract 432.

Laughlin, M. (1983) *Local government, the law and the constitution*, Local Government Legal Society Trust.

Leather, P. and Murie, A. (1986) 'The decline in public expenditure' in Malpass, P. (ed.) *The housing crisis*, Croom Helm.

Levitt, D. (1982) 'Housing standards: standards are not enough', *Architects Journal*, November.

Littlewood, J. and Mason, S. (1984) *Taking the initiative*, HMSO.

MacGregor, J. (1965) 'Strategy for housing' in *The Conservative opportunity*, Batsford.

Malpass, P. (1983) 'Residualisation and the restructuring of housing tenure', *Housing Review*, 32, pp. 44–5.

Malpass, P. and Murie, A. (1982) *Housing policy and practice*, Macmillan.

―――― (1987) *Housing policy and practice* (second edition), Macmillan.

Mann, E. (1986) 'Private rescue', *Building*, March, pp. 16–18.

Marshall, G., Rose, D., Vogler, C. and Newby, H. (1985) 'Class, Citizenship and distributional conflict in modern Britain', *British Journal of Sociology*, vol. XXXVI, no. 2, pp. 259–83.

Means, R. (1977) *Social work and the 'undeserving' poor*, Occasional paper no. 37, CURS, University of Birmingham.

Merrett, S. (1979) *State housing in Britain*, Routledge and Kegan Paul.

―――― (1982) *Owner occupation in Britain*, Routledge and Kegan Paul.

Miliband, R. (1974) 'Politics and poverty' in Wedderburn, D. (ed.) *Poverty, inequality and class structure*, Cambridge University Press.

Ministry of Housing and Local Government (1953) *Houses: the next step*, Cmnd 8996, HMSO.

―――― (1961) *Homes for today and tomorrow*, HMSO.

Mishra, R. (1981) *Society and Social Policy*, Macmillan.

Moore, R. (1980) *Reconditioning the slums: the development and role of housing rehabilitation*, Polytechnic of Central London.

Murie, A. (1975) *The sale of council houses: a study in social policy*, Occasional paper no. 35, CURS, University of Birmingham.

—— (1983) *Housing inequality and deprivation*, Heinemann, London.

—— (1985) 'What the country can afford? Housing under the Conservatives 1979–83' in Jackson, P. (ed.) *Implementing government policy initiatives: the Thatcher administration 1979–1983*, Royal Institute of Public Administration.

Murie, A. and Forrest, R. (1980) *Housing market processes and the inner city*, ESRC, School Publishing House.

Municipal Journal (1980) 'Stanley will use powers to beat house sales defiance', 17 October, p. 1199.

Nabarro, R. (1980) 'The impact on workers from the inner city of Liverpool's economic decline' in Evans, A. and Eversley, D. (eds) *The inner city*, Heinemann.

National Council of Social Service (1980) *Rural housing in East Hampshire*, NCSS.

National Federation of Housing Associations (1985) *Inquiry into British housing* (chaired by the Duke of Edinburgh), NFHA.

Nationwide Building Society (1986) *Local area housing statistics — Hampshire*.

Nevitt, A.A. (1968) 'Conflicts in British housing policy', *The Political Quarterly*, vol. 39, pp. 439–50.

Niner, P. (1975) *Local authority policy and practice: a case study approach*, Occasional paper no. 31, CURS, University of Birmingham.

Office of Population Censuses and Surveys (OPCS) (1972 onwards) *The general household survey*, HMSO.

O'Higgins, M. (1983) 'Rolling back the welfare state: the rhetoric and reality of public expenditure under the Conservative Government' in Jones, C. and Stevenson, J. (eds) *The yearbook of social policy in Britain 1982*, Routledge and Kegan Paul.

Orbach, L. (1977) *Homes for heroes: a study of the evolution of public housing*, Seeley Service.

Pahl, R. (1975) *Whose city?*, second edition, Penguin.

Pahl, R.E. (1986) 'Social polarization and the economic crisis', Draft paper prepared for seminar organised by the Hungarian Academy of Sciences, Budapest, March.

Phillips, D. (1985) *What price equality?*, Greater London Council.

Phillips, D.R. and Williams, A.M. (1982) *Rural housing and the public sector*, Gower.

Pinker, R. (1971) *Social theory and social policy*, Heinemann.

Pirie, M. (1985) *Privatisation*, Adam Smith Institute.

Praks, N. and Priemus, H. (eds) (1985) *Post-war public housing in trouble*, Delft University Press.

Pugh, C. (1980) *Housing in capitalist societies*, Gower.

Rossi, H. (1977) 'Adding to the stock of human happiness', *Roof*, July, p. 123.

Salt, J. (1985) 'Housing and labour migration', Paper presented at Conference on Housing and Labour Market Change, Parsifal College, London, 12/13 December.

Samuel, R., Kincaid, J. and Slater, E. (1962) 'But nothing happens', *New*

271

Left Review, 13.14.

Saunders, P. (1980) *Urban politics*, Penguin.

—— (1981) *Social Theory and the Urban Question*, Hutchinson.

Sewel, J., Twine, F. and Williams, M.J. (1984) 'The sale of council houses — some empirical evidence', *Urban Studies*, vol. 21, pp. 439–50.

Showler, B. and Sinfield, A. (eds) (1980) *The workless state*, Martin Robertson.

Shuksmith, M. (1981) *No homes for locals?*, Gower.

Simpson, A. (1981) *Stacking the decks*, Nottingham and District CRS.

Sipila, J. (1985) 'The traditional and the new poor (excluded)' in Riihinen, O. (ed.) *Social policy and post industrial society, basic report, 13th Regional Symposium on Social Welfare*, International Council on Social Welfare, pp. 89–102.

Skinner, M. (1980) 'Send a commissioner to sell houses says council', *Local Government Chronicle*, 17 October, p. 1091.

Smith, N. (1984) *Uneven development*, Basil Blackwell.

Spencer, K., Taylor, A., Smith, B., Mawson, J., Flynn, M., Batley, R. (1986) *Crisis in the industrial heartland*, Clarendon Press.

Stonehouse, P. (1981) 'The viewpoint of the private housebuilder', *Housing Review*, July/August.

Swenarton, M. (1981) *Homes fit for heroes*, Heinemann.

Szelenyi, I. (1981) 'Alternatives to capitalist development: an agenda for urban research', *International Journal of Urban and Regional Research*, 5, pp. 1–14.

Taylor-Gooby, P. (1982) 'Two cheers for the welfare state', *Journal of Public Policy*, vol. 2, pp. 319–46.

—— (1983) 'Moralism, self-interest and attitudes to welfare', *Policy and Politics*, vol. 22, pp. 145–60.

Titmuss, R.M. (1973) *The gift relationship*, Allen and Unwin.

—— (1974) *Social policy*, Allen and Unwin.

—— (1976) 'The social division of welfare' in *Essays on the welfare state*, pp. 34–55, Allen and Unwin.

Townsend, P. with Corrigan, P. and Kowarzik, U. (1987) *Poverty and labour in London*, Low Pay Unit.

Usher, D. (1987) 'Housing privatisation: the sale of council estates', Working paper 67, School for Advanced Urban Studies, University of Bristol.

Waldegrave, W. (1987a) Speech to the Institute of Housing, annual conference, June, mimeo.

—— (1987b) 'Some reflections on housing policy', Conservative Party News Service, 28 August.

Ward, C. (1983) *Housing: an anarchist approach*, Freedom Press.

—— (1985) *When we build again*, Pluto Press.

White, P. (1983) *Long term unemployment and labour markets*, Policy Studies Institute.

Wilding, P. (1972) 'Towards exchequer subsidies for housing 1906–14', *Social and Economic Administration*, vol. 6, no. 1, pp. 3–18.

Wilensky, H.L. and Lebeaux, C.N. (1965) *Industrial society and social welfare*, Free Press.

Williams, N.J., Sewel, J. and Twine, F. (1986) 'Council house sales and residualisation', *Journal of Social Policy*, vol. 15, no. 3, pp. 273–92.

Williams, P. (1982) 'Restructuring urban managerialism: towards a political economy of urban allocation', *Environment and Planning A*, vol. 14, pp. 95–105.

Winter, H. (1980) *Homes for locals*?, Community Council of Devon.

Index

Printed in Great Britain
by Amazon